W9-BVJ-443

ARNULFO L. OLIVEIRA MEMORIAL LIBRARY
1825 MAY STREET
BROWNSVILLE, TEXAS 78520

P. B. YOUNG

NEWSPAPERMAN

Race, Politics, and Journalism
in the New South

1910–1962

P. B. YOUNG

NEWSPAPERMAN

Race, Politics, and Journalism
in the New South

1910–1962

HENRY LEWIS SUGGS

University Press of Virginia
Charlottesville

ARNULFO L. OLIVEIRA MEMORIAL LIBRARY
1825 MAY STREET
BROWNSVILLE, TEXAS 78520

THE UNIVERSITY PRESS OF VIRGINIA
Copyright © 1988 by the Rector and Visitors
of the University of Virginia

First published 1988

Design by Diane Nelson

Frontispiece: P. B. Young in 1950. (Photo in the possession of the author)

LIBRARY OF CONGRESS
Library of Congress Cataloging-in-Publication Data
Suggs, Henry Lewis.
   P. B. Young, newspaperman : race, politics, and journalism in the
New South, 1910–62 / Henry Lewis Suggs.
      p.   cm.
   Bibliography: p.
   Includes index.
   ISBN 0–8139–1178–8
   1. Young, P. B. (Plummer Bernard), d. 1962.   2. Afro-American
journalists—United States—Biography.   3. Journal and guide—
History.   4. Norfolk (Virginia)—Biography.   5. Norfolk (Virginia)—
Race relations.   6. Afro-Americans—Virginia—Norfolk—Social
conditions.   7. Civil rights movements—Virginia—Norfolk.
I. Title.
PN4874.Y59S84   1988
070.4′1′0924—dc19
[B]   88-14200
                                                                  CIP
Printed in the United States of America

To the memory of
Edward Younger
Alumni Professor of History
University of Virginia

Contents

Preface

When the black journalist P. B. Young, Sr., died in October 1962, his death merited only a passing mention in national publications, when it was noted at all. For many white Virginians, Plummer Bernard Young had never really existed. For example, in 1947, when the circulation of his Norfolk *Journal and Guide* was close to 70,000 copies and the paper was at the height of its success and power, a book devoted to the press in Norfolk and the Hampton Roads peninsula accorded Young and the *Guide* only a few paragraphs. Even in Norfolk, where he lived for fifty-four years and became a force in the legal, political, and journalist spheres, he was given the most perfunctory recognition—a city park named in tribute to him. It is rare to find more than a few paragraphs on P. B. Young in histories of Norfolk during his lifetime. Although Young served for ten years as chairman of the board of trustees of the two leading black educational institutions in America, Howard University and Hampton Institute, neither institution has named a scholarship or building in his honor. This study of Young's life and work, it is hoped, will be a first step in correcting these oversights in the historical record.

Although P. B. Young is the central focus, the book also analyzes the strategy and ideology of many of his contemporaries, outstanding black leaders such as C. C. Spaulding, James E. Shepard, Mordecai Johnson, and Luther P. Jackson, as they worked to invest the black community with a sense of pride and accomplishment. The debate between Young and others over strategy in the South and their disagreement over the Afro-American dilemma concerning migration, World War I, and the NAACP offer insight into a previously neglected chapter of southern history while simultaneously providing a framework for analyzing the social history of Norfolk and tidewater Virginia. This volume depicts Young as a public figure and a complex personality. He could be both liberal and conservative on the same issue or a pragmatist who exhibited impatience with his contemporaries' inflexible approach to race relations. Young was not a theoretical statistician or a critical thinker but rather a man of action. He fought southern racism not because of some abstract reasoning but because of its effect on what he termed "a proscribed people."

Protest, politics, and journalism in the New South form the theme of this book, which is the first comprehensive study of the black press and black leadership in the South. Until recently, it was assumed that the black press in the South was virtually nonexistent during the post–Civil War years. Moreover, the black newspapers that were published were considered "insignificant and unworthy" as primary instruments of research. The black press has been ignored in scores of books on the civil rights movement and monographic studies of the black family, black politics, and the transformation of black life and culture in the New South. On more than one occasion I have been asked indignantly: "What are you doing studying that mess? Ain't no white folks wrote on that." Regrettably, black scholars still have not determined the priority for research on the black experience. Consequently, they have overlooked the fact that the black press richly illuminates our understanding of the programs, ideologies, and tactics that black leaders employed in the past. It is a window through which historians can view black responses to oppression, for the press captures what is happening in a community and freezes it for posterity.

The black press in the South also functioned as a carrier and preserver of black culture. It was not only an advocate and a crusader, it was a mirror, a chronicle, and an encyclopedia of the black experience. It also completes our picture of American journalism, and an understanding of American journalism is essential to our understanding of American history. The black press, in sum, is inextricably woven into the fabric of American life, and any attempt to remove the thread will do irreparable harm to the garment itself.

Young published the largest black newspaper in the South for over fifty years, an extraordinarily long career. It has been my good fortune and, at the same time, a great challenge to have the exclusive use of his personal papers, documents, and artifacts. Dr. Milton Reid, publisher; Dr. Carlton Goodlett, chairman of the board of the Guide Publishing Company; and Mrs. Brenda Andrews, executive publisher, granted me access to Young's personal papers and patiently consented to scores of interviews. Mrs. John Q. Jordan granted me exclusive use of former editor-in-chief John Q.

("Rover") Jordan's personal papers, and Mrs. Alfonso Elder, Mrs. Louis Jaffe, Dr. Helen Gray Edmonds, Mrs. J. W. Maye, Sr., mailed valuable documents to me as did Arnold Taylor and Father Joseph Green. Historians John Hope Franklin, John Blassingame, August Meier, Darlene Clark Hine, Earl Thorpe, David Bishop, Edgar Toppin, William Crawley, F. Nash Boney, Alton Hornsby, Thommy Bogger, and my colleagues in the Department of History of Clemson University made valuable suggestions.

Portions of this book appeared in earlier form in my articles entitled: "P. B. Young and Changing Urban Politics in Norfolk, 1920–40," *Journal of Ethnic Studies* 4 (Nov. 1977): 1—16; "P. B. Young of the Norfolk *Journal and Guide:* A Booker T. Washington Militant, 1904–1928," *Journal of Negro History* 64 (Fall 1979): 365–76; "Tidewater Virginia's Editorial Response to Changes in the Bi-racial System, 1945–1955," *Virginia Social Science Journal* 15 (Nov. 1980): 40–47; and "Black Strategy and Ideology in the Segregation Era: P. B. Young and the Norfolk Journal and Guide, 1910–1954," *Virginia Magazine of History and Biography* 91 (April 1983): 161–90, and are reprinted here by permission.

Historians Andrew Buni of Boston University, Jack Kirby of Miami University (Ohio), and Alan Schaffer of Clemson University read the completed manuscript and suggested revisions. William ("Bill") Crawley and Otho Campbell of Mary Washington College and Fred Regan, Henry Ferrell, and Mary Jo Bratton of East Carolina University revealed neglected archival resources on the New South. Tyler Blethen, Jerry Schwartz, Jim Lewis, John Bell, Max Williams, Jim Anderson, Alice Matthews, Constance Head, and Ellerd Hulbert of Western Carolina University offered invaluable suggestions and always encouraged me to complete the book.

But it is Professor Edward Younger, the Alumni Professor of History at the University of Virginia, to whom I owe the most credit. He was an inspiring teacher and adviser, patient but firm as a critic, and unstinting with his time—a warm and true friend. He was a father figure who often admonished me to seek "excellence without excuse" and to make the University of Virginia's Honor Code a part of my everyday life.

A special tribute is accorded the Department of History of the University of Virginia. I never realized that so many books existed on the Civil War and Reconstruction until I enrolled in Professor Willie Lee Rose's courses on these subjects. Equally challenging was Paul Gaston, who introduced me to Dan Carter's *Scottsboro* and extended my interest in the American South. Richard Ellis, who rivaled Norman Graebner as a lecturer, and Robert Dawidoff helped to improve my writing skills. Others in the department to whom I owe much are W. W. Abbot, Norman

Graebner, Joseph Miller, Merrill Peterson, Joseph Kett, John Craig, and William Harbaugh. Departmental chairman Martin Havran inspired me especially; he acted as my adviser following Edward Younger's death in 1979. It was Havran who recommended me for the job at Clemson.

The University of Virginia was my first integrated educational experience. I was the second black American to earn the Ph.D. there. When the degree was awarded in 1976, it never occurred to me that eventually I would integrate two universities and four departments of history. It has been a long, winding, and mountainous road from Pitt County, North Carolina, to the University of Virginia and thence to Clemson University. I am proof that the South is not monolithic.

I am indebted to the librarians and archivists of many institutions, among them: the University of Virginia, the Library of Congress, the National Archives, the University of North Carolina, the Virginia State Library, Howard University, the North Carolina Division of Archives and History, East Carolina University, North Carolina Central University, Virginia State University, and Clemson University.

Finally, I am grateful to my family and friends, who have supported me throughout the years. A special tribute to my mother Mary Suggs, my sister Addie, and my brothers Paul and John Robert, and the families of Henry Martin, Charlie, Sidney, and David Suggs. To Don Langston, Mrs. Louise Stocks, J. J. Worthington, Dexter Whitehead, William Elwood, Houston Baker, Emma Carr, Earl E. Thorpe, Helen Gray Edmonds, Caulbert A. Jones, Peggy Wiley, A. Knighton Stanley, Sophronia E. Baylor, Joyce Neal-Jackson, Queen Fountain, Berthalene Knox, Monte G. Givens, Fred McGuinn, Anthony J. Witkowski, Clarence Bunch, John Thomas Avent, James Robert Lewis, Alvin Frederick Anderson, Bobby Henderson, Amy Mills, Linda Reed, Lucinda Sullivan, Debra Witcher, William Henry Mitchell, Jacqueline Diane Neal, Robert Waller, John Wunder, Lovell Thornton, Nathaniel Evans, Stacey Hogan, Alan Grubb, Richard Saunders, Theda Perdue, Richard Golden, Dennis Paz, Joe Arbena, Elizabeth Carney, Don McKale, Leonard Greenspoon, Carol Bleser, William ("Bill") Maker, William Steirer, Thomas Kuehn, Jim Miller, John Johnson, Edwin Moise, Lawrence Estaville, Roger Leemhuis, Mike Heintze, Pamela Mack, Chuck Lippy, Larry McCollough, Ernest Lander, Bob Lambert, Cynthia Hunter, Flora Walker, Jan and Joy Dixon, Rameth Owens, Allen Jones, and Deborah Crocker. To Mrs. Edward Younger, a special thanks. Finally, to my American South and Western Civilization classes at Hampton, Howard, and Clemson, as you can see, I kept my word and individually listed your names in the preface.

THE PRESS

A NOTHER indication of the economic and social advancement of the colored people of Norfolk is the development of a weekly newspaper which is ranked by experts with the best
weeklies in America. While the Norfolk Journal and Guide aims to cover the Tidewater Virginia and North Carolina sections the paper has some circulation in every State in the Union.

The Norfolk Journal and Guide is owned by
The Guide Publishing Co., Inc. Occupies its own
buildings and operates its own modern plant, giving full-time employment to twenty-eight people
and part time work as agents, correspondents and
distributors to more than one hundred. A commercial printing business is operated in connection
with the paper.

The above is a facsimile of the front page of
the Norfolk Journal and Guide.
Average edition 12 to 14 pages.

Left to right—Mrs. Eleanor W. Young, Treasurer; P. B. Young, President and H. C. Young, Secretary of The Guide Publishing Co., Inc.

NORFOLK JOURNAL AND GUIDE BUILDING AND ANNEX

Norfolk Journal and Guide *building and annex, ca. 1915. (From* Norfolk's 36 Percent *[Norfolk, n.d.], pamphlet in the possession of the author)*

(All illustrations are from the Norfolk Journal and Guide *unless noted.)*

P. B. Young and wife Eleanor in Baltimore. (*Baltimore* Afro-American)

P. B. Young, Jr.; William Jones, reporter, Baltimore Afro-American; *and Scottsboro boy, at trial in Scottsboro, Ala., 1931.*

P. B. Young (4th from right) *at meeting of Virginia Commission of Interracial Cooperation, Virginia Union University, Richmond, Oct. 10, 1942. Gordon B. Hancock is on 2d row, extreme right.*

P. B. Young with FEPC members, November 1943. Left to right: Sara Southall, supervisor of employment and service, International Harvester Co., Chicago; Young; Samuel Zemurray, president, United Fruit Co., New Orleans; Malcolm Ross, assistant to the chairman; Rt. Rev. Monsignor Francis J. Haas, chairman; George Johnson, chief investigator; John Brophy, CIO; Milton P. Webster, international vice president, Brotherhood of Sleeping Car Porters, Chicago; and Boris Shishkin, AFofL. (National Archives, Washington, D.C.)

P. B. Young (4th row, extreme right), at Trustees Meeting, St. Paul College, Lawrenceville, Va., May 15, 1944.

P. B. Young, Sr., and Josephine Moseley Young on their marriage day, Feb. 11, 1950. (Courtesy of Mrs. Gladys Whitfield, Norfolk)

P. B. Young (first full figure) at inauguration ceremonies at Virginia State College, Petersburg, Oct. 21, 1950. In center is educator Mary McLeod Bethune.

P. B. Young at Virginia Negro Teachers Association awards ceremony, Norfolk, November 1950.

P. B. Young at greater Norfolk Elks ceremony, ca. November 1950.

P. B. Young at 4-H Club ceremony, Virginia State College, Petersburg, Aug. 26, 1950.

Emancipation Proclamation ceremony, Norfolk, January 1951. Mayor Fred Duck-worth at podium; P. B. Young at extreme right.

The Journal and Guide *in Detroit, March 1951. Detroit had a large Virginia-born population. Jethro C. Pollon (right) manager of Harry's Drug Store in Detroit, termed the* Guide *a "best seller." Satisfied readers are William Merriweather, Leroy Lewis, and Gertrude Ghosson.*

P. B. Young (right) *with Howard University president Mordecai Johnson* (center),
April 12, 1952.

Thomas W. Young (2d row, right) *at National Negro Newspapers Association ceremony at the White House with President Harry Truman, Nov. 22, 1952.*

P. B. Young and the management team of the Guide, 1961. Forefront: John Q. Jordan and John T. Belden. Left to right: William Hubbard, Francis Mitchell, P. B. Young, Jr., P. B. Young, Sr., Thomas W. Young, Robert Branco. (Photo in possession of the author)

P. B. Young awards 25-year plaques to Southall Bass III (left) and Alberto C. Carter (right), 1961. (Courtesy of Southall Bass III)

P. B. YOUNG,

NEWSPAPERMAN

Race, Politics, and Journalism
in the New South,

1910–1962

▪ 1 ▪

Halifax County, N.C.

In casting his lot with the Norfolk *Journal and Guide*, Plummer Bernard Young followed in the footsteps of his father, Winfield Scott Young, himself a newspaperman. The elder Young was born in slavery in 1848. He belonged to a white master of Halifax County, N.C., whose intelligent and compassionate wife tutored him, as she did her own children. By educating him, the master's wife provided the young slave with resources that would distinguish him from other blacks. Indeed, they altered his fortunes.[1]

The Civil War brought emancipation to the slaves but wreaked social and economic havoc throughout the South. In Halifax County survival for both blacks and poor whites was very difficult. The newly freed slaves wandered everywhere in search of employment, family, and friends. Believing that freedom resided in the cities, many drifted into the county's towns—Weldon, Roanoke Rapids, Enfield, and Littleton, where Winfield Young established himself after emancipation. Yet many blacks "shot free" by war could see no alternative but to leave Halifax County.[2]

Further complicating matters, Halifax County following the war had a large population of black orphans—mulatto children categorized as orphans because they were the offspring of white masters, many of whom were killed or dislocated by the war. A disproportionate number of these young people were classified by federal officials as "bastards."[3] Winfield Young, only twelve years old when the war began, was just such an orphan. His father was a white man on a neighboring farm.[4] Little else is known of Winfield Young's early years; the official records do not even reveal the date of his marriage to Sallie Adams, a beautiful twenty-five-year-old mulatto.

It is known, however, that Young was a quiet, unassuming man. His skin was almost white and his hair was black. He was a good family man. By 1880 he and Sallie were the parents of Walter W., born in 1872; John A., in 1875; Mary A., in 1877; and Winfield Scott, in 1878. By all accounts, he was handsome but a bit "too stiff" socially to be a ladies' man. Black people revered him as a person of honor and integrity. He owned two horses, two oxen, one cow, five pigs, twelve chickens, twenty-five dollars' worth of farm machinery, and six acres of woodlands. This was quite an achievement for a man only fifteen years removed from slavery, though there were a few blacks in Littleton's township who owned fifty to one hundred acres.[5] The white community likewise respected Young.

Young's fair complexion, passive social demeanor, land ownership, and, most important, his ability to read and write eased his transition from slavery to freedom. North Carolina's political, physical, and demographic characteristics also aided his passage into freedom. The white people of the small rural communities in this part of the state were independent and self-sufficient, and they tended to treat freedmen of similar bent, whom they knew as neighbors, less harshly than whites in larger cities did. The freedmen's fair complexion and familial relationships within the Halifax community also helped to ease their transition; nonetheless, freedom was extremely difficult for the freedmen of Halifax County. Winfield Young, with his unusual education, quickly emerged as a member of the black elite. Indeed, so ambitious was he that he and his bride considered leaving the county because of its limited economic opportunities, but they were encouraged to remain by James H. Young of Raleigh, a distant relative.

Having decided to stay in Halifax County, Winfield Young sought employment as a Freedmen's Bureau teacher. Like other southern institutions, the Halifax school system suffered disruption. After the war the Freedmen's Bureau attempted to establish schools on large plantations in response to the freedmen's thirst for knowledge. But by April 1868 the bureau's effort had resulted in only five one-room schools, each with an average daily attendance of thirty pupils. Young, one of twenty teachers appointed by the bureau from August 1868 until the fall of 1869, taught fellow blacks the three Rs in a segregated school system in the Rocky Spring community of Halifax County, for a monthly wage of five dollars. Federal authorities repeatedly complained of white apathy and the lack of community financial support, which in November 1868 forced the schools to close temporarily.[6]

During the early 1870s Winfield and Sallie Young moved from Halifax County into the town of Littleton, the county seat. There he operated a small dry goods store. Appointed justice of the peace, he interacted with both blacks and whites. At night and between sales he arbitrated disputes, fined violators of the law, certified legal documents, and officiated at marriage ceremonies. Young's store, in a dilapidated building, was like many a southern country store of the post–Civil War era. It was "the hub of the local universe-market place," serving as a banking and credit source, recreation center, public forum, and news exchange. Young's inventory included everthing from "swaddling clothes to coffins, from plowshares to Christmas candy, from patent medicine to corsets." Next to meat and molasses, he sold more turpentine and Tappan's Sweet Bye-and-Bye Tooth Powder than anything else. Johnny Reb Tobacco, Hoyt's perfume, wild-rose soap, and pewter spoons, knives, and forks were also popular. As proprietor, Young was all things to his community: adviser, holder of family secrets, teacher, funeral arranger, and, at times, an intermediary between estranged lovers. Among the hardships facing people in Halifax County were inadequate medical care and unhealthy working conditions. Here, again, the store proprietor filled the gap, offering an abundance of medicinal potions, including opium powder, Gray's ointment, Fletcher's Castoria, and Dewitt's Witch Hazel. Littleton's lone physician, Dr. Willis Wilcox, purchased these items from Young to treat boils, abcesses, and constipation.[7]

Winfield Young soon became widely known throughout the county. Regular churchgoers, he and Sallie attended Littleton's only black Baptist church, Enon Baptist; occasionally they also attended the black St. Anna's Episcopal Church. In April 1874 he was elected to Halifax County's board of commissioners, and his already heavy town duties now expanded to include the issuance of arrest warrants and eviction notices. He also certified jurors, authorized liquor licenses, and helped with the upkeep of the poor.[8] In 1875 he was reelected, surviving one of the most heated elections in Halifax County's history, in which James Monroe Grizzard, a white commissioner, lost to James E. O'Hara, a black Roman Catholic carpetbagger from New York City. Acrimonious debate and several ballot recounts followed.

O'Hara was not typical of black politicians in Halifax County. He was born in New York City on February 26, 1844. In 1862, in the company of New York missionaries, he visited Union-occupied eastern North Carolina, where he decided to make his home. After the war he served briefly in the state legislature (1868–69) and was elected as a county commissioner in 1874, the same year as Winfield Young. O'Hara's election in 1874 as chairman of the now predominantly black Halifax County Board of Commissioners generated controversy. White Halifaxians regarded him as a radical. A majority of the county commissioners in neighboring Jones and Edgecombe counties were black, and Republicans held most of the second district's other county offices as well. O'Hara dominated politics in Reconstruction Halifax (1865–78). Winfield Young had registered Independent at the beginning of the decade, but by the mid-1870s he, too, was an active Republican. The party named him postmaster of Littleton at an annual salary of $362 in 1877 (raised to $377 in 1879).[9] It is unlikely that he was appointed to such a post without O'Hara's approval.

But, unlike O'Hara, Young was not arrogant, crafty, and dishonest. Halifax County grand juries investigated the fiscal practices of the county commissioners several times between 1874 and 1876, but no one was indicted. In September 1879, however, a grand jury impaneled by the Halifax County Superior Court indicted the previous board of county commissioners—of which Winfield Young was not a member—on three counts of malfeasance in office. The culpability of Winfield Young was never an issue; in fact, the Raleigh *Signal*, published by and for whites, on October 15, 1891, praised him.[10] His contemporaries—James Robinson, Roger Boyd, Helena Harris—confirmed the *Signal's* characterization of Young. Nevertheless, opposition to black leadership was growing. The state's constitutional convention of 1875 ended the popular election of county commissioners, and voters approved the measure in 1876. It was implemented in 1878 as Reconstruction came to an end in North Carolina.

In November 1879 Winfield and Sallie Young traveled by train to Raleigh to attend the annual Negro Day Celebration of the North Carolina Industrial Fair. They marveled at the large crowd, which watched performances by the Oak City Blues, the Oberlin-Vance Guards, and the East Raleigh Guards and was addressed by North Carolina's Democratic governor. "You are now Freedmen," shouted Governor Thomas Jefferson Jarvis, and "your destiny is in your own keeping." "I wish," he noted, "that every colored man had his own home and piece of ground." He admonished blacks to "secure homes" and to "identify with the soil." His sentiments were later echoed by black Republican O'Hara, who in addition condemned migration from the South and chided blacks for complaining. O'Hara championed higher education and the establishment of a state university for blacks.[11]

Winfield and Sallie Young were frequent visitors to Raleigh, drawn by much besides the industrial fair—the annual Emancipation Proclamation Parade, for example, and Young's friendship with O'Hara and other black delegates from Halifax County in the North Carolina legislature. There were black social functions in Raleigh and at nearby Shaw University, a black institution. The Youngs' social network also included Charles N. Hunter, editor of the *Journal of Industry,* (1879–81), and distant cousin James H. Young, one of the most prominent blacks in Raleigh and later publisher of the Raleigh *Gazette* (1884–98).

Early in 1880 Winfield Young joined the True Reformers, a Richmond-based mutual benefit society whose purpose was to "break down crime, licentiousness, poverty, wretchedness and, at the same time . . . protect widows and orphans, in times of distress and want." The True Reformers nursed the sick and buried the dead, but unlike other black fraternal organizations they also paid the heirs an endowment. Moreover, they owned a small training school in North Carolina, a retirement facility in Westham, Virginia, a hotel in Richmond, real estate in Washington, D. C., and they founded the first black-owned bank in America in 1887. As the True Reformers expanded, new insurance societies arose to imitate and "refine" the system.[12]

In May 1884 Winfield Young launched his newspaper career when he established the *True Reformer,* a weekly newspaper in Littleton. True to its slogan, "victory is ours," the newspaper crusaded against crime, licentiousness, poverty, and intemperance. The *True Reformer* advocated "industry, economy, education and Christianity." Young, mindful of his role as a spokesperson for blacks, classified his paper as "non-sectarian." Because of his views on temperance, racial solidarity, and economic advancement, organizations in Halifax and the surrounding counties sought his services as a speaker and crusader. Meanwhile, the *True Reformer* slowly climbed to a circulation of 2,500—no small accomplishment in view of its being published in a community of 1,200 inhabitants.[13]

By 1884 Young had not only successfully made the transition from slavery to freedom, he had risen to a position of leadership in the black community. He exhorted fellow blacks to seek equalization, not integration. Again and again, echoing the words of black leaders across the South, he declared, "we ask but an equal chance before the law, no more, no less." He and other blacks in Halifax took a position unlike that of militant blacks like T. Thomas Fortune, editor of the *New York Age,* who advocated full citizenship for blacks. Young argued that blacks like Fortune could not speak for most blacks because they had never experienced slavery, because they lived in northern cities and functioned in a developing industrial society, whereas the majority of American blacks were illiterate former slaves who lived in the rural South. The capstone of Winfield Young's ideology was the theory of human rights as expressed in the Declaration of Independence. It was the source of his fierce national pride. Like other black newspaper editors and orators, he was proud to declare that he was a "native born American," a "loyal American," and that "this is our Country."[14]

When Fortune asserted that "the Negro should become an independent force in politics," Young and black Republicans in Halifax County demurred. "Ole Winfield could never bring himself to vote for a Democrat," one informant chuckled. But, at the same time, Young and other black party leaders were sensitive to the nuances in national black politics. They realized that "a movement for independence" was gaining momentum in the South.[15] Responding to Republican neglect, violence, and racism, blacks formed Democratic organizations in many northern states. In the 1884 elections T. Thomas Fortune, Monroe Trotter, Robert Purvis, Henry M. Turner, and other national spokesmen temporarily abandoned the Republican party and supported the Democrats. Yet Young and black Republicans in Halifax remained steadfast in their support of the party and of interracial cooperation.

In 1884 Winfield Young had pressing concerns of his own. His attention turned from credit ledgers, staples, and plows to twill, "sugar teats," and bottles in the summer of that year, for he and Sallie were awaiting the birth of another child. Plummer Bernard, the son who would become one of Halifax County's most outstanding black citizens and a national spokesman for southern blacks, was born in a comfortable whitewashed four-room cabin. It was well furnished by nineteenth-century standards. Near the fireplace in the parlor stood Sallie's lady barrelback chair. Crocheted shawls adorned the furniture, and the room boasted a Grafonola for playing Edison records. Sheffield candle holders and Betty lamps stood on the mantel, and Aubusson carpets covered the floor. A grog mug rested on a tier table, and an English gilt mirror adorned the wall.

According to contemporaries, Plummer Bernard Young enjoyed a happy childhood. Like other youngsters, he played marbles and foot-and-a-half, he accompanied his parents to St. Anna's Episcopal Church, and he attended grades one through twelve at the Reedy Creek Academy, a Baptist school, one of several black private schools established in the state by various denominations to fill the need created by the absence of public schools.[16] The Reedy Creek Academy not only gave its students a basic education but also reinforced the religious values of home. Mrs. Effie Hurd, a black Ohioan and the young Plummer Bernard's favorite teacher, often admonished him to "make something out of yourself." Her words were echoed by his father. Much to the delight of Mrs. Hurd and his father, the boy read prolifically at an early age. He devoured the *McGuffey Reader*, Webster's *Speller*, Ray's *Arithmetic*, and the Barnes *Universal History*, stocked in his father's store. Hunting and playing baseball relieved many youngsters from the daily tedium of this small-town life, but Plummer Bernard, not athletically inclined, preferred to read or watch baseball.[17]

During the long winter evenings Winfield Young tutored his son at the store. Years later, the son acknowledged the positive effects of his father's tutoring. He credited much of his learning to the *True Reformer* and to his employment as an errand boy for a local white daily. Additionally, his father's increased focus on the business of the *True Reformer* and consequent relations with black legislators Virgil Barnes, Henry Plummer Cheatham, and John Dancy as well as prominent blacks in Raleigh, North Carolina, and Emporia, Virginia, created an atmosphere in the Young household that affirmed the importance of education.[18]

Plummer Bernard used his bike to deliver the *True Reformer* every Wednesday. He was not known throughout the county, as were several other young men, for his ability to pick cotton or to "wear out a mule." He was occasionally seen in the grocery store and the pharmacy in Halifax, which, unlike Littleton, was "like a little city," full of ox carts, wagons, and buggies from midweek to Saturday but, like Littleton, was "rough" on Saturday night. Neither Plummer Bernard nor his brothers, Winfield and John, were remembered for causing "Donnybrooks" in either community.[19]

Halifax County and the town of Littleton remained predominantly black during Plummer Bernard's early years. Many blacks' homes in Littleton were two- and three-room shanties with outdoor toilets. Seemingly, every home had a pig in the backyard and farm equipment in front. Muddy streets, uncovered food, and unscreened windows invited flies. Although housing was segregated, Littleton's business community was diversified. Blacks owned barber shops, fish markets, cafés, and dry goods stores; whites owned meat markets, variety stores, and livery stables. Hawkins Grocery, Mayo's meat market, Peter Pigford's Fish Market, the Davis Café, and Bob Plummer's Barber Shop were among the best-known black businesses. All of the town's professional barbers were black, but they catered exclusively to white clientele. However, a change in fashion spawned a cadre of white barbers "because white men objected to black men trimming white females hair and massaging their face."[20]

Life in Littleton was dull, especially on weekends. Enon Baptist, the black community's lone Baptist church until the early 1900s, offered some respite. Although services were held during the week, Sunday was the time to "step out." The parishioners came early and stayed late to hear Pastor E. A. Taylor condemn alcohol, licentiousness, loose women, and sin.

Church membership stratified Littleton's black community during the late 1880s. Only ten or fifteen families attended the black St. Anna's Episcopal Church. The paucity of black Episcopalians may have been the consequence of Episcopalian rituals, which required a literate congregation. G. E. Harris, Young, Henry High Faulcon, Cheatham, and O'Hara were leaders in the church and the catalyst behind the movement to establish St. Anna's Episcopal Day School. The church functioned as an instrument to uplift blacks economically and to improve race relations, while channeling students to St. Paul College in Lawrenceville, Virginia, and St. Augustine College in Raleigh, North Carolina, both of which were supported financially by the predominantly white Episcopal Conference of the South. Academically and culturally, black Episcopalians in the South deemed themselves to be "members of the elite," and Young's family were part of that group. [21]

Plummer Bernard Young enjoyed visiting the railroad depot and watching the departure of the northbound trains. Years later he remembered daydreaming of faraway places like Baltimore, New York, and even Boston. Once, while accompanying his father to an emancipation celebration in Raleigh, he rode in the same car with white folks. But what Young remembered most clearly was the tipsy soldiers who loudly exchanged stories about Geronimo, buffalo, and outlaws. He also was excited at the sight of men in cowboy boots from Oklahoma, Texas, and North Dakota, but he attached no significance to their presence, not realizing that they were in all likelihood Populists, members of the Southern Farmers Alliance.

The Young household was probably more inclined than other black Halifaxians to converse about politics and the failure of the political alliance between blacks and Populists. As the century came to a close, blacks in North Carolina politics—both Democratic and Republican—were once again relegated to a powerless position. The breakup of the black Republican and Populist coalition made an indelible impact on Plummer Bernard Young. He listened as his father debated Republican ideology and strategies for survival with black legislators George White, Cheatham, Thomas A. Fuller, and others. He heard his father discuss the Populist candidates with W. H. Warwick, principal of the Reedy Creek Academy, and with Josh Austin, a local businessman. When the black strategy of "I-tickle-you-you-tickle-me" disintegrated at the end of the century, Winfield Young warned blacks "to look out for race as well as party." He admonished them "not to vote for Populists who are not in favor of suffrage." Soon the Republican-Populist alliance collapsed, and blacks in North Carolina were disfranchised. [22]

Between 1900 and 1906 Plummer Bernard attended the predominantly black St. Augustine College in Raleigh, a school funded by the Episcopal church. Young later had "pleasant memories" of his college days. He recalled that in 1903 he was a student in the print shop under "The Reverend Mr. Marvin," and that between 1904 and 1906 he supervised the printing office and attended classes in the "normal" department part time, taking mathematics and history. According to Young, college president Aaron Burtis Hunter considered him a "special student" in charge of printing and so did not list his name in the annual catalog because he was not a full-time student. Young wrote that he received "much inspiration during his matriculation from messers Boyer, Delaney, and Wright." He said he always contributed to the United Negro College Fund, of which St. Augustine was a charter member in 1944, and one year was a campaign cochairman.[23]

St. Augustine advertised itself as "a Normal School and Collegiate Institute with Industrial Department for Colored Students of both sexes." Applicants for admission had to present a certificate of good nature, show a mastery of common and decimal fractions, and be functionally literate. All communication between the sexes, except by permission of the teacher, was strictly forbidden. The objective, according to the catalog, was not only to cultivate womanly qualities in the young girls but "to throw the mantle of protection over all whom parents may entrust."

Young, who was listed in St. Augustine's Annual Catalogue, 1899–1900 as "third year prep," probably had not graduated from Littleton's Reedy Creek Academy. Interestingly, the Thirty-Ninth Annual Catalogue, 1905–1906 lists Young's father as "teacher of printing." Apparently Young successfully completed the preparatory curriculum; he began classes in the normal department on September 25, 1902. At the time his future wife, Eleanor White, the adopted daughter of the college president, was a teacher in the preparatory department. Plummer Bernard studied arithmetic, English, composition, physiology; he read Longfellow's "Evangeline," Tennyson's "Enoch," and Scott's "Lady of the Lake." At the time of his matriculation St. Augustine enrolled 325 students. They rose each morning at 5:30 and were required to attend both morning and evening prayer services.[24]

In 1906 Young married Eleanor Louise White after her graduation from St. Augustine College. His name does not appear on the graduation list or as an alumnus in official university records. Shortly thereafter he returned to Littleton with his bride. In 1907, after the birth on February 15 of their son, Plummer Bernard, Jr., Young accepted a position in Norfolk, Virginia, at twelve dollars a week as a plant foreman for the Journal *and Guide,* the newspaper of the Supreme Lodge Knights of Gideons, a fraternal order to which his father belonged. In early June 1907 Young and his little family made their way to Littleton's railroad depot and boarded Seaboard railroad's 8:30 A.M. Shoofly for the trip to Norfolk and a new career. "Yeah," observed James Robinson, "I remember the day that he left."[25] The Shoofly chugged and coughed its way through Weldon, Rocky Mount, Emporia, and Petersburg, to arrive in Norfolk in the early afternoon.

■ 2 ■

Church Street, Norfolk

When P. B. Young arrived in Norfolk in June 1907, he found "a busy, bustling place." The city of 67,452 was 37 percent black. With its majestic harbor, strategic location on the Chesapeake Bay, and naval base, it proclaimed itself the "Queen City of the South." Norfolk boasted ten railroad lines, twenty steamship lines, and fifteen banks with resources well over $30 million. Not only did it have the largest convention hall and the most beautiful, fully equipped hotel in the South, the Lynnhaven, there were seven other modern hotels accommodating visitors to the city. Employees from the city's eighteen lumberyards, ten fertilizer plants, two breweries, six brick plants, three paper-box factories, nine barrel factories, and numerous railroad facilities traveled to work on fifty-four miles of paved and sewered streets. The city was proud of its 8,131 telephone subscribers, three daily newspapers, race track, and seventy-six churches. Its public school system had an annual budget of $50,000, employing seventy teachers for 3,500 pupils. The city funded eighteen public schools, seven of them black. Norfolk Academy was a private school serving the white community; Norfolk Mission College, a private school serving the black.[1]

The government of this bustling southern city was controlled by whites, led in 1907 by Mayor John G. Riddick. Blacks had been virtually disfranchised by the state constitution of 1902. For blacks, housing was scarce, run-down, and segregated, and there was little economic mobility. But they survived through what historian Louis Harlan calls "deliberate compromise" with whites, with whom they "constantly and cannily" cultivated friendship and goodwill. A booming Norfolk, then, was an ideal town for an enterprising young white man and perhaps for a black one as well.

As the trolley car carrying Young and his family made its way from the railroad depot to the Eureka Lodge on Church Street, the "tallest skyscraper" in Virginia, the thirteen-story National Bank of Commerce, came into view, as well as the heights of the Taylor Building, the Board of Trade, and the Virginia Club Building. However, as the trolley neared Church Street and Norfolk's black community, the streets and lanes became unpaved and muddy. Teeming with black people, noisy Church Street was the only thoroughfare by which motorized vehicles could enter or leave the city. Nevertheless, it had "class"; it represented the lifeblood of Norfolk's black community. One observer rightly remarked, "Church Street had something for everybody" in the black community.[2]

Black business activity in 1907 was centered on Church Street's mile-long business district. There were dry goods stores, shoe shops, grocery stores, and restaurants. The street was always crowded with horses, carriages, carts, and people. It also had a reputation of being rough on Saturday night, when pimps and prostitutes rubbed shoulders with shipyard workers, laborers, and the black elite. Large crowds frequented the Manhattan Theater to watch *Uncle Tom's Cabin;* smaller audiences laughed at *The Smart Set* and *The Grip of Evil* at the Palace. Black sailors and merchant seamen consumed five-cent glasses of Pabst Blue Ribbon and Hoster's beer in Barney Jones's and Sam Lester's saloons; the ladies sipped Reinbran, a malt beverage with low alcoholic content. The noise of the crowd, the loud music, and smells of moonshine, fish, and chitterlings all added to the excitement. But across from Yeargan's Beauty Shop, the "Saints" inside of the Weeping Mary Soul Saving Station remained indifferent to the street noise and crowd. At their nightly revivals, the white-robed saints cakewalked around the pulpit singing "Sign Me Up for the New Jerusalem, Etch My Name on the Stone."

Meanwhile, both men and women surreptitiously jammed the dope dens and "bamas" inside the back rooms of various businesses to snort cocaine. Here a man could meet a nice "filly" or a "tenderloin." Black sailors and merchant seamen patronized Church Street's numerous honky-tonks, saloons, and dance halls where they could show off their skill at dancing the buck-and-wing, the juba, the pastry, and the cakewalk. Inside Lemuel Bright's Mount Vernon Hotel the sailors often attempted to imitate the "jig piano" technique employed by Harry ("Squirrel") Crosby, George ("Sparrow") Kimbrough, Joe Jordan, and "Jelly Roll" Morton, as they sang Ernest Hogan's "All Coons Look Alike to Me." Ragtime music was still in vogue in Norfolk in 1907.[3]

Store windows displayed large cardboard posters announcing forthcoming appearances at Hampton Institute's Ogden Hall of the Ethiopian

Dancers, the Fisk Jubilee Singers, and vaudeville shows from New York. Storefront churches proudly displayed pictures of Tuskegee Institute's Phelps Hall Bible Training School. Huge cardboard advertisements appeared on light poles each August to announce excursions to Cape May, New Jersey, and to the "Great Negro State Fair" in Raleigh, North Carolina.

Church Street was a black business center of regional importance. On a typical weekend shoppers from Portsmouth, Suffolk, Elizabeth City County, Virginia, and Gates County, North Carolina, rubbed shoulders in Pender's Grocery, the Riddick and Romanii beauty parlors, and Wiliams's Fish Market. Farmers from the surrounding area sold fresh vegetables in the open-air market while hucksters hawked everything from the divine message to the latest medicinal concoctions. At Madam Law's Beauty Shop on a typical Saturday morning, the clientele might include both the wife of Norfolk's most prominent black attorney and the daughter of an Elizabeth City County sharecropper.

Norfolk's black lawyers, doctors, and dentists patronized Charles S. Carter's Tailor Shop, Charlie Hardy's Barber Shop, Sim's Shoe Repair, and Lincoln's Optical Shop. Norfolk's black bourgeoisie often described the Church Street strip as "ugly and grotesque"; however, because white merchants in the main business district refused to serve blacks, elite blacks mingled with those well below their station at J. J. Corprew's Shoe Repair Shop, Stevenson's Jewelry, and Sam Tucker's Restaurant. White merchants, however, recognizing the purchasing power of Norfolk's rising black middle class, did operate black-managed and -staffed clothing outlets on Church Street. Generally, whites operated the grocery stores, pharmacies, and the butcher, jewelry, and specialty shops, while blacks almost exclusively owned the cafés, barber shops, funeral parlors, and banks.

The merchants of Church Street suffered the plight of black businessmen throughout the South. Although they championed black capitalism and a separate black entrepreneurial class, they often complained of discriminatory business practices that limited their clientele and reduced profits. Some, like their counterparts in New York and Chicago, served more than an exclusively Negro market. Such enterprises as tailoring and shoemaking also catered to whites; Miss Goldie Garrett's Millinery, Alston's Rubber, and Charles S. Carter's tailoring shop are examples. A few of the Church Street merchants had a "tremendous volume" of business, and their profit margins often equaled, and probably in a few cases exceeded, that of the downtown white merchants.[4]

The leading Church Street merchants were also leaders in the black community. Charles S. Carter was named to the vestry of Grace Episcopal Church in 1902. Others were ministers, and a good number served on boards of deacons for such churches as Bank Street, First Baptist, St. John's AME, and First Calvary. Most businessmen maintained interlocking memberships in elite black social organizations like the Odd Fellows, Royal Knights of King David, Knights of Pythias, and True Reformers. Their wives were active Tents, Daughters of Bethel, and Lady Elks. Their children played together at church picnics, the junior YMCA, and the Girl Scouts of America. The city's black merchants formed a cohesive community. By word of mouth, church bulletins, and flyers, they matched wits and prices with white merchants, as both attempted to corral customers. The merchants, mainly mulatto, appealed to race pride, telling fellow blacks to buy black. They visualized a separate entrepreneurial class with three purposes: economic uplift, racial solidarity, and patriotism.

Norfolk's leading black doctors, lawyers, dentists, and pharmacists maintained offices on Church Street. They, along with black postal employees, domestics, and letter carriers, were looked up to by the merchants because of their affluence. Some of the more wealthy professionals aided the merchants with interest-free loans. The merchants, in turn, offered employment to wives and children of the black professionals, thereby shielding them from the full force of southern racism.

The merchants of Church Street perennially complained about crime, the absence of proper drainage and sewage, and the shortage of qualified help. But whites often turned a deaf ear, viewing black businessmen as inept and their businesses as inefficient. Though they may have acknowledged that the lack of operating capital, the tighter bank loans, and inexperience were obstacles for blacks, they could point to the captive market as an advantage. Blacks monopolized certain occupations, which explains the immense wealth enjoyed by a few black merchants. To whites, this was proof that black complaints of the debilitating effects of segregation were untrue, and they challenged blacks to learn better business methods, particularly accounting and bookkeeping. But Church Street merchants persisted, complaining about a lack of sewers and insufficient police protection from shoplifters. They believed that their businesses, with but few exceptions, were not only equal to white merchants but much better.

Sociologist E. Franklin Frazier described Negro businesses as perpetuating a social myth, propagated by the Atlanta University Conference on the Negro in Business in 1898 and by Booker T. Washington's book *The Negro in Business* (1907). Norfolk's black businessmen were very much a part of this world of make-believe. Their interlocking memberships in numerous civic, fraternal, and social organizations shielded them from some of the harsh economic and social realities of American life. This business circle would be the center of Young's world for many years to come. Economically and socially, the businessmen ranked below Norfolk's black professional elite but well above shipyard workers and unskilled laborers. They feared the loss of their status and sought to assure their future by encouraging their offspring to seek professional careers in medicine, dentistry, and law. Most had attended college or were graduates of Howard University, Hampton Institute, and Norfolk Mission College. Most, like Young, were Republicans. They championed the conservative self-help philosophy of Booker T. Washington, which they extolled at annual meetings of the National Negro Business League and during Norfolk's annual emancipation celebration. Indeed, Norfolk's most prominent black businessmen in 1907, W. H. C. Brown, owner of Bute Street's Brown Savings Bank, was a personal friend of Washington and often a member of the local entourage that entertained the Tuskegeean on his visits to tidewater Virginia.[5]

Black capitalism, generally, reflected Washington's ideas concerning racial self-help. Such black enterprises as the Richmond-based Southern Aid Society of Virginia, Inc., the Norfolk Home Building and Loan Association, and the Brown Savings Bank were highly successful businesses in 1907, selling life insurance, burial certificates, and retirement policies to blacks throughout the South. Previously, black social and religious societies had issued such policies, but many had been forced out of business by a new Virginia law of March 25, 1904, that required insurance companies to deposit a minimum of $10,000 in bonds with the state treasurer.[6] One of the first things P. B. Young did when he arrived in Norfolk, like many a rising black man of the time, was to purchase a burial policy from the United Order of True Reformers. When that organization folded a few years later, Young moved over to Southern Aid's archrival, the North Carolina Mutual and Provident Association of Durham, North Carolina.

Norfolk's black business community, criticized by W. E. B. Du Bois for its lack of leadership and poor support for racial progress, nonetheless took great pride in its achievements.[7] It helped to sponsor the Emancipation Proclamation Parade and Celebration, an annual black event, and the 1907 Jamestown Exposition Day Ceremony, a public, segregated event that among other things honored the arrival of blacks in America in 1619. The highlight of the week-long emancipation celebration was a parade down Church Street, followed by a speech and a mass rally at a church. Norfolk's blacks used the event to express their patriotism and loyalty; black entrepreneurs, to highlight the success of Washington's philosophy of self-help and solidarity.

For a black businessman, affiliation with the National Negro Business League, spearheaded by the Tuskegeean, meant increased recognition and possibly even political patronage. Businessmen reasoned that associating with a national Republican such as Washington might help end the schism within the GOP between whites and blacks, who were angered by white leaders' continued neglect of black interests. Norfolk's black business community frequently cooperated with league officials in other tidewater cities to assure support whenever prominent blacks visited the area. Washington himself visited Richmond in 1902 and Norfolk in 1907 and 1908.[8]

Prominent black Norfolk businessmen were members of the Negro Development and Exposition Company, one of the sponsors of the Jamestown Exposition in August 1907. Richmond attorney Giles B. Jackson, a black, organized the Norfolk exhibit and worked quietly with Washington and President Theodore Roosevelt to obtain a $100,000 federal appropriation to pay for the display. Overall, the exposition was a huge success; "approximately 750,000 persons, at the rate of from 3,000 to 12,000 a day, by actual count," visited the exhibit. Dozens of displays touted Norfolk's black businesses, along with musical scores, needlework, inventions, and other "evidences of black progress from throughout the South." Black financiers W. H. C. Brown and William Rich of Norfolk, along with black attorneys James M. Harrison and J. Eugene Diggs, were in the local entourage welcoming President Roosevelt and Washington to Norfolk.[9]

The Jamestown Exposition made an indelible impression on P. B. Young, youthful reporter for the lodge's *Journal and Guide*. It was held at Norfolk's White City (advertised as the largest Negro amusement park in the South). It attracted scores of blacks from the surrounding areas, from as far south as Alabama, and from as far north as Boston. The *Star of Zion*, a black newspaper, called the exposition a "tremendous outpouring of beauty, brilliance and brawn."[10] J. H. Reynolds, Norfolk businessman and minister, and J. J. Mainor, Young's employer and publisher of the lodge's *Journal and Guide*, briefly addressed the crowd. Enthusiasm intensified when the exposition's president, H. St. George Tucker, introduced Booker T. Washington as the "greatest American in America."

Prolonged applause and waving flags and handkerchiefs greeted Washington as he approached the flag-draped podium. He extolled the virtues of self-help, industry, and morality. In a trembling voice he cried, "Whatever victory the Negro has made, has been a peace victory, and not a victory of violence or war." He was repeatedly interrupted by applause and fervent cries of "Amen." Following his address, his alma mater, Hampton Institute, regaled him with its thirty-piece band, and 250 students marched in review. Hundreds thronged forward to greet the native son. Such a dramatic display of support for Washington and his philosophy surely impressed Norfolk.

The young newcomers Eleanor and P. B. Young found the Norfolk of 1907 to be a very sociable community. News of social events spread rapidly in the black community—by fliers and church bulletins, by word of mouth, and by its only black newspaper, the lodge's *Journal and Guide*. The Odd Fellows, Royal Knights of King David, Knights of Pythias, and Daughters of Bethel were among the more prominent social groups. The Bayshore Hotel and Hampton Institute's Ogden Hall, both located in nearby Hampton, functioned as centers of black culture, where elite blacks like Young and his wife and their friends could hear black soprano Myrtle Moss, black pianists David and Clara Manners, and the Fisk Jubilee Singers. They could travel by ferry to the Hampton Roads peninsula to cheer at the traditional football game between Norfolk Mission College and Hampton Institute. Horse racing was popular among all elements of the black community, and in fact, several wealthier blacks owned some of the faster race horses.[11] Other events that attracted Norfolk's blacks were Negro Day at the Rocky Mount, North Carolina, Tobacco Fair and the Great Negro State Fair in Raleigh. The latter was a major social event for blacks in the upper South during the first decade of this century.

The social organizations kept blacks informed of important social and political events and upcoming visits of prominent blacks. They also served as reception committees for visiting members. In Norfolk they competed by producing stage shows and by giving awards for the best poetry and literature.

Eleanor Young, like her husband, would find much to do in her new community. Elite black women, like their white counterparts of the time, were expected to contribute time and energy to philanthropic activities. Moreover, they hoped to boost the morale and social acceptance of black women; they, too, functioned within the elite black hierarchy. The women organized clubs and schools to teach sewing and cooking and founded lending libraries.

Mrs. Laura Titus, the best known of the group, taught hundreds of women to cook and to sew in her Norfolk home. An 1876 graduate of Hampton Institute, she established a home for wayward girls and worked on behalf of black female migrants who often arrived in Norfolk without food or shelter. "It's time to dip down our buckets among the masses,"

ARNULFO L. OLIVEIRA MEMORIAL LIBRARY
1825 MAY STREET
BROWNSVILLE, TEXAS 78520

she once asserted, and her concern led her to establish the Southern Industrial School to teach the migrants how to cook and to sew.[12] Many of the women she taught were later employed by white families. Boys, too, were taught that the "thumb is not the thimble finger," and a "running stitch is not a walkover stitch." When Young arrived in Norfolk in 1907, Mrs. Titus, then a retired public school teacher, was the most prominent woman in the black community. Her home, with its large collection of books, served as a library and museum. She encouraged black mothers to join the Mary S. Peak Book Club and to read books such as *Kind and True, Peep of the Day,* and *For Mother.*

The motto of the Virginia Federation of Colored Women, "Lifting as we climb," expressed its goals to improve city streets and sewage; to house wayward girls; to assist the old, poor, and orphaned; and to uplift black women. Working for similar goals were the Norfolk Association of Colored Women, Colored King's Daughters, the women's auxiliary of Lott Carey, the YWCA's Christian Temperance Union, and the black National Nurses Association.

The church was another of the many centers of black social life. The Youngs found a thriving religious community when they arrived in Norfolk in 1907. Each of the thirty black churches in the city had a hierarchy of its own. Because meeting places were limited, the churches in 1907 were the center of Norfolk's black social life. Prayer meetings, benevolent society meetings, socials, festivals, religious revivals, oyster suppers, ice cream sales, weddings, funerals, and courtships—all took place within the walls of the church.

Most of the churches were Baptist, including New Hope and Macedonia. Lone Star and St. Mark also served the black Christian community. The one black Catholic church, St. Joseph, was headed by Edward J. Houlihan, and there was no black Presbyterian congregation, even though the United Presbyterian Church, USA, funded Norfolk Mission College's 500 black students. Next to the black Baptist community, the African Methodist Episcopal Church (AME) had the largest number of churches, among them, the Zion Mission, Metropolitan Zion, and John Brown AME. Grace Protestant Episcopal Church, one of the oldest and most prominent churches, located on the corner of Cumberland and Kent streets, was founded in 1883. Its pastor in 1907 was the Reverend William Patterson Burke. Its membership included a number of Norfolk's prominent black lawyers, dentists, and physicians.[13]

P. B. Young, Sr., and his wife, Eleanor Louise, joined Grace Episcopal Church on Sunday, July 1, 1907, thus becoming part of an organization that was already firmly established in Norfolk's black social, business, and educational community.[14] Young's affiliation with the Grace Episcopal Church accounted in part for his rapid business success. The church-business connection was evident, for example, when the Tidewater Bank was organized in 1918: Young was elected its president; Dr. G. Hamilton Francis, vice president; G. W. C. Brown, assistant secretary; and attorney J. Eugene Diggs, general counsel—all were members of the vestry of Grace Episcopal Church.

Norfolk's black churches were also a means for protesting inequities in the black community and dramatizing to whites the black community's loyalty and patriotism. Nearly all the ministers were Republican, and their sermons often reflected the Washingtonian views of self-help and racial solidarity. They believed that material advancement achieved through thrift, hard work, Christian charity, and economic chauvinism would bring recognition of blacks' constitutional rights and would break down oppression and segregation. The underlying militancy was presented in a conciliatory manner to the white South, as the clergy tended to soft-pedal blacks' grievances.

In 1907 most blacks in Virginia could not vote, and at the time Young arrived in Norfolk, black influence had been effectively eliminated from state politics. The Republican party had begun to reshape itself into a party of whites. In 1907 Governor Claude A. Swanson summed up the white conception of the black's place in Virginia politics: "We have no Negro problem here. . . . The suffrage question has ceased to be a subject of discussion or agitation."[15]

Richmond, a center of black political activity in Virginia in 1907, had a larger and more militant black community than Norfolk, with a longer tradition of national involvement. Richmond attorney Giles B. Jackson and John Mitchell, editor since 1884 of the Richmond *Planet*, the largest Negro weekly in Virginia, fought disfranchisement. Yet, when it became a reality, they seemingly resigned themselves to the hopelessness of the situation and eschewed politics. Mitchell's editorials tone became "more conciliatory" as he began to identify more with Washington's economic uplift approach to race relations. In the presidential election of 1908, candidates of both parties ignored black voters. Nevertheless, Booker T. Washington urged the remaining few thousand black voters in Virginia to vote for Republican William H. Taft; the Richmond *Planet* counseled blacks to "practice individualism."[16]

Despite the obstacles, Young found black political leaders in 1907 who were loyal and active members of the national Republican party under Theodore Roosevelt's leadership. They believed that Washington "had the president's ear" and that the best people still voted Republican. They had good reason to try to stay active in Republican politics, where they could forge relationships with leaders in the white community, especially the leading industrialists. One was Homer Ferguson, president of the Newport News Shipbuilding and Dry Dock Company, the largest single employer of blacks in the area. It "not only hired Negroes in all capacities but even took Negro boys as apprentices to the trades." There were no blacks in the highly skilled jobs, electricians or bell hangers, but many of the over 3,300 employees in 1902 were black semiskilled laborers, hired as caulkers, riveters, bolters, drillers, carpenters, and chippers. Ferguson was a pioneer who employed "more blacks in more occupational classifications than any other shipyard" in the nation. His employment practices followed a "paternalistic" pattern for many years; "the duty" to employ blacks was part of this policy.[17]

Young met Ferguson in 1907 while serving as a reporter for the lodge's *Journal and Guide*. Ferguson that year used his influence to make the Jamestown Exposition a success. Not only did he endorse Washington's philosophy, but the industrialist met often with the Tuskegeean when he visited tidewater Virginia. Washington challenged others in Norfolk to emulate Ferguson and urged the black shipyard workers to cooperate with the management. By 1909 Young and Ferguson were collaborating to make Norfolk the headquarters of a proposed Semi-Centennial Exposition.[18]

The Norfolk that P. B. Young found when he arrived in 1907 was a city of contrasts. Whites had the most and the best. Blacks had resources, though almost entirely within their own hierarchy. Norfolk was controlled by whites. But the black community had its own elite group, and P. B. Young was to become a leader among other leaders. He rolled up his sleeves and set out to make his fortune in Norfolk—to make a way and to find a place.

During his first years in Norfolk, Young worked hard to establish himself. He acquainted himself with his father's friends in the True Reformers, the Royal Society of King David, and the Knights of Gideons. He corresponded with Booker T. Washington, forming an association that would last more than a decade and would fortify his economic conservatism. He espoused the fundamentals of Washington's philosophy for the rest of his life. Indeed, he adopted "Build Up, Don't Tear Down" as the motto of the Norfolk *Journal and Guide*.

The *Guide* had its origin in a fraternal organization. Although such "secret" groups were supposed to look after the sick and bury the dead, many had far greater vision. They founded banks, newspapers, mercantile establishments, real estate companies, and other enterprises, many of which have survived.[19] The *Guide* was originally christened the *Gideon Safe Guide;* then it became the *Lodge Journal and Guide;* and later it emerged as a secular newspaper, simply the *Norfolk Journal and Guide.*

The Supreme Lodge Knights of Gideon, a benevolent fraternal club, was organized and chartered in Norfolk in January 1897. Aside from its fraternal and insurance features, it had interests in journalism, banking, education, and child welfare. The Gideons were the pioneers in launching black businesses in Norfolk. In 1900 they formed the Guide Publishing Company, which operated a job printing office and printed the official lodge organ. The first office was located on Bute Street. The equipment was meager, consisting of a small hand press and a few fonts of type. Young would later carry on for a while at this location and then move to larger quarters at 733 Church Street.

Even in its early days the newspaper was a creditable sheet, consisting of four six-column pages. The first editor was J. Henry Cromwell, regarded as a militant. As an editorial writer, he was admired for his pungent prose and feared because of his lack of objectivity. Georgia Brooks (later Mrs. Leon S. Roberts) was the city editor, and John Nicholas Brown was the Portsmouth representative and associate editor. Charles H. Butts, the foreman of the mechanical department, was regarded as a first-class printer, although the equipment he manipulated was antiquated.

The January 14, 1905, edition of the *Lodge Journal and Guide* is the only known copy in existence. It mirrors black journalism in the South and offers a peek at Norfolk's social history. The columns of page one are entitled: "Smithfield Dots," "Sewell's Point News," "Philadelphia Intelligence" and "Dan Cupid Again—The Victor Is." By happenstance, the article on Dan Cupid details the marriage of the grandmother of P. B. Young's second wife in Norfolk's Bank Street Baptist Church. But more important perhaps, this issue contains the Knights of Gideon's Lodge Directory listing the location and the membership of the various lodges in Virginia and North Carolina. Somewhat equally important in this extant issue are publisher Cromwell's editorials and the newspaper's Business Directory.

In an editorial entitled "Education and Conduct," Cromwell criticized Hampton Institute students for their "deplorable conduct" and "bad taste" aboard a Seaboard passenger train. Cromwell admonished the students "to take heed" and to restrain themselves. Such conduct by students from one of the black community's most elite educational institutions clearly perplexed him. Five years before P. B. Young, Sr., assumed control of the Lodge's *Journal and Guide*, the paper demonstrated a social commitment to the community.

In February 1907 the *Guide* had a circulation of 600 copies weekly, most of which went to lodge members. In the spring of that year, the Jamestown Exposition was to open in Norfolk, and business was looking up. When Butts resigned as foreman of the plant to enter the postal service, the owners engaged the services of Plummer B. Young, just out of St. Augustine College, to take charge of the plant.[20] Young on his arrival was confronted by equipment the likes of which he had never seen. One was a Prouty newspaper press, a hand-operated device that printed two small pages at the rate of 300 an hour. He persuaded the owners to discard this contraption and to install a Babcock drum cylinder power press. Although it, too, printed only two pages, it did so faster and better. Young made other minor improvements, including the addition of a power-operated job press and editorial improvements in the paper. The circulation increased to 1,000 by the end of 1907.

In the spring of 1908 the general conference of the African Methodist Episcopal church met in Norfolk, bringing not only more than a thousand visitors to the city but new business to the *Guide*. Many candidates for bishop and general offices flocked to the *Guide* office to have their campaign literature printed. The conference itself contracted with the *Guide* to produce a four-page, five-column paper, to be delivered to the church at ten each morning. To meet the schedule, the Gideons employed additional manpower: four fast hand compositors, who averaged two galleys of 8-point type a day (the output in 1920 of the average Linotype machine in an hour and a half), a pressman, and two other staffers. The staff was later augmented by Iverson R. Quick and Henry Cheatham Young.

In the spring of 1909 when editor J. Henry Cromwell resigned, business manager Frank E. Puryear called in the plant foreman and mentioned the matter of finding a new editor. "I'll take it," replied Young. Without further ceremony he was made editor of the lodge's *Journal and Guide* in addition to his duties as foreman. The twenty-four-year-old editor embarked immediately upon an effort to bring the paper closer to community life. It would publish more news of local activities, and its editorial policy would be directed to building a cohesive community sentiment. By the end of 1909 circulation had reached 1,500 copies weekly.

The years 1908 and 1909 were hard business years for fraternal organizations. The state insurance department imposed new regulations that required them to restrict operations largely to their insurance features. The Gideons, who would also liquidate their bank in 1910, decided to go out of the printing and publishing business. They told Young of their plans to sell the property. "I'll take it," was his reply. Papers were drawn up and the sale consummated. For $3,050 he purchased the job printing plant and the newspaper, by this time a thriving four-page sheet with a circulation of 500. It is unclear where Young obtained the money to purchase the paper. He may well have borrowed it from a local white banker who was impressed with the youthful and ambitious P. B. Young and his wife Eleanor. The banker was probably familiar with the social and economic philosophy of the True Reformers and recognized that Young would use the *Guide* to champion Washington's philosophy throughout Virginia. Young knew that the physical plant was overpriced, but he was eager for the opportunity. He immediately took into partnership his brother, Henry Cheatham Young, whom he made plant foreman. For a year the business operated under this partnership, after which it was chartered with P. B. Young as president, his wife as treasurer, and H. C. Young as secretary. Young substituted "Norfolk" for "Lodge" in the title of the paper. Thus was born the *Norfolk Journal and Guide*.

Once it was incorporated, the company could launch its first real expansion. A larger press—a Babcock drum cylinder large enough to increase the page size to seven columns—was installed, as was a folding machine. Then, in early 1913, Young undertook a daring step for a small newspaper with the installation of a $1,800 Unitype typesetting machine that set movable foundry type. It speeded up production considerably, but the Unitype never was as successful as the Mergenthaler machines, and it was soon declared obsolete. Despite this slight setback, Young remained interested in labor-saving capital improvements. By 1930 his would be a fully modern plant.

The first real setback the *Guide* suffered under its new owners occurred in the morning of December 28, 1913, when its Church Street plant was nearly destroyed by a fire that originated in the lodge and dance hall above it. Almost all the machinery, stocks, records, and files were lost. Young quickly made arrangements for getting out the paper while the plant was being restored, and the *Guide* never missed an issue. The fire destroyed all the newspaper files up to and including December 1913, an irreparable loss. As much of the old machinery as could be salvaged was removed to 620 Queen Street. Much equipment, including a Mergenthaler Linotype and two Chandler and Price platen presses, was added, and the business operated there until January 1917, when the Youngs purchased a brick structure at 711-719 East Olney Road.

Meanwhile, the *Guide* gradually grew. The number of copies sold weekly in 1919 was 4,000, by which time the paper had increased to eight pages. Its circulation then extended throughout tidewater Virginia and northeastern North Carolina. The Youngs adopted the trade name Guide Quality Printing for the commercial printing department of the Guide Publishing Company.

It was not Young's political astuteness alone that accounted for the success of the *Guide* and his own rising prominence. A *Guide* columnist, on a visit to the office in February 1917, asked, "What is the secret of the *Guide's* success?" Young's wife Eleanor was one reason. Moreover, he wrote, "These young men" (P. B. Young and his sons Thomas and P. B., Jr.) "come from old stock." He reminded readers of his father's career as a newspaper publisher. Winfield Young was now the *Guide's* circulation manager, having joined the staff soon after the disastrous fire of 1913, and he also edited a column entitled "Notes from the Field." On trips to South Boston, Virginia, in April and June 1917, Winfield Young reported that the *Guide* was "much admired" and that "every prominent businessman reads the *Guide*." In September 1917, at the 37th Zion Union Conference in South Hill, Virginia, the elder Young wrote, "It took them only a short while to hand over $21.00 for subscriptions to the *Guide*." The *Guide*, in short, was a family business.[21]

Early in his career Young resolved that the *Guide* would be a link between the leaders of both races. The role of the black newspaper, he wrote in 1917, was to effect social and economic changes in the black community. He repeatedly reminded his readers that "in the assertion of one's rights, it is not necessary to be vulgar or bumptious. Let us make the most, not the least, of the splendid opportunities we have."[22] Because of his convictions, Young quickly established himself as the spokesman for blacks in Norfolk. The most influential blacks—the Church Street merchants—were too reticent, he thought, and the black clergymen were too otherworldly. Young was able to maneuver himself into a position of leadership in part because of his affiliations with the *Guide*, the Grace Episcopal Church, and various civic and business organizations. His newspaper was an important disseminator of social, civic, and religious news. The Grace Episcopal Church—he was elected to the vestry in April 1910—was a bulwark in the black community in Norfolk.[23] It was a congregation that included the Church Street merchants and officials of the Norfolk chapters of the True Reformers, Knights of Pythias, and the Royal Knights of King David. When he assumed ownership of the *Guide* in 1910, Young promptly also became associated with the Norfolk chapters of the Negro Business League and the Negro Organization Society, a black civic organization. Young was well on his way to establishing himself not only as a respectable member of the community, but as a leader as well. He had found a place.

▪ 3 ▪

Washingtonian Thought

P. B. Young's rise to prominence was due in large part to his approach to race relations, which was strongly rooted in the accommodationist philosophy of Booker T. Washington.[1] Washington's ascendancy coincided with one of the most heightened periods of overt racial intolerance in America since the Civil War. As Booker T. Washington's philosophy of land ownership, economic self-help, and racial solidarity gradually achieved acceptance by many blacks, Young's father, Winfield Young, adopted Washington's philosophy as a temporary substitute for political activity. Undoubtedly, the conversation in the Young home during P. B. Young's adolescent years championed the efficacy of Washington's philosophy.

At age twenty, P. B. Young founded, edited, and published the *Argus*, a monthly magazine devoted to religion, morality, education, and industry. In a letter to Washington dated April 19, 1904, Young termed the *Argus* "a new enterprise" and requested Washington's assistance in order to secure its financial stability. Washington responded favorably a few days later. Also, P. B.'s wife, Eleanor White Young, firmly identified with Washington's beliefs. Shortly after their move to Norfolk in 1907, Young met Washington, and he was usually a member of the entourage that accompanied Washington during his numerous visits to tidewater Virginia between 1908 and 1915. Their friendship lasted until Washington's death in 1915.

Washington visited twice in 1912, and on each occasion Young was a member of the delegation that met privately with him. Following Washington's address at the Hampton Negro Conference in July 1912, Young accompanied him as he toured Norfolk and later as he addressed black and white workers at the Newport News Shipyard. The entourage then escorted Washington to a dinner at the "We-Us" Hotel (black), where Washington urged the National Association of Colored Workmen and Skilled Laborers of America to cooperate with the white shipyard management. "You are lucky to have Homer Ferguson, owner of the Newport News Shipyard, as your employer," he declared. He asserted that "black laborers in Virginia receive more pay in a week than white workers in southern Europe earn in a month." His remarks were designed to foster interracial goodwill and to solidify the position of black workers at the shipyard.[2]

The *Journal and Guide* endorsed the speech and urged other industrialists to emulate Homer Ferguson's progressivism. Young also alluded to the loose agreement between the shipyard management, the unions, and the *Guide*. Management recognized the potential of the black union as a source of labor in case of a strike by white workers and gave tacit approval to the black union. The black workers, realizing their precarious position, muffled their criticism of racial practices at the shipyard. Young and the *Guide* were looked upon by both groups as a mirror of black opinion. Young, like his Tuskegee mentor, tempered his criticism of shipyard management and the exclusionary policies of the white union in exchange for the better employment for black workers. Unskilled laborers initially constituted the bulk of the black union membership, but a few blacks were employed as carpenters, welders, machinists, and in other skilled trades. Young reasoned that a black union might curb the erosion of black skilled jobs. The young editor hoped better wages would help build an independent black entrepreneurial class and enhance the purchasing power of Norfolk's black community.

Young knew that an independent black industrial class could not develop without a prosperous commercial and financial group to provide the capital. The increase and prosperity of Norfolk's black entrepreneurs coincided with Young's dual approach to the race question. The economically functional Negro would be in an excellent bargaining position from which to demand his full rights and protection under the law. Black industrialist and entrepreneurs would gradually mitigate a prejudice against blacks that could never be legislated away. If everything else failed, there would always be the alternative of total segregation within Norfolk's self-sustaining black community. As Washington spoke in Norfolk, Young had already set into motion forces designed to transmute the social ideologies of economic individualism into concrete results. Economic developments in Norfolk during the 1920s would prove his wisdom.

Washington's visits to Virginia were occasionally sponsored by the Negro Organization Society (NOS), whose self-help philosophy resembled that of the True Reformers, the Knights of Pythias, and similar black organizations. Washington was a pillar of the NOS, and Young, along with the Church Street merchants and black professionals in Norfolk, sanctioned the group's activities. Its motto, "Better homes, better schools, better health, and better farms," appealed to whites as well, including Hampton's president, H. B. Frissell; President Woodrow Wilson; Edwin Alderman, president of the University of Virginia; and Virginia governors William Hodge Mann, Henry C. Stuart, and Westmoreland Davis. They supported the NOS because it was not a threat to the South's racial balance.[3]

Young championed the NOS because it functioned primarily through the black church, the Negro Business League, the Negro Farmers Organization, and black civic organizations. He probably visualized increased circulation for the *Guide* and the enhancement of his own image as a leader. To accentuate his attachment to the society, Young frequently featured Allen Washington, its president, on the front page. Allen Washington, much older than Young, became one of his closest advisers. Undoubtedly, it was he who was responsible for Young's meteoric rise in the NOS during the war years. Young, who represented the Virginia State Negro Business League at the NOS annual convention, was usually a featured speaker.

In response to a request from the NOS, Booker T. Washington returned to Virginia in May 1913 to tour the tidewater counties of Northampton, Accomack, Mathews, and Gloucester on what the New York *Evening Post* called "A Trip of Race Adjustment." Accompanied by black educators R. R. Moton, the Reverend A. A. Graham of Phoebus, and Young, at every stop Washington was hailed as the "Moses of Negro people." Interracial capacity crowds heard Washington preach the doctrine of reliability to Negro labor. After Washington returned to Tuskegee, Young wrote to him, observing "We are doing all in our power to further the movement in this territory."[4]

In November 1913 in Richmond, Young and Washington met again at the first annual convention of the NOS, which met jointly with the Negro Business League. Young was a delegate. The Richmond *Times-Dispatch* called the convention "the greatest audience of colored people ever assembled in Virginia."[5] A number of prominent whites also attended. Besides Washington, Young, and Governor Mann, the conferees included S. C. Mitchell, president of the Medical College of Virginia; J. M. Gandy, president of the State Normal School, Petersburg (later Virginia State College); Maggie Walker, founder of St. Luke Bank; and John Mitchell of the Richmond *Planet*. The conference also attracted white delegates from the Southern Sociological Congress, a liberal interracial group, and the University Commission on Race Relations, an interdisciplinary organization of southern white college professors, and was sponsored by organizations representing every phase of black life and culture.

Washington admonished the 4,000 delegates to "stay down South and get close to the soil." "Make yourself industrious," he said; "let your promise be as a law." Several hundred white delegates gave him a thunderous ovation. Other prominent speakers addressed the objectives of the conference—better homes, better schools, better farms, and better health. The delegates and their leaders actively sought the sanction and approval of whites. In their view, the best way to improve the condition of blacks was to win the support of the best whites in the South. For their part, whites viewed the NOS as "purely benevolent and altruistic." It challenged no stereotypes; its sole purpose was "to weld all other [black] organizations into a solid unit for morality, health, and education." The NOS was, said the New York *Evening Post*, "proof of goodwill."[6]

Young called the convention an "unprecedented gathering" and, like both Governor Mann and Washington, thought that it was proof of interracial goodwill. The conferees lauded Governor Mann for his sympathetic understanding, and in turn the governor pledged his support to end lynching and to stem the tide of black migration to the North. Along with Washington, Gandy, and others, he too urged blacks to remain in the South, to become more industrious, and to seek the friendship of whites.[7]

Booker T. Washington was again the main speaker at the second annual NOS convention in November 1914. Not since William Jennings Bryan had spoken during the presidential election campaign of 1896 had Norfolk's Armory Hall held such a large assemblage. The crowd was conservatively estimated at 4,500 people, of which 1,000 were white.[8]

Washington lauded blacks' progress in the South and condemned black migration to the North. "The entire South is dependent upon the Negro," he shouted, as he challenged blacks to seek the cooperation of whites and to take advantage of the South's soil and climate. "Build up, don't tear down," he exhorted, "own land, build your own homes, and start a bank account." Waving his arms and pounding the podium, Washington asserted, "It is at the bottom of life that we begin, and not at the top." He noted the value of having "level-headed, conservative, and able colored leaders." He enthusiastically praised the NOS and Young and his *Guide* for their efforts "to remove saloons and dens of vice" from Norfolk's black community.[9]

After Washington's address, the *Guide* reported, several hundred admirers rushed forward to greet him. Women waved white handkerchiefs, and Hampton Institute's band marched in review. Young was "impressed" with Norfolk's splendid show of support for Washington and with the "efficient and useful men" of the NOS. To Young's thinking, "a warm and personal letter" from President Wilson and the presence of such distinguished whites as Virginia's governor Henry C. Stuart and such prominent blacks as C. C. Spaulding, Sterling Brown, and Thomas Jesse Jones were proof of interracial goodwill and the efficacy of Washington's philosophy.[10] Later, whites and blacks dined together at the Borough Club.

Young serialized Washington's address in the *Guide*. A typical headline read: "Dr. Washington Endorses Dr. Morris and *Guide's* Fight." In response to Washington's appeal for increased interracial cooperation, Young organized a "Get Together Conference" of distinguished citizens "to improve the life" of Norfolk's community. Young, the Reverend Charles Satchel Morris, Sr., William Rich, and the Reverend Richard H. Bowling regularly met with Herbert Cochron, A. T. Stroud, Robert Hughes, Francis M. Bacon, and other local whites for what the *Guide* called "a free and frank exchange of ideas."[11]

Young continued to see Washington from time to time. He accompanied Washington, Frissell, and Gandy to an annual convention of Negro farmers in Indianapolis. He talked with Washington again in late August 1915 at the fifth annual meeting of the National Negro Press Association in Philadelphia.[12] He and Washington continued to correspond until the latter's death in 1915. A year later, Washington's personal secretary, Emmett J. Scott, visited Young to request his assistance in organizing a Washington memorial fund.[13] Young gladly accepted the responsibility.

Not only was Young an enthusiastic Washingtonian, he was very much a businessman. His affiliation with the NOS provided him both with a platform and also with an opportunity to increase circulation of the *Guide*. Young distributed complimentary copies of the paper at conventions of the NOS, the Negro Teachers Association, the National Negro Business League, the Laymen's Missionary Baptist Convention, the Royal Society of King David, and scores of other organizations. He highlighted their activities in pictures and words in his newspaper. At the same time the Guide Publishing Company printed the programs, constitutions, rituals, letterheads, and receipt books for the organizations; it also printed high school yearbooks, wedding announcements, church bulletins, and forms for black colleges and businesses throughout the region. Moreover, Young's affiliation with the NOS enhanced his reputation as a rising spokesman for blacks and extended his political support within the Virginia chapters of the National Negro Business League.

Young nevertheless realized that Washington's philosophy was blind to many realities of southern life. He lamented the violence, the lynchings, and the increased social proscription of blacks in the South. He condemned disfranchisement, the resultant black voter apathy, and the plight of black students in Virginia. Blacks, disfranchised by the state constitution of 1902, no longer had a voice in politics.[14] As the Democrats slowly "closed the door" on black political participation in Virginia, the Republicans offered no recourse; instead, they organized themselves into a party of whites. Many blacks, resigned to the hopelessness of the situation, eschewed politics. Meanwhile, southern lawmakers enacted Jim Crow laws in housing, education, and transportation, racially segregating blacks in every aspect of southern life.

As the situation on the eve of World War I worsened, Washington's strategy of conciliation and compromise seemed obsolete to many blacks, both north and south. Opposition to his philosophy first emerged with the publication in 1903 of *The Souls of Black Folks* by W. E. B. Du Bois. Dissatisfaction with Washington intensified with the founding of the Niagara Movement in 1905 and the establishment of the National Association for the Advancement of Colored People (NAACP) in 1909. By 1915 the success of the NAACP and the combination of Republican neglect and deteriorating race relations were forcing Young to reevaluate his thinking. Like Washington, he hoped that the Republican party would end its lily-white policy and restore equal rights in the country. But the age of black Republican hopes had ended, and Young would soon turn to the NAACP to develop a sense of pride and accomplishment in Norfolk's black community.

The establishment of the NAACP in 1909 signaled the climax of a protest movement against the political and civil subjugation of blacks, anti-black violence, and Washingtonian philosophy. The NAACP represented the future; Washington, the past. Although Washington conspired to take "the wind out of the sail" of the NAACP, the organization continued to experience "phenomenal success." It seemed that "nothing Washington could have done would have prevented the rise of the NAACP."[15] Young saw in its growth among the South's business and professional class an opportunity to enhance his own image as a race leader and thereby soldify support for the *Guide* as well.

Young accepted the NAACP, knowing that the South was not yet prepared to bestow suffrage or economic uplift on blacks. Even before joining the NAACP, Young had been periodically shaken out of his political complacency. As early as June 1913 he published a "forceful protest against the iniquitous separate car law." He editorialized: "We do not object to separate cars, but we want equal accommodations."[16] He came to believe that the increased acceptance of the NAACP among the business, professional, ministerial, and fraternal groups enhanced racial solidarity and laid the foundation for an independent entrepreneurial class. More important, perhaps, as a national body the NAACP provided a quick and effective channel to publicize local grievances.

Although Young was a disciple of Washington, his own philosophy was more reflective of social developments and rapid technological advances in American life after Washington's death. Washington's philosophy was in tune with the commercial character of an earlier age, while Young's outlook mirrored the dramatic changes that took place in life and in American society after World War I. He respected the ideals of Washington's philosophy but feared that the continued political subjugation of black voters might jeopardize the increasing needs of a "proscribed people." Increased proscription of blacks, expanded acts of violence, and the continued exclusion of blacks from the Republican party engendered a moral dilemma for him.

James Weldon Johnson, a national NAACP branch organizer, visited Young in December 1916, seeking his assistance in organizing a Norfolk chapter. Young accepted this responsibility, and in January 1917 black Norfolkians elected him as president of the new chapter. At the first meeting Young expressed concern over dilapidated housing, intolerable streets, and the increased tension between the races brought about by a large influx of black migrants, military personnel, and shipyard workers. Other officers worried about the lack of housing for black female domestics, lynching, and black apathy. The organizers agreed to hold their first public meeting on Tuesday, April 24, 1917, and to invite Johnson to be the principal speaker. Johnson delivered what Young called "a splendid address" at a mass meeting at the First Presbyterian Church. Johnson was an ideal choice. He was not only an effective organizer, he was charismatic as well. Young's efforts to organize a Norfolk branch of the NAACP coincided with the national organization's strategy "to build a strong chain of branches" in the South. Johnson visualized the NAACP as a magnet that would attract into "united action" the scattered social and political forces of a community. A month later Young traveled as a delegate to the NAACP national convention in Washington, D.C., where Johnson introduced him to W. E. B. Du Bois, editor of the *Crisis*.[17]

Young and his newspaper became closely associated in Norfolk with the NAACP. His home became the favorite meeting place for Johnson, Joel Spingarn, William Pickens, Walter White, and other NAACP leaders whenever they visited the tidewater area. Although the Norfolk branch had its own office, its early correspondence was written on the *Guide's* stationery. In bold type the letterhead urged Norfolkians "to cooperate in the work of racial uplift along lines that we hope to undertake."[18] Young used the *Guide* to call mass meetings to outline strategy in response to local grievances.

In March 1917 the *Guide* called a meeting at the John Wesley AME Zion Church "to secure relief from the intolerable street conditions" and to protest the lack of police and fire protection. The protestors formed the Colored Civic Welfare Association and selected Young president. He declined, however, saying that "this movement needs leadership of a legal character." Black attorney James M. Harrison was chosen. The *Guide* called for "vigorous action" because "we can no longer endure in silence." One month later Young and the Reverend C. S. Morris, Sr., addressed a "mass meeting" and a "patriotic demonstration" at the Metropolitan AME Zion Church. The NAACP, said Young, was the only medium in America for making known the plight of blacks. As an advocate of racial solidarity and interracial goodwill, Young was now popularly referred to as a "race man." City fathers were turning to his editorials to learn of the "impending crisis" in the black community.[19]

Johnson, White, and other NAACP officials embraced Young because they viewed the *Guide* not only as a reliable disseminator of information but also as an effective instrument for organizing membership campaigns and for pricking the conscience of the white community. Young found the NAACP acceptable because its membership, its campaigns against disfranchisement and lynching, and its objectives did not conflict with his Washingtonian views about self-help and racial solidarity.

Undoubtedly, national NAACP officials at times disagreed with Young's expressed conservatism, but they withheld public criticism for a number of reasons. First, Young owned a newspaper which the NAACP needed to disseminate information. Next, he was linked throughout Norfolk and Virginia through an intricate web of church, fraternal, and civic organizations; but more important, the white power structure had anointed him as "an able and safe Negro leader." Also, whenever, White, Johnson, and others visited Norfolk, they used Young's Norfolk home to plot strategy. Young's wife Eleanor was an excellent hostess and an excellent strategist as well. Young's son Thomas W. Young was a practicing attorney, and his other son Plummer Bernard Young, Jr., had one of the most brilliant minds in black journalism. Needless to say, the conversation at the dinner table was interesting.

Norfolk's chapter was structured the same way as NAACP chapters in Boston, New York, and Chicago were, but in order to survive NAACP chapters in the post–World War I South temporarily abandoned the national NAACP strategy of an open "vote and fight." Many blacks believed that the "vote and fight" strategy was too militant and a symbolic obstacle to the recruitment of new members. Local NAACP members used their interlocking memberships in the NOS, the National Negro Business League, the Federation of Colored Women Clubs, and the Negro Press Association to advance the new organization. NAACP meetings always paralleled their meetings. The announcement of a speaker's last name followed only by his initials and another meeting place held no significance to the white community, but to blacks it was the signal they could "go hear something good." Also, because the mass meetings were always held in churches and showed no signs of protest, whites assumed that they simply were revivals.

Thus, at first the black church insulated the NAACP in the South from political attack. But Norfolk's first NAACP chapter was ineffective, and it had disintegrated by 1921. The problem was not Young's leadership; personality conflicts between the members of the various denominations, fear of reprisal, the growing image of radicalism, and apathy owing to economic prosperity generated by the war were the chapter's undoing.

Young envisioned blacks as permanent dwellers of a rural South; through contribution to the region's economic progress, they would improve race relations. He opposed migration because there were "too many Negroes in cities" in both the North and the South. He challenged blacks to remain on the farm. Farmers, he wrote, "are unwarlike, industrious and . . . in a class by themselves." He believed that cities were decadent and that race problems in the North were "more acute than the South."[20] Young also welcomed black migrants into metropolitan tidewater and intended for the *Guide* to serve as an instrument to acquaint them with urban living. However, he was opposed to immigration by foreigners into the area lest they take away jobs from black refugees from the tobacco and cotton fields of eastern North Carolina and the coal mines of western Virginia.

Despite a heavy influx of shipyard workers and domestics, by the spring of 1917 industrial Virginia was experiencing serious manpower shortages. The Du Pont Munitions Plant in Hopewell and the shipyards in Newport News were seriously affected by the activities of labor agents, who had induced a large number of employees to abrogate their contracts for work in northern states. The Newport News and Hampton Railway and the Gas & Electric Company estimated that from forty to sixty black employees were leaving each week. The *Guide* complained that wages in industry had averaged only 22 cents an hour for the past fifty years. By the summer of 1917 the labor shortage in the city of Norfolk and on the Hampton Roads peninsula, especially in the shipping industry, had reached a critical level. Perishable crops were rotting on the docks.[21]

The exodus to the north generated special problems for Virginia farmers. Their initial reaction to black migration was relief that a potentially incendiary element of the population was being dispersed, but their feeling changed to anxiety as the full extent of the exodus manifested itself in an acute labor shortage in 1917. Headlines in the *Guide* mirrored the crisis: "South Views with Alarm Negro Exodus," "Dangerous Phases of the Migration Movement," "Labor Shortage Grows Worse," "Inquiry into Negro Exodus."[22]

Throughout the war, the *Guide* campaigned aggressively to stem the tide of black migration. Young enlisted the help of the national NAACP, the National Urban League, the National Negro Business League, the NOS, the Negro State Teachers Association, and the Negro Farmers Organization. He used cartoons and letters to the editor to dramatize the hazards of northern migration, and he asked field agents of the *Guide* to highlight "the Great Opportunities for Negro Labor in the South." He forwarded questionnaires to employers to survey their wages and working conditions and then chronicled their results in editorials.[23]

Young advised blacks "to shun the uncertain inducements held out by northern labor agents." "There is no problem . . . or question between employers and employees in the South which cannot be satisfactorily adjusted in conference," he wrote. He reminded laborers that they were accustomed to "Southern habits and tradition," that in the North they would become "misfits and set adrift." Black migrants were "herded" into labor camps and "housed and fed like cattle." To prove his accusations Young printed "Some Startling Affidavits" from men who had recently returned from northern labor camps. They had been recruited by agents of the New York, New Haven, and Hartford Railroad Company. They told of filthy penlike sleeping quarters, lice-filled blankets, boxcar bunks, and "beans in the morning and beans at night." They had been forced to live in boxcars and to "sit up like dogs." Alongside the affidavits Young published a letter from "a prominent Norfolk minister" who praised Young for sounding the alarm. He also reprinted columns from white newspapers that were critical of northern migration and front-page endorsements from popular blacks such as Mrs. Booker T. Washington, who advised blacks to remain in the South because of its "wholesome, clean atmosphere." Young, like Mrs. Washington, believed that blacks were about "to throw away" what he termed "a golden opportunity."[24]

Young knew how to make the most of publicity to direct public opinion.

He cultivated the image of *Guide* reporters as always being on the scene. He provided readers with what a headline in the March 30, 1917, edition called "Inside Information" on labor wages in the North. Such headlines were but a more visible side of his constant search for a wider platform. Behind the scenes, he sent field agent A. M. Vann to agricultural and educational conferences throughout the South during the fall of 1916. At a conference in Laurinburg, North Carolina, in November, more than 1,000 black farmers heard discussion of the question: "Is it best for the Negro to remain in the South?" According to Vann, the farmers believed that black migrants were "worthless, indolent, and thriftless." The campaign helped boost circulation, as well. In early November at a famers' meeting in Greenville, North Carolina, Vann reported that he "placed the *Guide* in 600 hands and collected $500." Later, at a meeting of several hundred blacks in Kinston, North Carolina, he reported that "nearly every man gave me a subscription to our paper." He planned to attend similar conferences in the South Carolina towns of Bennettsville, Darlington, Florence, Sumter, and Columbia and the North Carolina communities of Fayetteville, Dunn, Red Springs, and Maxton.[25]

The *Guide* churned out cartoons depicting the notorious labor agent. One portrayed a recently arrived black migrant at a northern railroad depot; he is confronted by a sign reading: "Breakfast, Beans and Water; Dinner, Beans; and Supper, Water and Beans." Another cartoon showed a migrant out of work in both the North and South after the war; yet another contrasted the old, northern promises with the new, southern accomplishments.[26]

Young's condemnation of migration was unlikely to have been motivated by purely humanitarian concerns. As a businessman he also recognized that the laborers were an important resource for himself and other business people. His condemnation of migration was surely both economically and politically motivated.

Young blamed labor agents for the "hysteria for going north." In a front-page editorial in April, he interviewed a representative of one of the largest transportation companies in Norfolk and concluded that Norfolk's wages compared favorably with those offered by northern labor agents. Whereas unskilled northern laborers—dock workers, freight handlers, railroad workers, and others—received 20 cents per hour or $2.00 per day for ten hours' work, black Norfolkians averaged from $1.50 to $2.50 per day, and in some cases, they earned from $15.00 to $18.00 per week. Also, workers were employed on a full-time annual basis and were "well protected" from inclement weather.[27]

The massive migration of blacks to Washington, D.C., and the North clearly indicated that Young's antimigration campaign was unsuccessful. It is also clear that Homer Ferguson, the largest employer of blacks in Virginia, supported him. Although white leaders generally refused to admit the existence of black grievances, this was an issue the town councils and committees from the white community were willing to discuss with black leaders. The Richmond *Times-Dispatch* even reluctantly admitted that wages and living conditions would have to be improved if the state intended to retain much of its black labor.[28] The most far-reaching effect of the crisis was to quell lynching, for it laid the foundation for an antilynching crusade by the *Guide* and the Norfolk *Virginian-Pilot*. Its more immediate effect was to widen the gulf between Young and John Mitchell, editor of the Richmond *Planet*. Before World War I the *Planet* had been the leading black weekly in Virginia, but after the war Young's *Guide* had assumed the leadership. Mitchell and Young disagreed on the migration issue.

Mitchell charged that the basic reasons for migration were unfair treatment, especially Jim Crow legislation and unequal legal protection. He asserted that these were creations of whites, and that whites would have to change them.[29] Mitchell articulated the views of a more urban, alienated, and aggressive populace. In contrast, Young used the *Guide* to direct rural readers, who were older and more conservative. Whereas Mitchell advocated a militant approach and urged blacks to organize and to protest unfair treatment, Young was more conciliatory. Mitchell championed migration because it represented an opportunity for blacks to earn higher wages, to obtain an education, and to develop an economic and political power base. Young counseled blacks to remain in the South where their numbers would eventually enable them to gain economic independence and political privilege. Mitchell encouraged migration because he was resigned to the hopelessness of the situation after the constitutional disfranchisement of Virginia blacks in 1902 and the black leadership's inability to evolve an effective black strategy after World War I. Young opposed migration because he had faith in the historic goals of the Republican party and in the New South.

At the height of the labor crisis in 1917 weekly editions of the *Planet* and the *Guide* rarely failed to comment on the migration issue, but migration was not really the issue. The editors' differences and the most persistent source of conflict between them arose from their contrasting opinions concerning the speed and direction that the black leadership should take. Young, a Washingtonian conservative, advocated self-help and racial solidarity and remained a Republican until 1928. Mitchell, because of the Republicans' continued neglect of black interests and deteriorating race relations, abandoned the Republican party and aligned himself with the dominant Democrats before World War I. Undoubtedly Young's conservatism, his tactics during the migration controversy, and the ascendancy of the conservative *Guide* angered Mitchell. Mitchell remained Young's nemesis until Mitchell's death in 1938.[30]

Although Young's *Guide* wholeheartedly backed the entry of the United States into World War I, it also mirrored the increasing frustration of black soldiers in military camps throughout the South. Young supported James Weldon Johnson's belief that the war would crystallize black demands for equality of opportunity even as it reinforced white fears of social equality. Like Johnson and Du Bois, Young saw the war largely as a struggle among Europeans for colonial empires. When similar opinions appeared in the Washington *Bee*, the Chicago *Defender*, the New York *Age*, and other black newspapers, the *Guide* quickly endorsed their comments. Yet Young also endorsed Du Bois's controversial editorial "Close Ranks," in which he urged blacks to "Forget your grievances for the moment and stand by your country." Throughout the war the *Guide* stood with NAACP leadership, which counseled restraint, and with others of the black press who championed "racial solidarity" while soft-pedaling black political grievances.[31]

When the New York *Herald Tribune* alleged that German agents were seeking to instigate violent dissension among southern blacks, Young agreed with the national NAACP, calling the charges "absurd," and with Du Bois, who characterized the allegations as "cock and bull." The NAACP in a confidential memo urged the black press "to stamp out this insidious rumor"and to dramatize the Negro's loyalty to the flag.[32]

Generally, blacks throughout Virginia reacted favorably to Young's philosophy and supported the war effort in the hope that their loyalty would be rewarded by an improvement in their conditions. Many blacks enthusiastically supported the Liberty Loan and thrift-stamp drives. In the fourth loan drive in 1918, Young reported, blacks in Virginia contributed more than $80,000. Victory gardens dotted the black community, and many of its homes were proudly marked with red crosses and the national flag.[33]

On January 9, 1918, the Norfolk *Virginian-Pilot* headlines read, "Greatest terminal in America to be built in Norfolk." The federally financed terminal would employ 10,000 workers and would serve both as a port of embarkation for troops going to Europe and as a rifle factory. Two days later the *Pilot* announced the proposed construction of 500 new federally subsidized homes to house 1,000 new shipyard workers for the Newport News Shipbuilding and Dry Dock Company. Almost overnight

Norfolk became the center of government activity involving the expenditure of millions of dollars. Ironically, the boom in tidewater Virginia created labor shortages in other areas of Virginia and the South and helped to thrust the *Guide* into a bitter controversy over the merits of southern labor and northern migration.

Meanwhile, as both white and black migrants from the eastern North Carolina and the Virginia piedmont moved into Norfolk, the city's population expanded from 67,452 in 1910 to 115,777 in 1920. Its black population increased from 25,039 in 1910 to 43,392 in 1920. Young's *Guide* warned the black newcomers about the social hazards of urban living and counseled them about health and hygiene. Young was especially sensitive to the plight of single black females, who often arrived without either employment or lodging. Many sought employment as domestics, but they also worked on truck farms and in tobacco, textile, and furniture plants. Others were employed on the Norfolk Naval Base, the Newport News Shipbuilding and Dry Dock Company, and in paper-manufacturing plants. The wages for black migrants varied from a few dollars per day on the truck farms to $175 per month for skilled welders and mechanics at the dry docks.[34]

Black migrants and soldiers overtaxed local recreational facilities, and black soldiers stood in block-long lines at soda fountains and in front of the Eureka Lodge at 626 Church Street, which functioned as a USO for black servicemen. A scarcity of housing generated high rents, and boardinghouses and hotels were filled to overflowing. In March 1917, in response to the housing crisis, the Newport News Shipbuilding and Dry Dock Company initiated a project to build a black housing development for its employees and to sell the houses individually at cost. The rapid influx not only aggravated an already critical housing situation but, in Young's words, "changed viewpoints on all questions affecting race." In an editorial entitled "The Negro and the War," Young applauded "tangible benefits" such as the willingness of white factories and mills to use black labor, but he also urged the white South "to lift the burden of social and economic oppression" and to eradicate the double standards of wages and working conditions. Young angrily complained that black migrants were "disrespected, disregarded, Jim Crowed, segregated, and treated with every human injustice" by white merchants. He noted that white merchants "don't spend a dime with black enterprise" and "do nothing" to support black self-help.[35]

By 1917 and 1918 Young's editorials were becoming more forceful and direct, but he was careful to remain within boundaries dictated by the white community. Because he was a "race man" and a conservative, his condemnation of "social and economic oppression" and of the white merchants' failure to reciprocate was acceptable. The white merchants knew that they were respected by Norfolk's black community and that the *Guide*'s flaming editorial about "Graft and Grafters Everywhere" would not hurt their business.[36] But in December 1916 Young began evolving an economic theory that was later to be popularized by *Guide* columnist Gordon Blaine Hancock as the "double-duty dollar"—buy where you work. On December 1 Young editorialized: "Charity begins at home. Colored people who have money to spend should discriminate with whom they trade. They should spend money with white merchants who in return will spend some of their money on black enterprise." He counseled blacks to "wake up" or face the possibility of always being "servants of servants."

The other issues that provoked more decisive editorials were unpaved streets, intoxicated servicemen, and racial violence. In a series of editorials called "The Dirt Roads of Norfolk," Young joined black activist C. A. Palmer to "vigorously protest" the intolerable conditions in the Hunterville and Barboursville sections of Norfolk. These black neighborhoods were furious because the Norfolk City Council had allocated $40,000 to repair roads in a predominantly white section. Young characterized the situation as "a grave injustice." He pointed to the high fire insurance rates and criticized merchants who had discontinued deliveries. He further claimed that residents could not purchase health insurance because of the unsanitary conditions.[37]

Norfolk's designation as the principal port of debarkation for military personnel bound for Europe dramatically increased the number of uniformed servicemen on the streets of the city. Their presence heightened tension between the races, and there were frequent fistfights between civilians and servicemen, servicemen and police. After one sailor's assault on a Norfolk policeman, the mayor, police chief, and Board of Control demanded that the Fifth Naval District place a permanent shore patrol in the city to maintain order. The black community was also aroused; the *Guide*'s editorial "Sailors Run Amuck Again" reflected black anger. Young lamented the assault but was "glad that something had happened to arouse the mayor and the police to decisive action."[38]

Fear and tension gripped Norfolk's black community during the war years. After the infamous riot at East St. Louis, Illinois, on July 2, 1917, Young claimed in a front-page article that "Decisive Action—Averted Trouble" in Norfolk. He alleged that "lawless" U.S. soldiers had almost precipitated race riots several times in Norfolk. After the East St. Louis riot, Young, S. S. Morris, J. McDonald, N. D. King, G. Jarvis Bowens,

and Richard Bowling caucused at the black YMCA and organized themselves into the Colored Citizens Committee (CCC), to deal with the
safety of Norfolk's defenseless black community. Although an armed mob
had committed an "atrocious" and "brutal" act against defenseless blacks
in East St. Louis, they heard "no strong public voice in Norfolk." They
challenged whites "to exert influence" and "to prevent bloodshed and
riots." The CCC was clearly disgusted with Norfolk's white leadership.
Nevertheless, the CCC urged blacks to resist violence and "to be patient
and to refrain from incendiary remarks to or about sailors." A bloody riot
would taint Norfolk's image as the "Queen City" and disrupt what CCC
leaders saw as harmonious race relations, thereby jeopardizing their role
as "able and safe Negro leaders." But more importantly, a bloody riot
would give what they termed "new and powerful arguments" to rival
northern communities that wanted the proposed terminal and might convince the government to cancel further expansion of the Norfolk Naval
Base. A riot thus might hasten migration and accentuate the labor shortage in tidewater Virginia. Although the CCC's concerns were published
in the *Guide,* a more detailed resolution signed by Young, Bowling,
McDonald, Morris, King, and Bowens appeared on the editorial page of
the *Virginian-Pilot* under the title "An Ounce of Prevention." The resolution asked that "colored citizens refrain from all incendiary remarks to
or about Sailors" and that "white citizens . . . raise their voices and assert
their influence."[39]

East St. Louis was only the beginning. During the "Red Summer" of
1919, at least thirty-eight riots took place. The worst occurred in Chicago,
Washington, D.C., New York City, Longview, Texas, and Knoxville, Ten-
nessee. The underlying causes were "profoundly economic, social, and
psychological," but the immediate cause was white racism. The black rioters were sensitive to acts of racial discrimination and disgusted with the
moderation of black leaders; they were aware of such publications as the
Challenge, the *Messenger,* and the *Crisis,* "which minced no words"
about black grievances and favored direct action to redress them.[40]

The black press united in the face of the threat of social violence. Young
and the Chicago *Defender* called the racial outbursts "a national shame
and disgrace." Young editorialized that "the black masses were driven to
desperation," and like the editor of the Kansas City *Call* and the Savannah *Tribune,* he blamed the racial unrest on violence, peonage, and discriminatory legal practices. Young's response to the Red Summer resembled that of more militant editors such as Mitchell of the Richmond
Planet, Robert Vann of the Pittsburgh *Courier,* and Du Bois of the *Crisis.*
Mitchell ascribed the violence to "lawless elements" of both races; the

Courier worried over the effects of the riots on blacks. Du Bois urged blacks "to reason together . . . don't seek reform by violence." The New York *Age* warned that it was "senseless" to denounce all whites. When the Washington *Bee*, the St. Louis *Argus*, the Savannah *Tribune*, and others demanded that the "government act at once" and "take vigorous methods" in order to make riots "less likely to occur," Young agreed. He and the California *Eagle*, the Indianapolis *Freeman*, and the Cleveland *Advocate* all condemned the violence and urged whites to give blacks "a fair chance." They counseled blacks to adopt a "sober and intelligent position toward whites."[41]

Unlike many other southern communities, the Norfolk City Council planned an elaborate ceremony to welcome home the returning black veterans. "Well done true and faithful warriors," the Norfolk *Virginian-Pilot* (white) editorialized. Virginia's second largest daily called the black veterans "patriots" who had "earned the gratitude of the community" and who had "met trials with steadfastness and courage." However, on the first day of the week-long celebration the arrest of a black soldier sparked a clash between blacks and police. Both the *Virginian-Pilot* and the *Guide* described the black mood as "ugly." One black yelled, "You showed you could fight in France . . . what are you afraid of now?" When the melee ended, two policemen and five blacks lay wounded. Nevertheless, "The Big Parade of Colored Vets" and the Armory Hall banquet were held as scheduled. The Norfolk *Ledger-Dispatch* (white) observed that the disturbance "wasn't a race riot," but "an ordinary riot," "a disturbance growing out of a crowd."[42]

In contrast to the extreme violence in Washington, D.C., Chicago, and other cities, the so-called Norfolk Riot seems rather pale. Young's specific response is unavailable, but he probably condemned the violence for fear that it would jeopardize the planned expansion of the Norfolk Naval Base and disrupt harmonious race relations between the races. Young, Bowling, and other black spokesmen often interpreted social passivity and the absence of an expressed racial identity as a sign of good race relations. Previous incidences of violence in other southern cities led Young to have premonitions about violence in Norfolk two years before it occurred. In an open letter to his friend publisher Louis Jaffe of the Norfolk *Virginian-Pilot* on August 9, 1917, Young warned that racial violence generated by the war would "discredit the city" and give "powerful argument" to rival northern cities who were opposed to what he termed "extensive local improvement." Young challenged whites to use their influence "to forestall bloodshed and riot" and urged black Norfolkians "to refrain from incendiary remarks about black soldiers and sailors."

Scarcely a month after the riots in Washington, Chicago, Longview, and Norfolk, an anti-red hysteria gripped America. Emanating from the government, the press, and patriotic organizations, it focused on "Bolsheviks," aliens, the NAACP, and the black press. U.S. Attorney General A. Mitchell Palmer and South Carolina congressman James S. Byrnes blamed the summer riots on Du Bois, A. Philip Randolph, Chandler Owens, and other national black leaders, labeling them Bolsheviks.[43] Black publications such as the *Crusader*, the *Challenge*, the *Negro World*, the *Messenger*, the Chicago *Defender*, and the *Crisis* were singled out as radical and seditious.

Young was stunned, even though his newspaper, along with the Pittsburgh *Courier* and a few others, escaped government scrutiny. He agreed with NAACP's Johnson, who protested that propaganda against lynching, disfranchisement, and Jim Crowism did not constitute radicalism, arguing that such tactics were necessary to advance the race.[44] Like Johnson, Du Bois, and others, Young attributed the hysteria to fear, suspicion, and the urge to retaliate. He agreed with editors Vann of the Pittsburgh *Courier* and Fortune of the New York *Age*, who asserted that blacks' loyalty to America was unquestionable. Young also agreed with Fortune that "real radicalism has not yet touched the Negro masses."

Young believed that Attorney General Palmer was poorly advised and "unequal to the situation." The riots, in his opinion, were caused by the "immunity from punishment" of lawless lynch mobs. "Pity the Attorney General," he editorialized; "he cannot see it." The title of a subsequent editorial reflected Young's mood: "The Negro Will Not Again Be Tame."[45]

Admist this controversy the NAACP sponsored a conference at New York's Carnegie Hall to discuss "Africa in World Democracy." Young warmly endorsed attempts by Du Bois and Johnson to end black factionalism. As Du Bois, Johnson, Joel Spingarn, John Hope (president of Atlanta University), and others arrived in Paris to open the First Pan African Congress in 1919, the *Guide* referred to them as "intelligent wide-awake men governed by wisdom." Young terms self-determination "proper and fair" and was optimistic that the League of Nations would judiciously administrate Germany's former African colonies. In addition, he was gratified that "the radicalism of Du Bois was happily tempered" by sober rationalism. One year later, Du Bois was awarded the Spingarn Medal, the NAACP's highest award, for organizing the congress. Young called him a "Genius."[46]

Throughout the turmoil of these years Young appeared to act independently, but in fact he maneuvered carefully within boundaries dictated by the white community. Still very much an accommodationist, he espoused a philosophy that matched that of the white political leadership in the South. When World War I ended, the *Guide* had the largest circulation of any black-owned newspaper in the South. Its editor-in-chief had emerged as the leading spokesman for blacks in tidewater Virginia and beyond.

As the decade ended, the NAACP had become the largest black protest organization in America. Ironically, it had more cautious southerners than militant northerners as members—42,588 in the South, 38,420 in the North.[47] The association held its 1920 annual conference in Atlanta, its first yearly meeting south of Baltimore. Young attended the Atlanta convention reluctantly, for his support of the NAACP was slowly waning. Internal dissension had already rendered the Norfolk branch ineffective, and the Red Summer and the red scare of 1919 eroded his commitment. The controversial June 1919 convention of the NAACP in Cleveland, Ohio, had further alienated him. At that meeting Du Bois, Colonel Charles Young, Archibald Henry Grimké, and others had vehemently condemned segregation and demanded a federal antilynching bill. Young, already uncomfortable with the convention's theme of "fight and vote," had aligned himself with the conservative faction that rejected the resolution because he feared a white backlash. The Brooklyn *Eagle* lamented, "a lack of unanimity . . . affected the failure to suppress lynching."[48] But Young and others had condemned the "all-or-nothing" element of black thought. They viewed middle-class white southerners as allies and in part blamed blacks for their own lack of achievement. The condemnation of lynching by prominent whites (including Virginia's governor Westmoreland Davis), the increased state funding of black colleges, and the support of such liberal white organizations in the South as the Southern Sociological Association were proof enough to Young of interracial goodwill.

Young was optimistic about the South and about the future status of blacks in the South. His optimism was shared by R. R. Moton, president of Tuskegee Institute, James E. Gregg, president of Hampton Institute, and James E. Shepard, president of the National Religious Training School, who believed that the South was "tired of lynching" and eager to cooperate with "wise, progressive, and conservative" blacks. Along with A. A. Graham, J. M. Gandy, and others, they believed that blacks determined their own fate. They conceded that they needed guidance from whites, but they boldly rejected what they termed "special privileges." Moton mirrored the sentiments of Young and the others when he declared: "The Negro Asks Just an Equal Chance."[49]

Young, Moton, Gandy, and other black southern leaders regarded Virginia, and themselves, as pioneers in the search for interracial goodwill.

They were men of character and integrity who had the ear of the best people of the South—both black and white—and who were respected as "able and safe" race leaders.[50] They believed that the character of blacks was patterned after that of whites. Accordingly, they focused on the fundamentals of life—education, health, and cleanliness—in order to make blacks more efficient and self-respecting. In so doing, they believed, they would reduce racial friction, uplift blacks economically, and advance interracial goodwill.

Young and the others regarded the suspension of their civil liberties and the abrogation of their suffrage as temporary. Young editorialized that the South was "waking up" to the truth enunciated by Lincoln and enlarged by Booker T. Washington: Americans cannot exist half slave and half free.[51]

By 1920 Young had established himself as a member of Norfolk's black business and social elite, emerging during the war years as a conservative spokesman of the black community. He would remain an ardent Republican throughout the 1920s, despite the party's lily-white proclivities. But he also faced a dilemma. He knew that the *Guide* could help bring about social and economic changes, but also that militant condemnation of segregation would invite white reprisals and even jeopardize the *Guide*. In the years ahead he would agonize over the Republican party and over the strategy he should adopt as both editor and leader in the black community.

▪ 4 ▪

Washingtonian Militance

Young had expected that the patriotism demonstrated by blacks to make the world safe for democracy would earn them a place in the Republican party. Instead, the party in Virginia adopted lily-whitism, and blacks responded with lily-blackism. To Young, both were equally repulsive, but because of the continued neglect of black interests and the increased proscription of blacks in the South, he was forced to qualify his support of the Harding-led Republican party, though his faith was temporarily revived with the election of Calvin Coolidge. When Coolidge refused to commit himself to a positive black policy, Young condemned the party and its leaders. By the late 1920s Young was to adopt "individualistic Republicanism."

The 1920s were a time of enormous growth for the *Guide*. Reaching fewer than 500 subscribers in 1910, it was circulating to approximately 29,000 by 1935, a readership that was spread throughout the eastern seaboard and even into areas of the Midwest. Although the *Guide* increased its employees from eight in 1910 to forty-two in 1935, it remained a family business well into the 1960s. Its success during the 1920s resulted from local interracial cooperation and from its location in Norfolk, which had a large and stable black community that looked to Young and his newspaper for leadership and direction.[1]

In 1920 the Guide Publishing Company purchased the two buildings at 721-723 East Olney Road, and in 1926–27 they were remodeled and occupied entirely by the business, editorial, and mailing departments. The mechanical plant remained in the building at 711-719 East Olney Road. The Youngs built up their business steadily. From an antiquated, homeless plant that could have been housed in a fair-sized living room, it grew until its properties, mechanical and real estate, were valued at $100,000 in 1930. The company furnished not only regular employment to a growing staff but part-time employment to hundreds of others as agents and correspondents. The annual payroll in December 1930 exceeded $50,000.

By 1923, when circulation had grown to 6,500 eight-page papers weekly, the volume taxed the capacity of the press and folding equipment. In the spring of that year a Duplex web press capable of turning out 5,000 eight-page papers an hour, printed and folded, was installed. After this, circulation and size of the paper gradually increased until the spring of 1929, when the new twelve-page tabloid reached 14,000. Circulation jumped again in the spring of 1929 when Young installed a thirty-two-page Hoe rotary press and stereotyping equipment; the sixteen-page *Guide* now went out to 25,000 readers. Nearly two-thirds of the circulation was by paid subscriptions, and 40 percent was in Norfolk and the tidewater.[2]

The *Guide* was dated on Saturday of each week. Its editorial page in 1920 served the highest purpose of journalism—the education of the people. It was more temperate, better organized, and factually more reliable than its Virginia rival, the Richmond *Planet*.

Fully two-thirds of each editorial page featured three to six editorials that ranged over a variety of topics, from international law and lynching to public morality and complex questions of economics and public policy. Many were devoted to race relations. All were well researched, couched in clear, forceful, and persuasive language, and were especially well organized. Each began with an explanation of a problem followed by a discussion of alternatives or various viewpoints. These led to a concise yet powerful statement of the *Guide*'s position. The final paragraph was often the most interesting and quotable. Because it was Young's custom to place his opinions within the broader framework of his general philosophy, these concluding paragraphs not only offered the reader a means of quickly extracting the heart of each editorial, but they were instructive homilies. These morsels of advice, addressed to friend and foe, were never offensive, arrogant, or self-righteous. They were compelling and designed to provoke thought. Often, they were eloquent. They appealed to the people's sense of decency, fair play, and reason; they condemned the irrational and demagogic. Long editorials on matters of particular importance were set off with large headlines on the front page under the banner "Review and Comment."[3]

Because white dailies so rarely carried social items of interest to the black community, much news in the *Guide* was "personal." The eager response of blacks throughout the eastern seaboard to the *Guide* confirmed the importance of such news to its readers. Where else could a black graduate from high school or college receive a write-up, or the marriage of a sharecropper's daughter be made known? How else could blacks send news of sickness and the effects of calamities to distant relatives and friends? The *Guide* highlighted local and national black business ventures, heralded the ability of black businessmen, and advertised their products. It offered birth announcements to the most lowly black and expressed condolence upon his death.[4]

Young often lamented the difficulty of making correspondents understand that most of their contributions ought to be news, opinion, and advertising. Although he realized that they could not ignore social activities, he nevertheless ordered them at times to "cut it down." He once commented, "If our newspaper keeps feeding them this kind of stuff they will develop atrophy of the brain."[5]

Along the eastern seaboard in such places as Exmore, Virginia, and Winterville, North Carolina, the local *Guide* offices served as travelers' aides. Local reporters helped blacks who were lost, penniless, or seeking direction to the home of a prominent black person. Many also served as character references for local blacks in need of loans or installment credit and aided new schoolteachers or ministers in finding a place to live. They served as neighborhood counselors, helped to ameliorate racial disputes, and served as character witnesses in courts of law. Although field correspondents often disagreed with Young's conservatism, their dedication and loyalty were unfailing.

The increase in the *Guide's* circulation during the 1920s paralleled the growth of Young's prominence as a race man throughout Virginia and beyond. Increasingly, Norfolk's rising middle class—black and white—read the *Guide* as a reflection of their own opinions and as a source of accurate information.[6] The Church Street merchants, domestics, mailmen, federal workers, businessmen, and a slowly expanding corps of military officers constituted the black middle class. They exaggerated their economic well-being and cultural achievement. The *Guide's* insistence that "interracial goodwill was steadily improving" despite growing violence and increased social proscription sanctioned their emphasis upon Negro "Society" and shielded them, to some extent, against the "contempt and terror" of a segregated society. Plummer Bernard and Eleanor White Young, members in good standing of Norfolk's black middle class, published a newspaper that, in large part, reflected their own standards and aspirations.

Because bickering rendered the Norfolk NAACP branch ineffective during much of the 1920s, Young devised a strategy called "Forward Together" to foster "greater self-respect, self-trust, and mutual confidence." It was designed to bring together representatives from all segments of the black community at regular intervals for a frank exchange of opinions on issues that affected black life "most emphatically." Young cautioned that the Negro Forward Movement (NFM) was not a grievance committee. He put emphasis on the word *forward*. The NFM's aim, he announced, was to create a spirit of "contagious helpfulness toward another." Representing the new movement, leading blacks visited fraternal, social, and civic groups to explain its objectives.

The NFM was in part a surrogate for political activity. First, it would boost business and enhance the commercial appeal of Norfolk's black enterprises. Second, it would serve as a platform to propagandize self-help and racial solidarity. Young knew that black industrialism needed a prosperous commercial and financial group to provide the capital. Only the economically functional Negro would be in a position to demand full rights and protection under the law. Young, like Booker T. Washington, urged the growth of an industrial "talented tenth." Black industrialists and entrepreneurs would gradually mitigate a prejudice against blacks that could never be legislated away. If everything else failed, there would always be the alternative of total segregation within a self-sustaining black community. In other words, Young sought to turn discrimination and segregation to blacks' advantage.

The *Guide* initiated an annual Trade Week in April 1921, which took place each year until the late 1930s. The purpose was to highlight what Young termed Norfolk's chief asset, "its unlimited supply of dependable black labor." The March 1925 Trade Week was typical. Monday was Banking, Building, and Loan Day; Tuesday, Insurance Day; Wednesday, Tailors and Grocers Day; and so forth throughout the week. On Sunday ministers were encouraged to preach sermons on thrift and home ownership.

The local economy did hold promise for enterprising blacks. According to the *Guide*, Norfolk had the largest tobacco and peanut export market in the world, was the largest coal port, and led the nation in the quantity of seafood and vegetables shipped abroad. The American Cigar Company, which employed 500 black women as stemmers, epitomized Norfolk employers who, in Young's words, were "liberal and considerate" and who saw black workers as being "efficient, reliable, and stable." Young proudly observed that many blacks had held the same job for more than thirty years and that "wages and working conditions compared favorably" with those in other sections of the country. Labor trouble was infrequent, and "amicable relations existed between capital and the working classes." He predicted that "the outlook for better times are good."[7]

Young was far from alone in his espousal of Washingtonian ideas. Throughout these years many speakers—both black and white—exalted self-help and examples of interracial cooperation. *Guide* columnist Nannie Helen Burroughs, founder of the Afro-American Women Wage-Earners Association, championed "pride of occupation."[8] Norfolk's Metropolitan Bank, which advertised itself as the largest Negro bank in the world, promoted a campaign of thrift and frugality. The Norfolk chapters of the National Negro Business League and the National Negro Retail Merchants Association affirmed their support of self-help through advertisements in the *Guide*.

In conjunction with Trade Week, Norfolk's black Chamber of Commerce called a "monster mass meeting" at the Second Calvary Baptist Church to promote thrift and home ownership. Ministers and businessmen visited schools, industrial plants, theaters, and saloons "to preach the doctrine of thrift and good citizenship." "Home" became a magic word. In bold red type the *Guide* editorialized, "Own Your Home—Build, Be Thrifty." Young realized that it was impossible to increase black home buying immediately, but the "idea," he said, was "to start people thinking."

Although Young's views on migration, patriotism, economic advancement, and racial solidarity closely resembled Washington's, he differed on some issues. For example, the *Guide* campaigned vigorously for better streets and more healthful conditions in the city, and Young chastised the city fathers and urged blacks "to organize, agitate, insist and persist." Observing that heavy traffic had made many streets in the black section impassable, he called for paved streets and more water and sewage connections. He charged that blacks paid taxes but received few benefits. Afro-Americans were entitled to public services, he maintained, because they needed to safeguard their health and to beautify their neighborhoods.[9]

In the above instances, Young's views were forceful and direct. Young used issues such as the black migration to the North as leverage, suggesting it could be stemmed if the streets and municipal services were improved. He knew that editor Louis Jaffe and other prominent whites in Norfolk would support improved municipal services for blacks. At the same time, Young was always careful to remain within social boundaries that had been dictated by the white community. Also, it was politically safe "to organize, agitate, insist and persist" about impassable streets because many of the stores on Church Street were white owned.

Young's opposition to northern migration had brought him into conflict with John Mitchell, editor of the Richmond *Planet*, during the war years, and Young never wavered from his stance.[10] The editors' rivalry provides insight into the black side of the struggle for leadership and political power in Virginia. The continued exclusion of blacks from both major political parties kindled a fire of protest in Mitchell and spurred him in 1920 to form a separate black party. Young questioned the wisdom of a third, all-black party and formulated a strategy of "protest and resistance."

Richmond's "colored insurgents" had originally planned a separate party in March 1910 to protest the Republicans' lily-white policy, hoping to extract more patronage as a reward for remaining in the party.[11] The Republicans' lily-white policy had deep roots in the Gilded Age and was more or less formally established in 1908 by William Howard Taft, who, like earlier Republicans, hoped to win white votes in the South. Warren G. Harding continued lily-whitism in 1920, prompting the birth of Mitchell's lily-black movement.

The Richmond *Planet* became the voice for the lily-blacks. As the gap between Mitchell and Young widened, Young accurately predicted that the race issue would play a major role in the Virginia gubernatorial campaign in 1921. Following the Republican convention, which excluded blacks, the lily-blacks met in Richmond on September 6 and nominated Mitchell for governor, Theodore Nash of Newport News for lieutenant governor, and J. Thomas Newsome of Newport News for attorney general. Young was offered the lieutenant governor's post, but he refused. By now he was out of step with black politicians in Virginia and condemned the movement as political suicide. He charged that the third party was ill timed and unwise, and that the lily-black candidates had drawn a color line by excluding whites, thereby stirring racial antagonism.[12]

For the first time Young's political loyalty to his race, as well as his personal integrity, was seriously questioned. The lily-blacks, defending their bolt, insisted that for twenty years they had made no attempt either to lead the party or to gain social equality, as whites in both parties charged. They demanded "to be treated as other citizens with all the rights, privileges, and immunities accorded them, including the right to vote and to be voted for." Young did not challenge the political objectives of the lily-blacks, merely their tactics and strategy. He opposed the continued lily-whitism of the Republican party, but unlike Mitchell and the lily-blacks he favored a program that encouraged blacks to register and to vote for a major party. He saw the lily-black party as isolated and powerless. More could be accomplished, he counseled, by organizing statewide voter leagues and building up an organized black electorate. In the practical world of politics, votes, not petitions, carried weight with elected officials. Although professing sympathy with Mitchell and Newsome, Young claimed that "ample retaliation might be accomplished without committing political suicide." Young maintained that the lily-black platform should first be submitted through a referendum to the people.[13]

Moreover, Young believed that hostile political factions or rival economic interests could threaten the economic progress of a voteless people. The lily-black party's political impotence posed a threat to the economic advances that blacks had already made. Echoing the philosophy of Washington, Young maintained that economic gains were the best way to create respect and status for blacks and would lead to their political acceptance by whites. His strategy was to augment black economic strength so that they could support financially those whites who would work for their political interests. The "imperialistic and racial methods of Mitchell and Newsome would only exacerbate racial antagonism," he warned.[14]

Matters finally came to a head when Young and Newsome met face-to-face at a political rally in Portsmouth, Virginia, on October 16, 1921. From the speakers' platform Newsome condemned prominent blacks who opposed the lily-black movement and announced that he was going "to get them." His hostility was clearly directed toward Young, who was seated in the audience. Newsome realized that the predominantly black audience identified with the goals of the lily-blacks, and that this gave him an opportunity to embarrass a political opponent and garner support from blacks who had hung back.

Young was a proud man. He was furious with the lily-blacks not only because they had not offered him the governorship but because they had rejected his counsel and threatened harmonious race relations. Angered by Newsome's remarks, he stood up and demanded to be heard. Permission granted, he then defended himself against charges of disloyalty to his own race. But as he began to recite the "history" of the black race in Virginia under the leadership of such men as Mitchell, Newsome, and Joseph R. Pollard, several men in the audience yelled, "Stop him, stop him." Young and his supporters were enraged; a fistfight almost ensued. The following week the *Guide* headlined: "Mitchell, Newsome, and Negro Republicans Arouse Class Hatred in Race in Bitter Speeches."

Meanwhile, headlines in the Richmond *Planet* read, "Tidewater Newspaper Opposes Colored Republican Ticket." Mitchell asserted that the *Guide* had "jumped the track." He reminded Young that he had initially supported the lily-black movement. Mitchell asserted that this was a fight for "race and integrity." He challenged Young to "look at yourself." Mitchell believed that Young was angered over the party's selection of Mitchell to run for governor. The evidence confirms his suspicions.

In the gubernatorial campaign the lily-black politicians waged a relentless campaign of abuse and innuendo against Young and other blacks who disagreed with them. Young appeared to oppose not so much the lily-black movement as the nomination of Mitchell. He accused Mitchell of employing "imperialistic and racial methods in an attempt to impose without reservation [his] judgment in matters political upon the intelligence of the colored electorate."[15]

While blacks bolted the Republican party and argued among themselves and lily-white Republicans defended their position on race, the Democrats had little difficulty in sweeping the 1921 election with a substantial 70,000-vote majority. Norfolkians delivered a mere 90 votes to Mitchell out of a total registered black electorate of 1,600. Statewide, Mitchell received 5,230 votes, one third (1,953) of which came from his home district of Richmond. Young claimed that Mitchell's defeat was inevitable because blacks would never accept his radical leadership.[16]

After the 1921 election the lily-black movement ended as quickly as it had begun. Blacks in Virginia again faded into the political background, not to reappear until the white primary cases in 1929. Blacks' temporary political awakening in the early 1920s over the lily-black movement aroused insufficient enthusiasm in Virginia to sustain a permanent political drive.

Continued lily-whitism began to set Young adrift from the Republican party. He sharply criticized the Harding and Coolidge administrations for their apathy and lack of support. Ethel Waters sang a "blues song" entitled "I Ain't Nobody's Mama Now," he recalled, but the black voters of the South had acted as "the wet nurse of the Republican party." He implied that he was no longer a regular Republican and noted that the "spirit of independence is more prevalent now than ever."[17]

The lily-black movement left black Republicans splintered and confused. As campaign rhetoric abated, many withdrew from the political arena and vowed never to return. But Young stuck to the party of Lincoln. He sought to conciliate differences among black Republicans and to appease the Mitchell faction. More than anything else, he hoped that his attempts at compromise would allay the fears of whites, who had resented the all-black gubernatorial slate of 1921. Young also hoped that his strategy of conciliation would unite Republicans under the "Forward Together" banner.

In large part Young's political views remained consistent. For instance, in 1922 he opposed Marcus Garvey's Universal Negro Improvement Association, again exhibiting antipathy to black separatism. He agreed with Du Bois, who viewed Garvey as a "disoriented victim of the color line," and with the NAACP's Johnson, who was equally contemptuous of Garvey's "Back to Africa Movement." When nearly all of the black press, especially the Chicago *Defender* and the *Crisis*, demanded that Garvey must go, Young did likewise. He rejected Garvey's offer to debate with him the efficacy of his movement and protested his visit to Norfolk in 1922. Young called Garvey's ideology "misguided," while Du Bois referred to it as "bombastic, wasteful, and illogical." [18]

Young's aversion to black political separatism was again dramatically demonstrated a few years later. While attending the NAACP national convention in Philadelphia in July 1924, Young was stunned when James Weldon Johnson urged him to support the Progressive party's nominee, Robert La Follette. Young listened intently as Johnson chastised the Republican party for its refusal to build a viable political organization in the South and to fight vigorously for black suffrage. But Young still disdained third parties and lodged his hopes in the emergence of enlightened white southerners. He thought La Follette's position on black suffrage and civil rights was unclear and that an important segment of the Progressives' coalition, the socialists, were too weak and disorganized in the South. Whereas Johnson observed that Walter White, William Pickens, Du Bois, and other national leaders perceived a trend toward a national third party, Young clung to the only part willing to offer at least some aid to blacks, the GOP. [19]

Young at first greeted Harding's candidacy and election with high hopes. One issue that aroused his optimism was Harding's stance in regard to Haiti. The United States had intervened in Haiti in July 1915, sending in occupational forces for strategic and military reasons. American interests in the Caribbean region, including the Panama Canal and large business investment in Cuba, needed protection. Although the decision to intervene had been part of the long-term development of hegemony for the United States in the Caribbean, the threat of a German submarine base in the area had also been a key factor. [20] From the outset, Young was one of the foremost defenders of Haitian civil and political rights.

The occupation of Haiti endured as a campaign issue during the 1920 presidential race. Young was glad to be able to report in the *Guide* that year that James Weldon Johnson, a prominent black Republican, a member of the Republican National Advisory Committee, and an active opponent of the occupation, discussed the Haitian situation with the Republican presidential candidate Warren G. Harding. A short time later Young challenged blacks to "keep faith with Haiti" and criticized America's control of Haiti's customs and finances. [21]

Although some Haitians welcomed American intervention as a means of ending internal political and economic chaos, and a small number of the elite even collaborated with the Americans, the majority of Haitians were hostile toward America. The U.S. Marines in Haiti were racist; they looked askance at Haitians, seeing them all as "Niggers." Young was quick to praise the president for his condemnation of American occupational forces' harsh practices in Haiti. However, his optimism soon faded as Harding's indifference to black voters at home became apparent. Young's despondency was a result of several futile discussions between Johnson, the newly elected secretary of the NAACP, and Harding. Harding's knowledge of black problems was slight, and he was reluctant to make public statements or commitments.[22]

Calvin Coolidge, who assumed the presidency on Harding's death in 1923, seemed a different man altogether. Most blacks remembered Coolidge's vice-presidential speech to the Senate in which he promised "protection of rights of the minority from whatever source they may be assailed," and they cautiously renewed their allegiance to the Republican party. Young, on the other hand, remained aloof and criticized Coolidge for his appointment of C. Bascom Slemp, Virginia Republican chairman, as his private secretary. Young denounced Slemp as "notorious referee of Republican patronage in Virginia" and a "whip horse"of lily-whitism in the South at large. But Coolidge's flirtation with lily-whites in the South was less obvious than Harding's, and in 1924 he lined up black as well as white convention delegates.[23] Norfolk's white Republicans invited blacks to their district convention, and in February 1924 blacks attended the Republican state convention in Roanoke without incident. Young reported that a "spirit of reconciliation pervaded the convention." Black delegates from Petersburg were seated in preference to an all-white delegation; a black delegate, B. F. Crowell, seconded the party's choice, and black state chairman Joseph R. Pollard, formerly of the lily-black group, urged blacks to vote Republican in the 1924 election. Young's strategy of conciliation and compromise was finally succeeding, and his criticism of Coolidge abated somewhat.[24] Black Republicans were stuck. Where could they go? No one wanted them. It wasn't that Young and others like him were doing the GOP a favor; rather, they were hanging on for dear life to get whatever patronage they could.

A spirit of reconciliation marked the Republican national convention in Cleveland in June, when black delegates from Georgia and Mississippi were seated. Young, who was a delegate, noted that Slemp, the Virginia Republican chairman, "betrayed no lily-white proclivities," fraternizing with black groups in a way "that reminds one of the former days of Republican ascendancy." Still, Young qualified his support of the party and followed what he termed a more "independently Republican" course. He backed "silent Cal" because the GOP platform advocated an anti-lynching law and because the black vote was unwanted by the Democrats. Throughout the summer of 1924 the *Guide* urged readers to "keep cool with Coolidge." [25]

But the Coolidge administration and the Republican party did not live up to blacks' hopes. The Virginia state party organization, in particular, reflected the do-nothingism of the government. In March 1925 Young reiterated his position of independent Republicanism with the announcement that the *Guide* had "always been a Republican paper, but it has never been a slave to the Republican party and never expected to be." He explained his position: because voters make up the Republican party, they should criticize the party and vote against it when political leaders defaulted on their commitment to them; they must do so as "independent thinking citizens." [26]

In hopes of reconciling blacks with the GOP, Young and others in November 1925 led a black delegation to the so-called Washington Conference to meet with President Coolidge. The conference was called by Melvin J. Chisum of the National Negro Press Association to "sound out" the black press and to acquaint the president with black political and economic leaders. The conference discussed Republican apathy, lynching, and the paucity of black political appointees. Prominent blacks in attendance included Vann of the Pittsburgh *Courier*, Mitchell of the Richmond *Planet*, and C. C. Spaulding of North Carolina Mutual Life Insurance Company. William Walker, then editor of the Washington *Tribune*, recalled that Young conferred at length with Du Bois about the continued disfranchisement and the increased polarization of the races in the South. [27] Evidently, Young's strategy of conciliation and compromise was being put to a severe test. He joined with other leaders and demanded more black participation in national affairs and an end to the continued exclusion of blacks from the Republican party. [28]

The Washington conferees were not the only blacks during this period to insist unsuccessfully upon full citizenship. The February 7, 1925, edition of the *Guide* headlined: "Extra! Fisk Campus Place of Terror Because of Student Riot." The students had rebelled against the Code of Discipline, a detailed set of university rules that set hours for meals, sleep, and study. The rebellious students were a new breed of Negro on campus, different from Young's generation. They had a strong sense of race and insisted upon full citizenship and a curriculum that deemphasized vocational education. Young reluctantly supported the strike and called on Fisk's president, Fayette Avery McKenzie, to resign to "save his own dignity and the welfare of the University."[29]

The controversy at Fisk revealed much about the nature of Du Bois's and Young's leadership. Du Bois's dynamic words in the *Crisis*, in the Fisk *Herald*, and in his speeches to the alumni catapulted him to the forefront of the controversy. Young used the *Guide* to defuse the crisis and to explain controversial issues to people on both sides. Du Bois was a provocateur; Young, a compromiser. Du Bois protested that the students were "humiliated and insulted." In addition, he charged that McKenzie's policies undermined the students' initiative and self-respect. Although Young respected Du Bois, he nevertheless blamed him for the trouble at Fisk. Young acknowledged that the students had grievances, but he worried about the impact of the strike on public opinion and on the future careers of the suspended students. Du Bois hoped that the controversy would serve as a model for all black colleges and bring changes in black higher education. Young called for a quick settlement and predicted that the student strike would provoke southern white anger and hamper attempts to gain interracial goodwill.[30]

It was not long before riots burst out on the campuses of Howard University and Hampton Institute. Young was stunned. He angrily called the strikes "ill conceived." To him the much-heralded "New Negro" represented a "small, insignificant group" whose actions touched only the "illiterate adult masses of the South." He blamed the strike at Hampton on a lack of self-discipline and low admission standards. In both instances he used the *Guide* to present the college administration's side of the strike.[31] Clearly, Young was a product of the old school; he had grown up when all trustees and presidents of black schools were white; now Mordecai Johnson, a black, was to head Howard. Times were changing, and Young was not changing with them.

Young sided with the college administration during the student rebellion, but when his son Thomas W. Young encountered "flagrant discrimination" and "color prejudice" at New York University, Young privately condemned university officials. He kept the controversy out of the *Guide* but filed "vigorous protest" with NAACP Assistant Secretary Walter White and legal counsel Arthur A. Spingarn. Young was even more interested in the case of Reba McLain, a young black woman who was dismissed from a physical education class, than in the case of his son, who was refused a dormitory room. Race was the issue in both instances, but according to Young, McLain's case was more important because it affected the "vital opportunity" of black students to take courses in northern universities. He kept his mouth shut publicly, however, to keep blacks in white colleges, or possibly because he feared repercussions on his news-paper. The NAACP promised to do "everything within its power" to end racial discrimination at NYU and blamed the controversy on "a handful of Southern whites" in the administration.[32] White favored legal action, as did Young's son, but Young demurred.

Young's conservatism temporarily strained relations between himself and his son. Thomas believed that "the Negro must strike back at every injustice and mistreatment accorded him." To him, legal combat was the most positive way to assert one's stand. But his father reasoned that uni-versity officials were "on the record . . . and on the defensive." He agreed with Spingarn, who argued that NYU could not be forced to integrate its dormitories or its department of physical education. Instead, he suggested a conference, which the NAACP promptly arranged at its headquarters. White, Spingarn, Thomas W. Young, Reba McLain, and Harold A. Voorhis, assistant to the chancellor of NYU, met and decided against legal action because it might create "hostile sentiment" toward NYU's other eighty to one hundred black students.[33] The controversy was further abated by liberal NYU faculty members who circulated petitions to protest discrimination within the university. Thomas Young com-mented that he was "absolutely satisfied" with the results of the confer-ence. "A precedent was established," he remarked. Though he called it a "complete victory," he transferred the following year to Ohio State Uni-versity. One year after the controversy, NYU allegedly denied a dormi-tory room to Asa T. Spaulding, son of the president of North Carolina Mutual Insurance Company, and two years later benched a black football player before a game with the University of Georgia.[34] The *Guide* ignored the first controversy and made only scattered references to the other.

Young was forced to negotiate personally with White, Spingarn, and NYU officials rather than through the local NAACP because "internal dissension and conflict" had rendered the Norfolk branch ineffective since 1921. Young's political conservatism, a large cadre of well-paid workers from the Newport News Shipbuilding Company, an educated elite from Hampton Institute, and internal bickering for various offices within the local branch contributed to the NAACP's ineffectiveness. Also, the grow-ing popularity of both the national and the local branches of the NAACP challenged the leadership class within the black church and threatened the social status of local black civic and fraternal groups. Undoubtedly, many black Norfolkians were comfortably entrenched within the wall of segregation. Accordingly, when Dr. G. Hamilton Francis, a personal friend and a trustee of the Grace Episcopal Church, attempted to revital-ize the organization in September 1921, he found the task "impossible," and like Young, he resigned as president. Despite voluminous letters and many field trips to Norfolk by NAACP officials, the branch remained dormant from late 1921 until mid-1925. Dr. Francis attempted to revive it again in August 1925 but "found it impossible." Young did not attend the fall meeting, nor was his name among the list of "prospective members" forwarded to the national NAACP in New York. On September 18, 1925, the national director of branches asked Young "to help revive the dormant Norfolk Branch." He cheerfully accepted the responsibility, organizing a conference to discuss issues confronting Norfolk's black community.[35]

Aside from lynching, the most pressing problem facing Norfolk's blacks in 1925 was inadequate housing. As in Richmond, Atlanta, Montgomery, and other cities of the South, deplorable segregated housing in Norfolk often made life unbearable for blacks. The national NAACP expected Young "to crystallize public opinion" and to "organize opposition" to residential segregation. Although the editor assured NAACP officials of his "earnest desire to cooperate," seemingly he was not yet ready to violate the South's code. He considered it inexpedient to attack segregation openly. He believed that accommodation was necessary. Moreover, he believed that an assault on white supremacy would impair his effectiveness as a race leader. His strategy was to uplift blacks economically, to seek the friendship of influential whites, and to gradually wear away prejudice.

After black attorney David Edwards assumed the presidency of the Norfolk chapter, Young accepted an appointment to the committee on public relations.[36] Other leaders of the group were, in their words, "forward thinking men," whose view paralleled that of the national NAACP. Their first move was to have the local branch challenge Virginia's residential segregation law as illegal. On February 26, 1926, the national NAACP announced its backing of the move. The national NAACP was in a position to fight not only residential segregation but the white primary and regenerated Ku Klux Klan as well, for it had the use of money and legal expertise unavailable to individual black litigants.[37] As the national NAACP heaped praise upon the Norfolk chapter, Young found himself on the side of timidity during a crisis.

A few days before the national NAACP made its move against residential discrimination in Virginia, the Norfolk branch circulated a flier announcing a "Big Mass Meeting" at the Second Calvary Church. The *Guide* advised that the purpose of the meeting was "to present facts" surrounding the murder of Leroy Strother, a thirteen-year-old black youth who was fatally wounded during an altercation with Israel Banks, a white Jewish merchant. Banks, who had assumed that his gun was empty, had intended only to frighten Strother. After firing the weapon, Banks carried Strother's body next door to Strother's grandmother and surrendered. Young and reporters from the *Guide* arrived on the scene promptly and waded through a crowd of onlookers to interview witnesses. The mood was ugly; the black community was outraged. The *Guide* and the Norfolk NAACP launched a drive to raise funds to prosecute Banks.[38]

At a mass meeting attorney Edwards, G. W. C. Brown, Sr., and J. Thomas Newsome, along with James Weldon Johnson, Robert Bagnall, and other national NAACP officials, urged Norfolkians to protest the violence. But Young was again on the side of timidity and restraint; the *Guide* even failed to respond editorially. However, Edwards in a letter to NAACP official Johnson alleged that Strother was the third child fatally wounded by a Jewish merchant within the past ten months. He condemned Strother's killing and vowed to show whites that they could not kill blacks "without just cause" and "without militant opposition." Banks was subsequently convicted of involuntary manslaughter and fined $600. Black attorney J. Thomas Newsome prosecuted the case. The national NAACP criticized the "light penalty" but praised the conviction as a warning to "lawless whites" and as a model "to encourage the development of active branches" throughout the South.[39] Meanwhile, despite internal conflicts, the Norfolk NAACP went forward with plans to fight segregation.

Young responded more strongly to a march by 400 hooded Klansmen in Carrsville, Virginia, in May 1929. In this instance, his reaction epitomized his feelings about interracial violence. He quickly responded editorially and sent reporters "to weave the story together." He called the incident "typical" in the lives of blacks "ruled by fear, cowardice and prejudice" in rural communities. He believed that "justice resided in Virginia," and he called upon Virginians "to take note." Meanwhile national NAACP officials "confidentially" solicited his opinion of white attorneys Hugh L. Holland and J. Melvin Lovelace; they wished to know more about their "ability and faithfulness to Negro clients" arrested in conjunction with the case. Young called Holland and Lovelace "capable lawyers" but termed their case "difficult" because of Klan pressure.[40] He enclosed copies of confidential correspondence from the attorneys, numerous clippings, and a detailed account of the incident. Apparently, he was forwarding all this information because the Norfolk branch was again defunct. In turn, the national NAACP sent Young confidential depositions and correspondence from Holland and Lovelace.

Young devoted more attention to lynching than to any other issue during the 1920s. He exposed the Klan's dastardly acts in pictures and words. From the time of the birth of the new Klan in 1915 to the passage of

Governor Harry F. Byrd's state antilynching bill in 1928, weekly editions of the *Guide* assailed lynchings. Young tried to prick the conscience of white Christians, and he was especially critical of whites who merely condemned the Klan's violent deeds but attributed them to ignorant bigots and lower-class white men. He called such apathy inexcusable. Pointing out that whites monopolized law in the South, he challenged law enforcement officers to bring the offenders to justice. To Young, lynching and other acts of violence committed by the KKK affected whites as well as blacks. He declared, "No man escapes its contamination; . . . all of society is affected by the actions of a part of society."[41]

Black families in the rural counties of Virginia depended upon the *Guide* to expose Klan activities and violence. Oftentimes, blacks who were "rudely shocked" or under "intense mental strain" as a result of Klan activities personally visited Young in his Norfolk office. And yet Young had detractors who denounced the *Guide's* response to interracial violence. They forwarded clippings and letters concerning alleged Klan activity in Virginia to the Chicago *Defender*, Pittsburgh *Courier*, and the national NAACP, accusing the *Guide* of being "afraid" and of printing news "to suit Southern people." Because Norfolk's NAACP was defunct during the early 1920s, Young also sent newspaper clippings and reported incidents of violence to NAACP officials in New York. In turn, they requested that Young forward depositions from both complainants and defendants. The NAACP respected Young's judgment about the legalities and exchanged confidential information about black attorneys and possible strategy with him.[42]

Young and Louis Jaffe, editor of the Norfolk *Virginian-Pilot*, devoted more attention to lynching than to any other issue during the 1920s. Both excoriated those who would replace law and civility with mob rule and lynch law. Ironically, both opposed federal antilynching legislation as a violation of the principle of states' rights. Neither ever openly attacked the entire system of racial segregation; neither proclaimed the social equality of the races. Rather, they urged the extermination of lynching because it was an unlawful and unconscionable injustice to blacks and because it corrupted and debased whites as well. Jaffe was the first white editor in the South to speak out vigorously against lynching. In June 1928 he condemned this form of mob violence in an editorial entitled "An Unspeakable Act of Savagery" which earned him a Pulitzer Prize. As the 1920s came to a close, the shocking disclosures in the editorials of Young and Jaffe, the rationality of their powerful words, and their stature as spokesmen of their respective races helped to influence Governor Byrd to press for the enactment of a strong state antilynching law. Thus, Virginia became the first southern state to enact such a law. At the end of Byrd's term in 1930, both the *Pilot* and *Guide* characterized him as the greatest governor in modern Virginia history. Young prophetically asserted that the people of Virginia would recall him to high office.[43]

Meanwhile, the legal battles on behalf of blacks' rights continued in the courts. *Moore* v. *Dempsey* in 1923 rejected mob presence in the courtroom as detrimental to a defendant's right to a fair trial; a 1927 ruling, *Nixon* v. *Herndon*, legalized black participation in Democratic primaries. The *Guide*, New York *Age*, Richmond *Planet*, Pittsburgh *Courier*, and other black newspapers hailed the *Nixon* decision as significant, far-reaching, and "the beginning of a new era." They provided widespread coverage of the NAACP's role in the case; indeed, "the relationship between the NAACP and the black press was mutually beneficial."[44] The NAACP had its own press service and provided the black newspapers with important copy. In turn, the black press provided the NAACP with much-needed publicity.

Even though Young publicly supported the NAACP in the *Guide*, by the end of the decade his private commitment had waned. Dissent within the Norfolk branch along with a shake-up in the national office and the Pittsburgh *Courier's* charge of "malfeasance and gross mishandling of funds" affected his thinking. The controversy arose on October 9, 1926. When the *Courier* headline "NAACP Slush Fund Aired," the Norfolk editor was shocked. He was a personal friend of James Weldon Johnson, and he respected W. E. B. Du Bois, who was also implicated. The charges were serious, and the NAACP found itself on the defensive. The controversy filtered down to individual branches throughout the South and forced rank-and-file members to choose sides.[45]

Nearly every black newspaper entered the dispute. The *Guide*, Chicago *Bee*, Philadelphia *Tribune*, Baltimore *Afro-American*, and the Richmond *Planet* defended the NAACP.[46] But the Cleveland *Gazette*, Chicago *Whip*, Detroit *Owl*, and Tucson *Times* joined the *Courier* attack. Hostility between the NAACP and the *Courier* continued until 1929, when both publicly vowed to "bury the hatchet"and cooperate in the common cause. Young disdained the NAACP's inability to garner Republican patronage and was sensitive to the growing political power of the dominant Democrats in Virginia. The NAACP's legal attack on disfranchisement and the white primary further alienated him and accentuated the sectional and ideological differences between black leaders in the North and South.

Young and other conservative blacks questioned the NAACP's strategy of "agitation and protest" and, at times, even its efficacy. To Young, white support of the Southern Sociological Congress, the Council on Interracial

Cooperation (CIC), and the NOS was proof that "good white people" did not wish to disturb the tenuous harmony they had established with himself and other "able and safe" black leaders. When Virginia senator Carter Glass, S. C. Mitchell, Louis Jaffee, Homer Ferguson, and others who represented in Young's view "the best blood of the old South" and the most enlightened sentiment of the "new South" condemned the Massenburg bill, which prohibited public interracial assemblages, Young applauded because the bill was detrimental to the state's "happy race relations."[47]

Seemingly, Young and the "able and safe" black leaders interpreted a reduction or absence of overt violence as racial harmony. In the face of disfranchisement and continued Republican neglect, they continued to assert that "interracial goodwill was steadily growing." They assumed that they could change the character of race relations in the South through moral suasion. The NAACP's militance was antithetical to the southern way of dealing with race relations. In other words, observed Thomas Dabney, a career *Guide* employee, "southerners knew what was best for the Negro." Blacks like Young reasoned that the white South—good white people—were tired of violence and would eventually resurrect the postwar coalition of liberal blacks and whites and, they hoped, restore, Republican patronage. The NAACP was too polemical, too combative, an obstruction to interracial goodwill. In his paper Young consistently touted acts of goodwill by whites—from increased funding of southern black colleges to the employment of a lone black. Such acts, coupled with his own rise to prominence and Governor Byrd's antilynching law, proved to him the validity of his philosophy. By the end of the decade, the NAACP in Virginia was dormant; the Richmond branch was apathetic and the Norfolk branch defunct. When the Norfolk branch was revived again during the early 1930s by the Reverend B. W. Harris, rector of the Grace Episcopal Church, neither Young nor his wife Eleanor were members.[48]

▪ 5 ▪

Becoming a New Deal Democrat

In the presidential election of 1928 Young abandoned the Republican party. For the next few years he followed a course of "militant independence," finding himself in the same political camp with the NAACP and W. E. B. Du Bois. He urged blacks to vote for any candidate who paid back "individual dividends in justice, fair play, and full equality of all citizenship rights." He exhorted blacks "to hold to any independent mind politically," and he vigorously supported measures to increase the number of black voters. He advised blacks in Virginia to seek an accommodation with Virginia's young governor, Harry Byrd, and his emerging Democratic organization. He condemned President Herbert Hoover's neglect of blacks, voted for Franklin Roosevelt in 1932, and by 1936 had become a firm New Dealer. In the meantime his newspaper continued to flourish, and he earned plaudits for himself in the state and nation. By 1928 the *Guide*'s circulation exceeded that of the Richmond *Planet*, *Carolina Times*, *Carolinian*, Savannah *Tribune*, Atlanta *Daily World*, and other southern black-owned newspapers. It had expanded its circulation into New Haven, Chicago, Kansas City, Omaha, and major western cities.[1]

In January 1928 Young reflected upon Republican indifference and Democratic conservatism. He noted that black support of Coolidge in 1924 had been prompted by Democratic apathy and by fears that La Follette, whatever his virtues, could not win the presidential race. Ironically, four years later Young found himself in agreement with radicals A. Philip Randolph and Chandler Owens, who supported America's first Catholic presidential nominee, Democrat Alfred E. Smith, because "it might teach the United States a lesson in pluralism and tolerance." He aligned himself with other members of the black citizens' Democratic Club, which was originally organized as a "Smith for President" movement in early 1928. Like Du Bois, Young welcomed Smith's candidacy because it threatened the solid South. Also, he could not ignore the other influential black newspapers who had changed allegiance from Republican to Democratic. Du Bois called the 1928 presidential campaign "the most humiliating" that the black man had ever experienced. After weeks of racist propaganda, Young joined black leaders to issue "An Appeal to America" to end the epithets.[2]

By September 1928 black political preferences throughout the Commonwealth were in a state of flux, as indicated by the Buckroe Conference. Buckroe Beach, Hampton, was the site of a state conference of black voters convened to plot strategy after the Republican national convention of July 1928, which had excluded blacks.[3] Young, along with Newsome, Mitchell, and other former lily-blacks, shelved their differences. Although the conferees passed a resolution not to endorse either Smith or Hoover, the *Guide* recorded that Smith sentiment predominated.[4]

Following the Buckroe Conference, Young hastened to assure his white readers that most blacks were apolitical, interested only in economic improvement. He was a reluctant Democrat but, in his words, "partisan now and extremely so." He no longer thought blacks owed gratitude to the Republican party, claiming it had abandoned its traditional principles and embraced those who would deny blacks political and civil freedom. On October 27, 1928, Young announced his support for Smith and for an informal group of black dissident Democrats called "Smith for President." The *Guide* echoed the sentiment of many Virginia blacks when it declared that blacks did not desert the Republican party; the party had repudiated them.[5]

Young's political shift reflected the antipathy of black national leaders toward Republican lily-white policies. Despite the black campaign against him, however, Hoover received the second largest number of votes ever secured by a Republican.[6] A *Guide* headline attributed Smith's defeat to "Religion, Race, and Rum." Young was philosophical. Like Du Bois, he reasoned that the election presaged a new politics: the "solid South was smashed." Furthermore, he saw Smith's candidacy as promising because it had forced blacks to become "definitely independent" of the Republican party. He asserted that during the next campaign "the color of our skin will no longer disclose our political fate."[7]

Young expressed qualified approval of Hoover's inaugural address in which Hoover characterized a "disregard and disobedience" of the law as the greatest problem of the country. But he deplored Hoover's failure to mention blacks. It was not the blacks' desire to be separated from the "body politics," Young reasoned; rather, it was white prejudice that set blacks apart and blocked their participation in American life. The failure of the president and the lily-white Republicans to recognize blacks only reinforced their exclusion and deprived them of equal opportunity.[8]

The general shift of black voters to the Democratic party that Young had predicted failed to materialize, and his anxiety heightened after the final tally and the full impact of Hoover's victory was revealed. Hoover received 58.12 percent of the popular vote, exceeded only by the Harding vote in 1920. The solid South was cracked; the heaviest Democratic losses were in the South, where provincialism, prohibition, and Protestantism had proved stronger than party. Apparently, Young misunderstood Hoover. A recent study has characterized him as "racially progressive" and not "a lily white racist" who deliberately attempted to drive blacks from positions of leadership and influence in the Republican party. Young's misstatements about Hoover were probably inspired by Hoover's reticence and personality. Despite his Quaker background, Hoover displayed little sympathy for blacks and said less about the racial issue than any other modern president. Also, Hoover backed an all-white delegation to the 1928 Republican convention over an integrated one, and even though fifty-seven blacks were lynched during his administration, he offered no public protest. Hoover's successful invasion of the Democratic South doomed black influence in southern Republican organizations. According to one source, "lily-whitism" was given "a great fillip."[9]

And yet, Young later reasoned, Hoover's election and the lily-white movement in the South might ultimately work to the advantage of blacks. It would be a "ticklish strategy." If Republican racism continued victorious at the polls, it would offend the strategic black vote in the North and West.[10] Also, if the lily-white Republicans attracted disenchanted Democrats and critics of the New Deal, they could drive the opening wedge for a two-party system in the South. Ultimately this would benefit blacks. Prudence therefore dictated that blacks temporarily remain politically aloof.

Young regarded the election in Illinois of Republican Oscar De Priest, the first black elected to the U.S. House since 1900, as an "unmistakable vindication" of the *Guide*'s Democratic proclivities.[11] De Priest, like Young, had urged southern blacks "to cast their votes with the Democrats in certain situations" on the grounds that a friendly Democratic governor, mayor, or judge could enable blacks to consolidate their economic gains.[12] Young felt further alienation from the Republican party after Hoover nominated Judge John Parker, an alleged racist, to the U.S. Supreme

Court. He aligned himself with the NAACP and repeatedly blasted Parker's nomination in the *Guide*. He reminded blacks that as a Republican gubernatorial nominee, Parker had condemned the black in politics "as a source of evil and danger to both races." After the Senate rejected Parker's nomination, Young commented that blacks had exerted more political influence in the fight against Parker than at any time since Reconstruction.[13]

Before that controversy had settled, Young found himself at odds with Hoover over his inept handling of the European pilgrimage of Gold Star Mothers. In late February 1929 Congress passed an act that sponsored the visits of the mothers and widows of American servicemen interred in Europe to the graves of the deceased. As the first group prepared to depart on May 6, 1930, the Hoover administration arranged segregated transportation. The black community was outraged. Young accused Hoover of openly sanctioning segregation. Of the 450 black mothers originally scheduled to make the trip, only 58 sailed. The nomination of Judge Parker, the Gold Star Mothers issue, and Hoover's refusal to meet with Executive Secretary Walter White of the NAACP in October 1930 confirmed Young's belief that the party persisted in its lily-whitism. In May 1930 Young again asserted his independence by urging blacks to vote for "men and measures" regardless of party. Hereafter, he noted, "the term Republican and Democrat will assume only a relative importance to black voters."[14]

Any possibility of realignment with the national Republican party disintegrated in 1931 with the Scottsboro affair. Young sharply criticized the Hoover administration for its lack of concern over the most significant event of the year, which became a cause célèbre of the 1930s. The case arose when nine black boys were arrested and charged with the rape of two white women aboard a train in Alabama.[15] Despite overwhelming evidence of the boys' innocence, Alabama officials vigorously prosecuted the case. The *Guide* maintained that the Scottsboro trial was not an ordinary criminal trial but a struggle over whether blacks could have competent counsel, an unbiased jury, and an impartial trial in the South. Young charged that Hoover had succumbed to political pressure and inflamed public opinion. Hoover's lack of leadership, the inertia of his administration, and his capitulation to racism ended any possibility that Young might return to the Republican party.

The 1930s ushered in the worst economic crisis in American history. Blacks were the first to face hunger, joblessness, and despair. The burden of unemployment fell most heavily on the black female-headed households. Black women domestics lost their jobs to white competitors who had been displaced by factory closings. Black teachers, many of whom earned considerably less than whites, suffered salary cuts. Young was especially grieved at the displacement of black female domestics because of the high unemployment rate among black males. He attributed the low wages and the high unemployment to an overabundant labor supply. Washwomen in the Norfolk-Portsmouth area eagerly worked for half wages, and cooks once employed for fifteen dollars per week were paid three dollars. Black nurses received an average salary of three dollars per week. Nationally, in 1930 approximately four of every ten black women worked outside the home, compared with one of every six white women. In the South the proportion of married black women employed ranged from 20 percent in Arkansas to over 43 percent in Florida. Only 9 percent of married white women, however, were in the work force.[16]

Norfolk's Metropolitan Bank, which advertised itself as "the largest Negro Bank in the World," collapsed in January 1931. Black municipal service workers throughout the tidewater area were fired. Jobs traditionally held by blacks, garbage collection and street cleaning, were assumed by whites. Young complained that black teachers, businessmen, and professionals accepted jobs traditionally held by the poor and unskilled. He counseled both high school and college graduates "to accept the sad fact that no jobs are available." High unemployment and low wages demoralized Norfolk's black community and, in Young's view, were "making thieves of servants." "Decency cannot long be sustained," he concluded.[17]

Hoover blamed Europe for the crisis and insisted that relief was a local responsibility. "We have now passed the worst," he announced wishfully in May 1930, "and shall rapidly recover." Young retorted that Hoover was hallucinating. The editor refrained from blaming Hoover for the Great Depression, but he did condemn the president's relief policies and his reluctance to employ federal initiatives. He called Hoover a "master of evasion." As hard times gripped Virginia, Hoover's name became synonymous with hardship. The *Guide* caustically referred to this period as "Hoover Time."[18]

On the other hand, Young reasoned that unemployment and hunger might help to engender racial solidarity and economic security within the black community. Before 1930 blacks were "heedless and indifferent"; prosperity had lulled them into a false sense of security and accomplishment. Young explained, "the current depression may well be . . . our salvation." The lessons it taught might be of "incalculable value."[19]

Ironically, according to Young, black businesses on Norfolk's Church street thrived while white business establishments elsewhere in the city went bankrupt. There were a number of reasons for this. First, white establishments catered almost exclusively to whites, while black businesses were patronized by both races. Black businesses tended to be family owned and paid their employees, both black and white, less than white businesses; in addition, black businesses enjoyed a smaller margin of profit. Among the hardest hit was the dry-cleaning business, and throughout the spring and summer of 1932 white Norfolk cleaners engaged in a price war that at times erupted into violence. At the center of the controversy were two of the largest dry-cleaning establishments in the city of Norfolk, Rick and Scott. The white establishments charged that these "colored cleaners" had too many billboards, advertised too much, and forced whites out of business. Young used the *Guide* to alert city fathers to this effort to hinder black enterprise. He boldly defended Rick and Scott. They mirrored the success of the black self-help movement and epitomized Washingtonian thrift, self-help, and economic independence.[20]

During the Depression the *Guide* chronicled the plight of black business. Although black Virginians were the "first fired and last hired," unemployed whites received relief before blacks did. By the early 1930s the Norfolk NAACP was again defunct, the Norfolk chapter of the NOS was consumed with only "the head and heart," and the *Guide* was the only instrument of protest. The unwillingness of whites to employ blacks in businesses that served a predominantly black clientele infuriated Young. He criticized Norfolkians for their "complacency" and at mass meetings organized by the Negro Chamber of Commerce he called for what black educator and former *Guide* columnist Gordon Blaine Hancock later popularized as the "double-duty dollar"—"buy where you work." He had already thrown down the political gauntlet, and his editorial polemics during the early 1930s mirrored his changed political beliefs. He challenged black citizens to stop making excuses. He advised them to buy only from black merchants, to hire only black contractors, to let only black mechanics make repairs, and to permit only black artisans to beautify their homes.[21]

Young's hope for an independent entrepreneurial class fit his overall approach to the race question. The economically functional Negro would be in a position to demand full rights and protection under the law. Young, as Washington did before him, believed that black industrialists and entrepreneurs would gradually mitigate prejudice against blacks that could never be legislated away. Young further believed that if this strategy failed, Norfolk's blacks could still survive if they had built a self-sustaining black community.[22]

The hard times forced several black colleges to cut back or to close. The

Guide reported that Hampton Institute abandoned its summer program, and Morgan State in Baltimore temporarily closed. North Carolina College in Durham suffered a $30,000 deficit. Elizabeth City State College in North Carolina best epitomized the problems among black colleges. Teachers' salaries were cut in half, and the college and its faculty members accepted farm produce in lieu of money. Black suicides also threatened the survival of black colleges during the early 1930s. The *Guide* reported that schools in Virginia and North Carolina were plagued by a wave of suicides; three attempts alone occurred during February 1932, one successfully.[23]

The colleges were also plagued by student strikes and increased hostility between the faculty and the administration. But, unlike the black college rebellions of the 1920s, the disruptions now were nonviolent, and their chief thrust was economic. Protest now focused on injustices within society rather than on blacks' exclusion from society. Strikes at Howard, St. Augustine, North Carolina A&T, Kentucky State, Langston College (Oklahoma), and other black colleges occurred throughout the 1930s. Tuskegee was forced to close, and Hampton was again brought to the verge of social anarchy. Young angrily blamed the student unrest, suicides, and budget deficits on the Depression and "a changing social order."[24]

The suicides on black campuses dramatized the overall suicide rate for blacks in Virginia. The *Guide* reported that black suicides in 1933 doubled those of the previous five years. For example, there were 232 suicides in Virginia in 1928 and only 7 were black; yet, in 1933 there were 336 and 25 were black.[25] Young was appalled. He concluded that blacks were "weakening spiritually and physically" under the Depression. His response was to extol certain aspects of black life in order to elicit a sense of pride and accomplishment among blacks chilled by the bleak hand of the Depression. He gave front-page coverage to the admission of a black to an Ivy League university and the appointment of a black to a previously all-white police force. Typical headlines read: "Negro Student at the Naval Academy," "Historic White Church Founded by Negro Cobbler," "P. B. Young to Speak at White College."

There is a direct relationship between oppression in the black community, both real and imagined, and the quantity of social items in the black press; as oppression grew, social items proliferated. Young recognized that social items detracted from hard news, but he had no choice. He frequently ordered his field agents to "cut it down." "If we keep feeding them [blacks] this stuff, they will develop atrophy of the brain," he asserted. At the same time, Young realized that extended social items in the newspaper projected blacks as enterprising and resourceful and was thus responsible for his inreased circulation. The *Guide* offered advice on love, marriage, and speculations of all kinds. The society page was open to the public, and occasionally someone with an ax to grind would phone or send in an item to cause embarrassment. Laughter, too, was a form of therapy and recreation. "Oh! What a Lie," headlined gossip about a prominent black member of the community or news of an alleged love tryst between a popular minister and a choir member. The intimate details, sprinkled with gossipy comment and pictures, were included.[26]

The *Guide* initiated a series of articles on black Virginians in New York City, which had a larger Virginia-born population than Norfolk. The grace, charm, and sophistication of the "Daughters of Virginia," the "Sons of Virginia," the "Tidewater Girls," and the "Hampton Club" were exalted. Entire pages were allocated to announce stage productions from New York of *The Emperor Jones, Green Pastures,* and *Imitation of Life.* A black cartoon, "Little Moses and Phantom Island," the most clever colored character ever created, satirized black life. Serialized features such as "How to Become a Good Hostess" and "The Disadvantages of Teen Marriage" were carried weekly. Advertisements for products to "lighten the skin" and "straighten the hair" noticeably increased, as did advertisements for black businesses, funeral homes, and movie theaters.[27]

The increased ads of products to lighten the skin and to straighten the hair were probably reflective of self-hatred and emulation of whites. To a large degree, successful blacks resembled whites. Young did not deliberately exploit this type of advertisement, but as a businessman, he had no choice. The absence of black broadcast media gave Young a monopoly on advertisements within the black community. He championed black business advertisements because they paralleled his views about economic self-help and racial solidarity. Also, advertisements had a twofold strategy. First, they boosted local businesses and thereby exalted Norfolk's prosperous black middle class. Next, they extended the ideals of the Negro Forward Movement.

Mounting circulation attested to Young's continued success. From September 30, 1932, to December 31, 1934, the average net paid circulation of the *Guide* increased by a phenomenal 70 percent, to 26,105. Young proudly proclaimed that he owned the "largest" and "best edited" black newspaper in the South. On the *Guide's* thirtieth anniversary in 1930, its property and real estate were valued at $100,000 and it had an annual payroll in excess of $50,000.[28] Moreover, it had never missed an issue, and its price remained ten cents per copy.

Young initiated a bold campaign to extend suffrage to blacks; he called it "A Next Move Forward." The *Guide* stepped up its assault on the white primary, poll tax, and other obstacles to black voting in Virginia during the 1930s. Young urged blacks to "move forward" and "to participate," not in blind party allegiance, "but with political discernment calculated to consolidate and to advance black political and economic interest." He rebuked the Republicans for their loss of "democratic ideals and political foresight" and sought out what he termed "new political latitudes" in order to create a more favorable climate for black suffrage.[29]

Despite his enthusiasm, Young's voter registration campaigns were generally unsuccessful until the candidacy of black attorney Victor Ashe in the early 1950s. The phrase "Next Move Forward" presupposes that something of significance had happened before. Although black suffrage was an issue, the "Next Move Forward" was really an extension of the "Negro Forward Movement" that Young and other prominent black Norfolkians had evolved during the pre–World War I years. At that time, the issues were racial solidarity and economic uplift. The same issues predominated during the "Next Move Forward."

In December 1931 Young accepted an invitation to attend a nonpartisan conference in Washington, D.C., organized by Chicago's black Republican congressman Oscar De Priest. The purpose was to debate black political strategy and ideology. Over three hundred delegates from twenty-six states attended. Howard's president Mordecai Johnson urged the delegates "to band together; to keep the politicians guessing," while Robert Vann and Kelly Miller noted that black Republicans were riding a dead horse.

A few weeks later Young and other black leaders from throughout Virginia along with over three hundred delegates met in Richmond to organize the nonpartisan United Civic League. Its purpose was to promote voter enrollment and to oppose racial injustices. Young was the keynote speaker. The United Civic League later evolved into the Virginia Civic League after branches were established in Petersburg, Suffolk, Lynchburg, and other cities. This nonpartisan organization soon sprouted in other black southern communities, and in the late summer of 1932 Kelly Miller mentioned a National Nonpartisan League, which was launched because of dissatisfaction with "existing political conditions" and eleven years of Republican rule. The new organization was an alternative to the NAACP, which was defunct in many communities in the South. Many blacks belonged to both groups, and even though black enfranchisement was the objective of both, the league was more successful. Its title was less abrasive and did not conjure up the same image among local whites as did the NAACP. Accordingly, it was easier for blacks at the grass-roots level to meet and to organize under its aegis. Even though the stated purpose of the league was to encourage voting, meetings occasionally included discussions of civic improvements and outrageous acts of racial violence. On several occasions a National League Committee consisting of Oscar De Priest, Kelly Miller, Baltimore editor Carl Murphy, and black educator Mary Church Terrell interviewed candidates from the two major parties to "ascertain their attitude."[30]

Although black leaders like Kelly Miller, W. E. B. Du Bois, R. R. Moton, and others all favored a more politically independent black voter, they disagreed about strategy. Young and Luther P. Jackson favored a massive voter registration program and what the *Guide* called "Militant Independence." Miller favored registration and political independence but advised blacks to vote equally for candidates of either party. Also, Miller and others counseled that it was "good politics" for southern blacks to align themselves politically and financially with black candidates in Chicago, Philadelphia, New York, and other northern cities.[31] Young responded that Miller had lost "lucidity." "Why should blacks vote *equally* for the two major parties and destroy their opportunity for being a decisive factor?" he asked. In Young's view, neither then would be obligated to help blacks. Miller argued that an equal vote meant less retaliation from the losing party; Young retorted that blacks "owe no debt to any party" and should vote for any party or candidate as long as—only as long as—a solid vote supported black demands for equality of citizenship. Young's strategy of militant independence was based on the assumption that if blacks voted intelligently and consistently in their own interest, the parties would soon "learn their lesson" and respect the power of the black vote. Young believed that Miller's strategy would lead to a separate black party and a political debacle like the lily-black movement of the 1920s.

Although the NAACP was often the most visible protest organ in the South, the nonpartisan United League and the NOS were often the more effective means of inculcating blacks with a sense of political independence and galvanizing visible protest. The black church was a safe place for blacks to debate political organization; hence, the move for black political independence at the local level in the South depended as much on the black church as it did on the black press and local organizers, and not much on the NAACP.

For black leaders, partisan issues often became entwined with social and educational matters seemingly beyond the pale of politics. Young's interest in the affairs of the federally supported Howard University, founded in the nation's capital by leaders of the Freedmen's Bureau, is a case in point. Young met the black president of Howard, Mordecai Johnson, during the early 1930s at regular meetings of the NOS and the CIC. He would become one of Johnson's staunchest supporters, as again and again the black university became the focus of controversy, a perennial political football.

For example, in April 1931 the *Guide* reported that Johnson was "under fire" and "at war" for alleged wrongdoing, and it characterized the situation at Howard as a conflict between the "old and new." Johnson's problems emanated from his conflicts with board member Emmett J. Scott, the former personal secretary of Booker T. Washington, and from Johnson's decisions to dismiss the law school dean and to downgrade athletics. Young, in support of Johnson, angrily described the situation as a "calamity" and commended the board for stamping out "the ugly situation at our leading university." But Johnson remained "under fire" throughout most of 1931, as controversies erupted over his decision to suspend the dean of the dental school. The white faculty resigned from the law school, and there were charges of sexual harassment in the department of English. The *Guide* declared that Johnson's foes were out to get him.[32]

A few months later Johnson was again the target when a new dispute arose over his desire to mortgage university property worth $6 million for a $160,000 loan. Also, Johnson was accused of favoritism as he attempted to deflect criticism from a janitor who was accused of falsely certifying that his son had performed work and was entitled to compensation. After the university's architect exposed the alleged incident, Johnson attempted "to punish him."[33] Johnson's detractors induced Democratic congressman Robert Hall of Mississippi to call for a congressional investigation on behalf of "interested parties." Young dismissed the investigation as "a tempest in a teapot." In a speech to the Sons of Norfolk Social and Beneficial Association, he asserted that it was "time to close ranks." He alluded to the political jealousies at Howard and the "amusing ambitions for leadership." "Forget who is spokesman or leader," he asserted; "no one Negro will ever be able to lead all Negroes."[34]

In February 1932 Young caucused with black Republican congressman Oscar De Priest, in Norfolk to address the Independent Voters League. De Priest privately explained that "campus politicians" had supported Johnson, a black, for the presidency of Howard on the assumption that they could use him to support their "petty ends." However, when Johnson proved to be "a real man," they had turned on him. De Priest, like Young, believed that the "shakedown" at Howard was in response to a Roosevelt Democrat's "angling" for the presidency of Howard.[35] Their view was bolstered by black historian Carter Woodson's weekly column in the *Guide*, which suggested a similar thesis. Young conducted a friendly review of Johnson's administration in the *Guide* and listed its accomplishments. The congressional investigation quickly evaporated, as did charges of fraud against the janitor.

When the House later unsuccessfully attempted to slash $1 million from Howard's 1933 budget, in what Young called an "obvious injustice," Howard's students blamed "unwarranted and cheap" publicity. Meanwhile, the black press characterized Johnson's detractors as "troublemakers" and depicted Johnson as "able, fearless, and sincere." Shortly after the budget controversy Johnson had to defend himself against charges that he was a Communist.[36] They were unfounded, concocted to force his resignation.

Young was appointed to Howard's board of trustees for a three-year term in April 1934. Johnson remained "under fire" throughout the decade, amid charges of maladministration and unfair labor practices. But Young never wavered in his support. He asked his subscribers "to trust the Trustees" and warned that Howard would end up with a white president if controversy continued. He printed excerpts from the board's meetings in feature articles on the front page of the *Guide* and quoted a "reliable source," probably either Johnson or himself. He used bylines from the Associated Negro Press in response to what he called "pernicious criticism," and even printed a letter from an old nemesis, J. Thomas Newsome, the former "lily-black," a Howard alumnus who called Johnson's critics "exceedingly petty and vicious." Young regarded Howard University as the "capstone" of black education, and his objective was to embarrass Johnson's detractors and to expose his enemies. Southall Bass, former managing editor, recalled that Young often said, "I will never use the press to kill a man, but I will use it to tell the truth."[37]

Black education took a back seat to pure politics during the 1932 presidential campaign. From June through October, at the height of the campaign, Young's Democratic proclivities were revealed in a series of editorials. He acknowledged that the black vote was generally unwanted by the Democrats in the South, but Roosevelt's campaign exuded confidence, hope, and a New Deal and so attracted his support.[38] Besides, political power and patronage flowed through the now-dominant Democrats in Virginia. Moreover, influential blacks such as Du Bois, Walter White, and Mary McLeod Bethune, to say nothing of influential black newspapers like the Chicago *Defender*, the Baltimore *Afro-American*, and the Pittsburgh *Courier*, had switched their allegiance to the Democrats in 1928.

After an editorial in the Raleigh *News and Observer* suggested that blacks did not belong in the Democratic party, Young responded swiftly and with fury. He called the editorial "absurd" and charged that the *News and Observer's* editor, Josephus Daniels, had based his stand upon a false attitude. He boldly asserted that blacks did "not belong to the Republican party." He asked, "What is it in biology, anatomy, and civics which precludes blacks from becoming Democratic if that is their political choice?" One month later, in July 1932, Young again indicated his Democratic leanings as he borrowed FDR's campaign slogan, "Time for a New Deal," to demand, editorially and in person before the Norfolk City Council, more parks and more bathing beaches for blacks following several accidental drownings at isolated and unprotected waterfronts. A short time later he defused an effort by blacks to boycott Norfolk's 250th anniversary celebration because of segregated facilities. Young publicly endorsed Roosevelt for the first time at a civic rally in Rocky Mount, North Carolina, on the eve of the election. However, he still termed himself an independent. He reviewed the Republicans' lily-white policy since 1900 and indicated that the Democrats could best improve the lot of the masses, both black and white, and reverse the continued social proscription of blacks in the South. He predicted a gradual shift of blacks to the Democratic party and asserted that most blacks would cast their votes for "Mr. Roosevelt."[39]

Despite the Depression and Hoover's neglect of the poor, many older blacks approached the 1932 election with ambivalence, reluctant to desert the party of Lincoln. To those blacks who were unimpressed with Roosevelt and who yet wished to remain loyal to the GOP but were unwilling to vote for Hoover, Young offered his "militant independence" strategy. As for himself, Young lukewarmly endorsed Roosevelt. He heartily disapproved of Hoover, but he was unimpressed with FDR's inattention to black problems while governor of New York and his running mate, John Nance Garner of Texas. Nevertheless, he believed that Roosevelt would be a dynamic leader and could best end the Depression.[40]

Roosevelt scored a stunning victory in Virginia, amassing 203,980 votes to 89,637 for Hoover. Probably fewer than 20,000 blacks voted. The *Guide* calculated in a "liberal estimate" that approximately 13,168 of the 329,000 blacks older than twenty-one voted in 1932.[41] The election showed how little political clout blacks had in Virginia politics.

According to one observer, after FDR was elected Norfolk blacks danced the "Charleston Blue" on Church Street. Large crowds gathered outside the Attucks Theater; church bells rang and radios blasted the electoral count from store windows. Young and his wife Eleanor were seen celebrating at the Bon Ton Restaurant with other members of the

Eureka Lodge and the Royal Knights of King David. Later Young attended Roosevelt's inaugural, and he carried the text of FDR's address in the *Guide*. He predicted that blacks would desert the "party of emancipation." He termed FDR's election a mandate for change and the beginning of an era.

A few months after the election, black Republican Oscar De Priest visited Portsmouth's Zion Baptist Church and touched off what the *Guide* called "a verbal bombshell in local politics" by calling for nonpartisanism. But his strategy was short-lived. Young's "militant independence" also soon disintegrated, and the momentum for a separate black political movement gradually dissipated. FDR's New Deal symbolized hope, and Young now agreed with the Pittsburgh *Courier* that it was "time to turn Lincoln's picture to the wall." He aligned himself with Norfolk's black Citizens Democratic Club (CDC), which had been formed as a Smith for President club in 1928. He noted that "there was a time when we had to apologize for being Democrats"; "now," he observed, "nearly all Negroes vote Democratic."[42] Young's militant independence and the momentum that propelled the nonpartisan movement were in reality both reincarnations of the lily-black movement of the early 1920s. But this time the drive for black political independence did not leave black leaders and voters in Virginia "splintered and confused." Responding to the deepening Depression and the promises of FDR's New Deal, blacks united under the banner of the Democratic party as their independent movement collapsed. By the early 1930s Young had become a more effective leader, and the *Guide* was more potent than it had been in the early 1920s. Many of the blacks who had left the political arena in the 1920s vowing never to return had now changed their minds. Many black leaders and a variety of organizations had succeeded in inculcating blacks with a renewed sense of political effectiveness. Young had played a significant role in bringing about that change.

▪ 6 ▪

Battling the Depression

During the 1930s Young moved from reluctant to enthusiastic support of the Democratic party. He abandoned the Republican party because it continued its lily-white policy and because political patronage in the South now flowed through the dominant Democrats. He reaffirmed his friendship with Governor Harry Byrd and became what former *Guide* editor John Q. Jordan called "a kingmaker with the Democrats." He supported Roosevelt's reelection in 1936 and again in 1940 because he believed that FDR could best end the Depression and bestow a sense of pride upon American blacks. Increasingly, he used the *Guide* to call for basic reform. Even in the depths of the Depression Young remained optimistic. "There is no cause for discouragement," he editorialized; "FDR knows what ought to be done."[1] Soon, he predicted, under FDR's strong and courageous leadership better days would come.

Soon after Roosevelt assumed the presidency the Supreme Court declared the Agricultural Adjustment Act (AAA) of May 1933 unconstitutional. The act, designed to elevate farm prices, authorized benefit payments to farmers who limited their acreage. The Court held that Congress had no power to control agricultural production since it was a local business. The *Guide* agreed. Although Young championed the plight of illiterate sharecroppers and tenants, philosophically he was in the same camp with Harry Byrd and other southern Democrats. He called the AAA "an invasion of state rights." But he also believed that the AAA aggravated race relations and displaced blacks from the farm. The *Guide* and other black publications joined the NAACP in condemning the "shameless" stealing of government checks made out to sharecroppers and tenants under the AAA, and he supported Walter White, executive

77

secretary of the NAACP, when he chastised the government for ignoring complaints against maladministration, fraud, and dishonesty.[2]

Another New Deal program, the National Industrial Recovery Act, was declared unconstitutional by the Supreme Court in May 1935. To stimulate industry, the act allowed for a minimum wage and the abolition of child labor. Many desperate blacks had rallied in support of FDR's program for economic recovery; the *Guide* recorded mass demonstrations and parades in support of the National Recovery Administration (NRA) in Richmond, Norfolk, Petersburg, Atlanta, and other major cities in the South. Black fraternal, business, and religious organizations pledged "whole-hearted allegiance" to Roosevelt. Generally, the black press supported the recovery program, believing, to cite the Pittsburgh *Courier* as one example, that the act "is destined to be a lifesaver to black Americans."[3] The *Courier* had been the first black weekly to endorse Roosevelt, and its editor, Robert L. Vann, later received a federal appointment. Young was probably interested in a high federal job also but was too conservative to ask.

Young criticized the NRA because it excluded low-income farm workers and domestics. He charged that it stopped at the color line. Indeed, bitter complaints against the NRA from blacks throughout the South prompted the National Urban League to set up an Emergency Advisory Council.[4] Young was elected captain of the local council at a mass meeting in Norfolk; his son, Thomas W. Young, by this time the assistant business manager of the *Guide*, was commissioned to investigate job losses and determine the extent to which whites had replaced blacks in industry.

Meanwhile, the *Guide* initiated a vigorous campaign to organize the black community to fight job losses. At a mass meeting called by Young to debate strategy, acrimonious debate and threats of violence erupted between Young and Dr. Samuel Francis Coppage, a black dentist, over the issue of a separate wage scale for black workers. Young willingly accepted lower wages for black workers in exchange for their continued employment, but the militant Coppage faction charged that a separate scale would brand black workers as inferior. The NRA wage dispute polarized black communities throughout Virginia and the South, a fact that distressed the normally placid editor of the *Guide*. Young rejected Coppage's allegation that he did not want blacks to have "white folks' pay." He reasoned that "minimum wages are beneficial to individual workers only if workers are actually employed." In response to Coppage and to numerous other complaints against discriminatory wages, Young established a complaint desk and urged *Guide* subscribers to report violations of wage and hour codes. Like other black journalists, Young recognized that the NRA was "defective" and "corresponds to an incomplete diagnosis or treatment of a sick man." But he saw no quick remedy "except an appeal to Roosevelt's sense of fairness."[5]

Another New Deal relief agency, the Resettlement Administration (RA), had four divisions: land utilization, rural settlement, suburban resettlement, and management. Will Alexander, a native southerner, former director of the CIC, and Young's personal friend, was selected by FDR to head the Resettlement Administration in the spring of 1935. Rural settlement made rehabilitation loans or grants to destitute or low-income farm families. Young believed that Alexander was a good choice to direct the RA. Later as head of the Farm Security Administration (FSA), Alexander made better homes for the rural poor his first priority.[6]

Alexander's commitment to blacks was dramatically demonstrated early in 1937 when whites from Hampton and Newport News attempted to change a new federally financed suburban housing project in Newport News from black to white occupancy. The *Guide* responded angrily. Aberdeen had been planned, engineered, and built by blacks and was to be occupied by black tenants. It was specifically designed for "the resettlement of Negro shipyard workers, longshoremen, and other low-income Negro families" from the slum areas of Newport News, Hampton, Norfolk, and neighboring towns. Each of the four- to six-bedroom homes had brick veneer; each unit was priced at $5,523, to be paid in forty years. A community building, recreation center, poultry house, paved streets, electricity, and telephone service made Aberdeen one of the most modern housing projects in the South.[7]

Predictably, white real estate dealers and farmers who lived nearby protested to Congress. In an exclusive interview with the *Guide*, Alexander voiced his opposition to the proposed change in tenancy.[8] Like Young, he favored the employment of black personnel on resettlement projects designed for blacks. Alexander lobbied George Mitchell, regional director of the FSA; L. R. Reynolds, director of the North Carolina CIC; and other prominent liberal whites throughout the South for support of the Aberdeen project. The project generated sharp criticism throughout tidewater Virginia. The *Guide* observed that powerful southern Democrats were hostile to what they termed "The Unsettlement Administration" because it did not stop at the color line and threatened cotton's kingship with its ideas of diversification.[9]

In June 1937 the Newport News *Daily Press*, a prominent white daily, asked U.S. Senator Harry Byrd to look into the cost of Aberdeen and asserted that the "government was wasting huge sums of money." Young responded quickly, conceding that government programs invited some waste and inefficiency but insisting that Aberdeen was an exception. Abandonment was untenable, he charged, and he termed the project a "wise" investment. The issue was ultimately settled amicably in favor of black tenancy, and the project was dedicated in May 1938. Alexander, Young, Joseph H. B. Evans, and other leading black and white citizens from throughout tidewater Virginia were among those present at the ceremony.

Alexander, Mitchell, and other officials of the FSA regarded the *Guide* as "the leading Negro weekly in the South." The FSA employed a black assistant, Constance Daniels, in its information division to serve as a liaison to the black press. When the Department of Agriculture decided to appoint a black journalist to the FSA's information division, it sought out *Guide* employee Frederick S. Weaver. On several occasions the FSA prepared news releases "strictly" for the *Guide*, a "feeder" to the Negro press. The *Guide* explained FSA directives, countered anti–New Deal propaganda, and highlighted FSA achievements. One issue ran these headlines: "10,405 Negro Families Aided by FSA," "FSA Families Helping to Win War," "One Thousand Florida Migrants Helped by FSA." The articles were backed by an editorial extolling the New Deal as "Not All Waste or Charity." The pieces were clipped by FSA officials and forwarded to both white and black newspapers throughout the country.[10]

Young was a personal friend of educator Mary McLeod Bethune, William Hastie, Robert C. Weaver, and other blacks who were regarded as having "cabinet rank" in the Roosevelt administration. Will Alexander and Harold L. Ickes, secretary of the Department of Interior, were instrumental in having blacks appointed to important positions, but it is Eleanor Roosevelt who is credited with expanding the size of this so-called black cabinet. Young at first was critical of the black cabinet, at times even expressing indignation. He asserted that "Negro Affairs" were no different from affairs of any other group of American citizens caught in the vortex of economic collapse. Furthermore, he declared, no black held a policy-making position. "Always," he editorialized, "we are placed as an afterthought, and then not as an American but as a Negro." At the end of FDR's first term, however, Young praised the black cabinet officers for their splendid service. He was especially proud of Bethune, who in 1935 was awarded the Spingarn Medal, the NAACP's highest award.[11]

Young had at first reluctantly supported Roosevelt, but his support for Harry F. Byrd's election to the U.S. Senate in 1933 was firm from the start. Although Byrd, governor of Virginia from 1926 to 1930, was a conservative, Young characterized his tenure as one of the most progressive in modern Virginia history.[12] Byrd used state surpluses to upgrade black colleges and was the first governor in the South to support antilynching legislation successfully. He implemented voting and tax reforms and promoted rural electrification, which aided hundreds of black families.

When Byrd's Republican opponent, Henry A. Wise, charged that Byrd had paid the poll taxes of several hundred blacks in exchange for their vote in the 1933 senatorial campaign, Young angrily termed the allegation "ridiculous." He noted that a "gentlemen's agreement" of 1918 excluded blacks from participation in both major parties, but the Democrats allowed a few blacks (like himself) who met the legal requirements and "had risen in educational and economic status" to vote.[13] It seemed ironic to Young for the Republicans to denounce the Democrats for permitting blacks to vote.

When the *Guide* endorsed the nomination of Harry F. Byrd in 1933, Young characterized him as a man of honesty, courage, and integrity. "Why shouldn't black Virginians admire and wish to support Senator Byrd?" he asked. His backing not only reflected his Democratic proclivities but also his confidence in FDR's New Deal policies. Young asked, "What voter wants to dismantle the New Deal and return to the old order? or, What has any political party or candidate offered as a substitute for the New Deal?" Byrd won by a sizable margin.[14]

In the 1934 congressional elections the New Deal was the single issue. As the New Deal placed its distinctive stamp on the economy and the federal government, southern Democrats grew increasingly disenchanted with Roosevelt's policies because they threatened the old social order. Initially southerners had supported Roosevelt's programs out of party loyalty and a dire need for aid. However, when considerable portions of FDR's relief flowed to blacks, southerners began to voice strong objections. Senators Byrd and Carter Glass of Virginia were among the first opponents who urged a return to the pre–New Deal economic policies.[15] Young chided them only mildly and cautioned that dissension might result in a Republican Congress and thereby jeopardize their positions of leadership.

But not all blacks shared Young's confidence in the New Deal, and some members of the black press saw FDR as a vague and shifty politician.[16] Job discrimination, local channeling of funds to whites, and racial differences in education, housing, and public health subsidies alienated black leaders in both the North and the South. The national NAACP criticized Roosevelt for his failure to press Congress for an antilynching law and eventually broke with him over that issue in 1935. W. E. B. Du Bois concluded that the "NRA was a step either toward Socialism or Facism," and "the beginning of government control."[17] Southern discontent and the dissatisfaction of black leaders appeared to threaten Roosevelt's chances for reelection, but Young remained firm in his support of the New Deal. He acknowledged that it was somewhat unsuccessful and inefficient. He attributed the deficiencies to customs, prejudices, the structure of state and local government, and the opposition of influential financial and political cliques who feared increased taxation and loss of power.

During Roosevelt's first term black voters turned decidedly toward the Democratic party. Black Democrats were elected in New York, Philadelphia, and Pittsburgh. The extent of the shift was dramatically demonstrated in Chicago by the election of Congressman Arthur W. Mitchell, the first black Democrat ever to sit in the U.S. Congress. By 1936 black Virginians had proclaimed their "independence" and had deserted the Republican party. They had legally challenged the white primary, and their increasing political strength and loyalty to the Democratic party had assuaged the hostility of many white Democrats. Dr. J. M. Tinsley, former state secretary of the Virginia NAACP, and Roscoe C. Jackson of the Richmond Democratic Voters League confirmed that the 1936 election was the first in which the majority of blacks voted Democratic, according to one source.[18]

Young failed to realize that the New Deal contained no specific policy to help blacks and that FDR felt no strong commitment to them. As president, he was interested in ameliorating the poverty of all the economically stricken, a group that included most blacks. But because Young and others like him focused on FDR's successes in reviving the economy and restoring faith in government, they overlooked the policies that shortchanged blacks.[19]

On October 31, 1936, in a front-page editorial Young announced: "We Stand with Roosevelt." With this endorsement, he acknowledged his commitment to the Democratic party and its economic views. He still believed in the virtues of individual initiative and thrift, but less in laissez-faire Republicanism. He recognized that some government control was necessary to prevent a recurrence of economic disaster. Young's vote for Roosevelt in 1936 demonstrated his gratitude as well as his expectation that continued loyalty would bring additional benefits.

In Virginia FDR won by a sizable margin. The heavily populated 21st precinct of Huntersville, in Norfolk, which had never voted for a Democratic presidential candidate, cast 202 votes for Roosevelt and 131 for Landon. The *Guide* observed that the results signified the black man's faith in the Democratic party. Only once before had any Democrat won in that precinct—when Harry Byrd defeated his Republican opponent in 1934. Young called FDR's second inaugural address "brilliant." He

warned blacks that FDR's social philosophy was not an invitation to continue "utter dependence upon the government for the essentials of life."
The government did not owe anyone a living. He boldly asserted the need
for private initiative, hard work, thrift, and self-denial.[20]

The 1936 presidential election cemented Young's transition from independent to Democrat. He became an ardent defender of FDR's New Deal
and a cog in Harry Byrd's emerging Democratic political machine. His
objective, in his words, was to end "human misery," to advance interracial
goodwill, and to encourage black pride. He often reminded blacks that
they were an integral part of the political, social, and economic life of the
South. Prudence dictated that they align themselves with the dominant
Democrats to secure economic gain. "Mr. P. B.," as he was affectionately
called, was now an able, safe, and generous friend of the Democrats.

Young may have been firmly committed to the Democratic party in
1936, but he was not typical. Blacks were neither active in party affairs
nor welcomed locally as voters by white Democrats. Blacks in Virginia
were apathetic about voting.[21] Young attributed their attitude to white
racism, fear, intimidation, and an unfavorable political climate. Democrats exploited black apathy and effectively used the poll tax to disfran-
chise some whites as well as blacks; in so doing, they created a small
electorate and a political machine.[22] Young questioned the constitutionality of the poll tax and supported legal action by the NAACP to nullify
the law, but he remained pessimistic about its repeal. He couched his
editorial opposition to the poll tax and other obstacles to black suffrage in
clear and concise language; however, he was careful to separate his opposition to the poll tax from his support for Harry Byrd, Sr., and the
Democratic party.

Throughout the decade the *Guide* waged several campaigns to increase
the black vote. The right to vote was a precious heritage; suffrage, Young
often asserted, was the only barrier between freedom and reenslavement.
Despite the devices to restrict black suffrage, the political climate in Virginia began to change during the late 1930s.[23] For example, in 1937 the
organization headed by Byrd suffered a setback when a more liberal opponent, James H. Price, won the gubernatorial election. He reformed
the state's education and public health systems and restricted the administrative powers of various state agencies, thereby lessening the restrictions imposed upon blacks.[24]

The New Deal drove many southern Democrats in Congress into a
voting coalition with Republicans in 1937. They voted against further
New Deal legislation in fear of an unbalanced budget, increased federal
power, and a weakening of white supremacy. Roosevelt's attempts to en-

sure the defeat of certain anti–New Deal Democrats in Georgia, South Carolina, and Maryland were conspicuously unsuccessful—the incumbents had raised the race issue. Young bitterly wrote that white supremacy always carried elections in the South. According to him, vote-getting played a part in the 1940 defeat of a federal antilynching bill. The legislation covered kidnapping, bank robbery, and bootlegging, he wrote, but southern senators opposed the bill because they feared a loss of support. Young, ever mindful of his philosophy of "build up—don't tear down," only mildly criticized conservative Democrats. [25]

Young remained a firm supporter of the New Deal, despite militant opposition from other black leaders such as A. Philip Randolph, Walter White, and Robert Vann, who criticized Roosevelt for his failure to press Congress for civil rights legislation. Du Bois was one of the earliest and most vociferous critics of FDR's New Deal. In a speech before the NAACP annual convention in 1932, he remarked that blacks were "still faced with the necessity for a positive program." Young, however, wrote that blacks must meet and combat discrimination not through emotional outbursts but with carefully organized programs of economic and political pressure. Reiterating his stand against discrimination, Young reminded his readers that Roosevelt did not initiate discrimination and could not arbitrarily abolish it without incurring the wrath of Congress. [26]

Still performing a conservative role, Young urged the black leaders to temper their criticism of Roosevelt. FDR had enlarged the scope of black opportunity in the armed forces more than his Republican predecessors had. Young repeatedly headlined Roosevelt's recognition of black achievement: "Negro Officers to Command Negro Regiment," "FDR Makes B. O. Davis General," "FDR Passes through Harlem . . .," and "Negroes in Key Defense Posts." [27]

The *Guide* again supported Roosevelt in 1940. On November 2, 1940, Young moved "to thank and encourage" Roosevelt for his action in integrating blacks into the American society and for his efforts in helping to ease discrimination. A few days later Roosevelt carried Norfolk and the nation. Young was "heartened" by Roosevelt's reelection. In response to a query from Claude Barnett, director of the Associated Negro Press, he responded that "Negroes in Virginia, as elsewhere, shared to some extent the social gains of the Roosevelt Administration." He predicted that Roosevelt's election would have a "stabilizing effect upon business, industry, and agriculture" and reminded Barnett that the Roosevelt administration had provided blacks their first opportunity to serve in important government positions. [28]

"Mr. P. B." remained a firm, enthusiastic supporter of the Democrats.

And he did not relent in his belief that political rights and economic gains were the tools by which black Americans could gain full and equal citizenship. The *Guide's* editorial policy changed noticeably under the pressure of the Depression and New Deal politics. Young's editorials became more aggressive. He was still a Bookerite conservative, but the Depression, events like the Scottsboro trial, and the lack of more substantive aid for blacks in the New Deal worried him. The *Guide's* new editorial excursion into reform was intended to fight more constructively the battles of black schoolteachers, farmers, and domestics. High unemployment and rising taxes evoked unrest among the poor that threatened tidewater's image as the "Gateway to the South." The black press must be an advocate, Young explained. It must give more attention to the problems of the masses. He pleaded for "quickened social justice" and aroused public opinion. But militant blacks denounced the *Guide* as "jellyfish, ultraconservative, cowardly, and afraid to speak out." And yet, the *Guide* was barred from CCC camps in Virginia because it was "radical, antagonistic and red."[29]

Young allegedly went broke in 1929; however, by the mid-1930s he had apparently recovered. In 1933 he purchased a new photoengraving plant with the latest equipment. At the time, he remarked, "Only a few white dailies and weeklies have it." The *Guide* not only survived the Great Depression, it grew during the 1930s. Subscribers paid $3.50 a year, and their numbers climbed from 19,885 in September 1933 to 26,105 in December 1934, and to 28,500 in 1935. The number of pages increased from four in 1910 to sixteen by 1935. One year later the *Guide* became the first black newspaper in the South to offer an index. The paper had subscribers from Maine to California, but the bulk of them lived in the metropolitan areas of tidewater Virginia and eastern North Carolina. The staff, which numbered forty-two in 1935, had a payroll in excess of $100,000.[30]

The *Guide* was not a one-paper-a-week weekly. Its national edition, which went to press on Tuesdays, was augmented by separate editions for Richmond, Portsmouth, Hampton-Phoebus, Baltimore, and Washington on succeeding days of the week. At one time during the decade, according to former editor John Jordan, the *Guide* printed eight different editions between Tuesday and Saturday.[31]

John Belden, who served as circulation manager for over thirty years, recalled that although the newspaper was dependent upon circulation during the Depression, the paper never missed an issue or a payroll. Although Norfolk was portrayed in the media as a beacon of liberalism, "Segregation was so thick," he remembered, "you could cut it with a knife."[32] Accordingly, he explained, "Young walked a tightrope."

Among the special contributors whose articles enhanced the newspaper's popularity were Carter G. Woodson, a historian; Kelly Miller, an intellectual; Charlotte Hawkins Brown, an educator; Georgia D. Johnson, a feminist; and the Reverend Richard H. Bowling, minister and propagandist. To this wealth of special contributors, the regular staff added versatility with such features as P. B. Young, Jr.'s "The Melting Pot," a column on local and state issues; Gordon B. Hancock's "Between These Lines," on local, state, and national events; John Jordan's "Rambling Rover," on events in the Portsmouth area; and Thomas W. Young's "Windows of the World," on international events.

Throughout the decade Norfolk was plagued by what the *Guide* called "a wave of Banditry." On March 11, 1933, its headlines shouted "Extra! Extra! Gang War Breaks out in Norfolk." It reported that gangsters had visited Norfolk's Church Street in a seven-passenger car after a "Turf man argued with a Jug handler." A few months later a gang feud between the Charlotte Street Apes and the Downtown Horses allegedly resulted in the death of a black teenager. Bold daylight shootouts between bootleggers occasionally occurred, and incidents of chicken stealing, flimflamming, purse snatching, gin milling, bootlegging, and "hot stuff" were recorded almost weekly. "In nearly all cases," lamented Young, "the Negro is accused." His family did not escape the violence. His oldest son once fired a .38 revolver at a suspected bandit. Earlier, his daughter-in-law Undine was the victim of an attempted flimflam.[33] Even Young himself was the victim of an attempted extortion scheme called the "Snatch." But when the "ransom" note arrived at his private residence, 733 Chapel Street, Young alerted the police and later assisted them in capturing the alleged extortionist.[34]

The most persistent crimes throughout the decade were "yoking" (seizing around the neck and rifling the pockets), robbery, assault, pilfering, and malicious destruction of property. Lesser offenses, stealing auto parts and breaking windows, were committed with what Young called "reckless abandon." Urban areas throughout tidewater were plagued by what the *Guide* called "number fever." Occasionally, rivalry between numbers operators erupted into warfare. The numbers kings were apparently well heeled financially. One runner jokingly called for a "bank holiday" after he paid $21,000 in a single day in March 1933.[35] The facility with which major criminals operated in Norfolk led many to believe that "big shot" whites funded and protected the racketeers.

The *Guide's* numerous campaigns against crime in Norfolk were generally ineffective. Young was concerned that "number fever," gang feuds, and bootleggers represented a threat to harmonious race relations. He only rarely condemned the police for their inability to reduce the incidence of felonious offenses and black-on-black crime. Young and other prominent blacks periodically complained before the Norfolk City Council, but their objective was more to seek an explanation than to demand a grand jury investigation of violent crimes. At the height of a "crime wave" in June 1933, Young blamed the lawlessness on "too lenient public opinion" and "constituted authority." A few years later, the *Guide* editorialized that "gangs of thieves are operating in this city at random." Young this time blamed the "Dark Streets."[36]

On the eve of the war, in February 1939, the *Guide* lamented that "yoking" was now more prevalent than at any time in recent memory. He called crime in Norfolk "appalling" and characterized as "justifiable" the action of a local minister who killed one would-be "yoker" and wounded another.[37] He was particularly incensed at the high incidence of black-on-black crime and the youth of the offenders, most of whom were between sixteen and twenty-five. Because a disproportionate number of the assaults occurred on Church Street and the surrounding areas in the black community, city fathers and the police were not very responsive to black complaints.

Interestingly, Young praised Norfolk's police for their "Good Police Work" and blamed the rising violence on fertile incubators of crime such as high unemployment and slum housing. He challenged Norfolkians to rid their community of "divers," "joints," "numbers," "prostitution," and a concoction called "footwash." To buttress his argument, Young pointed to a housing survey that revealed that 12 percent of Norfolk's black population occupied only 1 percent of the city's total housing area. Yet Norfolk's slum area—1 percent—which was 95 percent black, recorded 35 percent of the homicides, 39 percent of the robberies, 35 percent of the assaults, and consumed $750,000 of the police budget. The *Guide* termed the statistics "startling."[38]

Norfolkians, blacks and whites, agreed that Norfolk slums were among the worst in the nation, but until 1940 establishment of an authority to remedy this situation was vigorously and successfully opposed by property owners, real estate firms, and other groups. Young; Louis Jaffe, editor of the Norfolk *Virginian-Pilot;* W. E. Dubnam, editor of the Norfolk *News Index;* Thomas P. Thompson, city manager; Colonel Charles Borland, director of public safety; and attorney Charles L. Kaufman (white) were in the forefront of Norfolk's biracial slum clearance movement between 1935 and 1940.[39]

Even though Young had waged numerous campaigns to rid Norfolk of its main incubators of crime, its slum housing, he was generally ineffective. But when his editorials were corroborated by the *Virginian-Pilot*, the *News Index*, and the Norfolk *Ledger-Dispatch*, and when his views were publicly supported by the Norfolk County Medical Society, the Tidewater Ministerial Association, the Central Labor Union, and prominent whites, he was more successful. As slum clearance evolved into a biracial movement in Norfolk and as whites assumed a more aggressive role in the fight, Young and the *Guide* tactfully withdrew, keeping a lower profile.

On January 19, 1935, City Manager Thomas P. Thompson announced the appointment of a Committee for Slum Clearance and Better Housing "to make a study of the slum districts of Norfolk." The appointees were all white. A few weeks later, attorney Charles Kaufman emerged with one of the most comprehensive examinations ever compiled for an American city. The result were shocking. Kaufman's thesis confirmed what the *Guide* had reported earlier, namely, "that crime increases and thrives directly in proportion to a city's slum."[40]

Kaufman's report initiated calls for slum clearance from Norfolk's white community. Perhaps its concern was best expressed by the *Virginian-Pilot*, which called the slum conditions "primitive" and demanded an end to this "natural asylum of mould and vermin." C. M. Gordon, pastor of the First Christian Church, called the slums "unspeakably filthy" and urged city officials to rid the city of these "abominable conditions." Norfolk's Kiwanis Club and the YWCA staged public debates on slum clearance, and the *Guide* organized "slum tours" for interested whites. On April 16, 1936, the Virginia CIC held a statewide conference at the Freemason Street Baptist Church in Norfolk. Its members, at Young's behest, issued an urgent plea for slum clearance.[41]

In response to an aroused public, City Manager Thompson and Public Safety Director Borland organized a Crime Conference in Norfolk in March 1937 that attracted noted criminologists and well over a thousand spectators. The conferees endorsed Kaufman's report and exhorted Norfolk's "intelligent leadership" to begin slum clearance. The Crime Conference, together with petitions from both the black and the white community and the serialized accounts in the *Guide*, the *News Index*, and the *Ledger-Dispatch*, enabled city officials to overcome the recalcitrance of the city council and strong opposition from property owners. In 1940 the city's housing authority was established. Young functioned as chairman of the Negro Advisory Committee for well over a decade. He helped determine the names, locations, and policies of pre–World War II housing projects such as Roberts Park, Merrimack, and Oak Leaf. Years later, in the

1960s, Robert C. Weaver, secretary of the U.S. Department of Housing and Urban Development and the first black cabinet official, acknowledged that Norfolk was "the first city in the nation" to initiate an urban development program. He noted, "Norfolk is where the story began of the rebuilding of America's cities," and he asserted that Young and the *Guide* were an integral part of the movement.[42]

Concomitant with Young's efforts to reduce crime and to abolish slums, the *Guide* waged a campaign for more jobs, fewer taxes, and more civic improvements. After 700 black women were dropped from the rolls of the Virginia Emergency Relief Administration in May 1935, Young responded angrily in a front-page editorial. He called for an investigation, and in a letter to the area administrator of the agency, he characterized the action of officials in Norfolk as "unjustified" and "virtual abandonment."[43] His resentment was fueled by the early morning transportation, by bus, of the unemployed women to work in the strawberry fields of Norfolk and Princess Anne counties. He organized mass meetings and formed a so-called Vigilance Committee, with himself as chairman, to explain the "Relief Tangle" to civic groups and to seek support. Young forwarded the petitions, "which represented every phase of Negro life in Norfolk," to the agency.

Young highlighted the activities of the Unemployed Council—a socialist organization—after it organized street demonstrations "to protest the Relief Decrees" and distributed fliers that read "All Black Women Cut Off Relief: Fellow Workers What Are You Going To Do?" Previously, Young had buried stories of earlier demonstrations by supporters of the council on inside pages of the *Guide*, while featuring free rent, equal employment, slum clearance, and the NRA on the front page.[44] On this occasion, however, he exploited the activities of the Unemployed Council in order to sensitize officials in Norfolk to the racial unrest. He forwarded newspaper clippings to city fathers.

Two weeks after Norfolk's "mass protest," the March 30, 1935, edition of the *Guide* carried the headline "Harlem Riot Worst in Twenty-five Years." It reported that "700 police and 25 radio cars were needed to quell the rioters." Negroes were the aggressors, whites the victims. Young editorialized that "the same situation that exists in Harlem, exists to an even larger degree in Norfolk." Speaking directly to city fathers, he wrote, "People will not indefinitely submit to exploitation and economic repression."[45]

A few weeks later Young headed the negotiating team that extracted a revised relief layoff order from city officials. Young attributed the modification to strong editorial protest. He was warmly applauded by the black Baptist Ministers Conference, the Aeolian Social and Beneficial Organization, and numerous other civic and fraternal clubs throughout the city.[46]

Unfair taxation of blacks was yet another issue that aroused the black publisher. He used strong editorial comment and social action to protest a decision by the Norfolk Board of Equalization to raise the 1931 real estate assessment on black property by $7,000 and, at the saem time, to lower the tax on white property by $46,000. He called the board's action "governmental despotism" because of the "precarious economic conditions" among blacks. Young fired off numerous letters of protest to city officials and formed a citizens' committee—the Norfolk Civic League— to protest the tax increase and to lobby candidates for city council. The *Guide*, the *Virginian-Pilot*, and the *Ledger-Dispatch* recorded that "never before in the history of the city have members of the race been so thoroughly aroused" as were those attending a mass meeting at the Bank Street Baptist Church in February 1932.[47]

Several years later, Young, in a detailed letter to City Manager Thompson, forcefully complained of the "excessive," "unjust," and high tax assessments in the black community. However, when individual assessments were questioned, he wrote, "they were immediately reduced." Young concluded by praising Thompson. He knew that Thompson was "only too glad to have this called to your attention" and that "lax methods" would not be "tolerated" by the administration.[48]

Norfolk, like many another jurisdiction, was unable to collect taxes with normal facility during the Depression. But unlike other tidewater communities, Norfolk had budgetary problems that were aggravated by what Paul Wilstach's *Tidewater Virginia* (1929) and the *Guide* called "The Great Wall," an "invisible barrier" of taxes and tolls that impeded the normal flow of traffic to Norfolk. "We are hemmed in on all sides by a maze of ferries and toll bridges," complained Young, who called Norfolk a "colossal blunder created by shortsighted government." Young's remarks were echoed by G. Leslie Hall, president of the Tidewater Automobile Association, who compiled statistics to show that Norfolk was the most expensive city in America in which to own and operate an automobile.[49]

The budget crisis necessitated the closing of city libraries, the elimination of summer school, and the curtailment of juvenile and domestic relations court. Young's wife Eleanor, who was the president of the Colored Library Association, responded quickly. She gathered petitions from the Norfolk Teachers Association and black religious, fraternal, and civic groups, and she challenged unsuccessfully the closing of libraries before the city council.[50]

But the issue that angered the black community the most, and that ignited militant cries of "Taxation without Representation," was the city council's decision to repeal the allocation of $14,000 for the purchase of a black beach. Norfolk's black community was outraged. A protest meeting at the Bank Street Church was "filled to overflowing." Young and his wife delivered riveting and dramatic speeches, heavy with portents of danger. "The strip of sand [is] not important," observed Young, but "justice" is. Moreover, "we should not have to submit to segregation for the sake of peace."[51] His wife observed that "blacks are drowning every week in isolated, unprotected, and unfamiliar waterfronts." Like her husband, Eleanor asserted that it was "Time for a New Deal." Cries of "Fight for Beach," "Fight to Finish," and "Taxation without Representation" filled the air. The group selected black attorney Charles Archer to articulate their grievances before the city council. The committee, of course, included P. B. Young.

Although the various speakers assailed city officials, they tempered their criticism of Mayor E. Jeff Robertson, Councilman S. Heth Tyler, and Police Chief S. W. Ironmonger, who supported the project.[52] "Many splendid [white] women," in Young's view, supported the beach project, as did tidewater's two leading white newspapers, the *Virginian-Pilot* and the *Ledger-Dispatch*. Louis Jaffe, editor of the *Pilot*, campaigned for the project, as did Colonel James Mann and other prominent white Norfolkians. Middle-class whites supported such issues, for they did not challenge the biracial system.

The beach project, like slum clearance, soon became a biracial effort. Jaffe spoke for the white community when he asked the city council to approve the beach project "for the sake of peaceful relations between the races." At Young's behest, Colonel Mann added his "distinguished legal ability" and cooperated with the black attorney—without pay—to guide the project through the city council after some whites procured an injunction. Over a thousand blacks jammed the council chambers in March 1932 as the city council voted to restore the funds. Young called the decision "a legal and moral victory" that would attract the attention of the nation. "Let us hope," he editorialized, that the "bitter struggle is ended."[53] He then sought to conciliate the various factions and to cultivate city council support for blacks.

The budget crisis and the beach controversy divided Norfolk along racial lines, apparently, but they did not do serious damage to the fabric of race relations. Both crises abated after officials agreed to a redress of grievances. Young's role is clear. He successfully projected himself as a concerned spokesman and emerged as a hero. Moreover, his sons, Thomas W. and P. B., Jr., proudly accompanied their father to public gatherings throughout the controversies and were regarded as rising conservative spokesmen as well.

By the mid-1930s Young had become what columnist Gordon B. Hancock called "A Coming Man," and the *Guide* was the most widely read black weekly in the South. Seemingly, Young lamented, editors Robert Vann of the Pittsburgh *Courier*, Robert Abbott of the Chicago *Defender*, and Carl Murphy, Sr., of the Baltimore *Afro-American* were insensitive to the racial problems of the *Guide*. He could not attack segregation without losing editions bound for New York, facing denials of loans for capital improvement, and, more important, forfeiting his status as a race leader.

Young's reputation and his newspaper's circulation were inseparable, asserted Southall Bass, the former managing editor. Just as a black attorney needed a white attorney to represent a black client in the courtroom, noted John Jordan, Young needed the support of white editors throughout the South. They alerted Young to newsworthy stories, leaked political gossip, and surreptitiously forwarded accounts of Klan violence. Both Jordan and Bass noted that the *Guide* survived because "whites respected it as a seriously edited paper, of, by, and for Negroes." In August 1933 Young remarked that "more influential white people today are subscribing and reading Negro newspapers than ever before."[54] Many white members of the Southern Interracial Commission, the Southern Regional Council, the Virginia Interracial Commission, as well as prominent white tidewater Virginians, regularly subscribed to the *Guide* until the mid-1950s.

The advertisements in each edition appealed to all segments of society, both black and white. As the *Guide's* circulation grew, so too did its income from national advertising. The Virginia Electric and Power Company (Vepco), Conoco Oil Company, the Norfolk and Western Railroad, and Norfolk's own "Southern Beer" took out full-page advertisements.

The *Guide* was concerned with not only social reform but humanitarian aid as well. After Walter Blow lost both legs in an accident, it related the story and raised funds for his artificial limbs from the community. Distraught mothers sought its editor's advice, and the trials and tribulations of weary travelers are immortalized in its pages. The *Guide* helped to raise the "colored quota" of Norfolk's Annual Community Fund and quietly organized "mass meetings" to give impetus to a tuberculosis sanatorium serving both races.[55]

While the *Guide* tackled hot issues like the Scottsboro case and slum clearance, Young "carried on quiet negotiations" with "influential political friends" to improve street conditions and municipal services. After two blacks were charged with the murder of Isadore Shockett, a Jewish merchant, the *Guide* "quietly investigated" and unearthed new evidence that led to a new police probe.[56] On the other hand, Young quietly fed information to prosecutors about blacks who were accused of hideous crimes and whom he deemed to be guilty.

During the 1930s many honors were bestowed upon the editor. In 1932 Young was elected to the Urban League's board of directors. Shaw University awarded him an honorary Doctor of Laws degree in 1935, and Richmond's Virginia Union University bestowed a Doctor of Humane Letters degree in 1937. He was chosen in 1940 by the Richmond *Times-Dispatch*, a white daily, for its third annual honor roll of Virginians who had conspicuously served the state during the year. Young's award noted that he had reflected credit upon the state through a display of courage, intelligence, generosity, and unselfishness. In an earlier survey Young was chosen as one of the "thirteen most interesting" blacks in the nation.[57]

During the late 1930s the *Guide* faced a new type of competition. White dailies, particularly the Richmond *Times-Dispatch*, began to include Negro obituaries and "Colored News" in their pages. Young believed this development to be harmful because its primary objective was commercial rather than cultural advancement. Moreover, the white press began to expand its market through the use of radio. In response to the increased competition, the *Guide* launched "Everybody Wins" subscription campaigns in which automobiles and large cash prizes were given to lucky subscribers.[58] It also sponsored cooking schools, fashion shows, and guided tours of its plant and equipment for interested church, fraternal and civic groups, both black and white.

Young believed that "*All* newspapers have a social responsibility," because they influence the life of a community daily. White Virginians' knowledge about blacks was limited to what they read in the newspaper; therefore, he editorialized, the press had to assume the responsibility for wiping out misunderstanding and injustices.[59] The press must help offset segregated public education, he believed. He pointed to a policy of the Richmond *Times-Dispatch* as an example of practices that needed to change. The *Times-Dispatch* included a special section on "News of Colored People." Young lamented that after enough editions were printed to serve black subscribers, the plate was removed from the press and the remaining editions, headed for white subscribers, were devoid of this section.

When blacks complained to him about their treatment by white dailies, Young dismissed their criticism in an angry editorial entitled "Up the Wrong Tree." There is more wholesome, constructive, inspiring news in the twenty pages of the *Guide*, he responded, than a local daily carries within a lifetime. When another subscriber complained about discriminatory employment practices, Young responded, "Tears Availeth Not; Votes Bring Results."[60]

Occasionally, in a display of liberalism, Young printed criticism of the *Guide* on the editorial page. On more than one occasion, noted Thomas Dabney, he was forced to retract stories and offer apology. Once, Young criticized a white superintendent who later stormed into Young's Norfolk office and shouted words that could not be printed in a family newspaper. "P. B. turned red as a beet," chuckled Dabney. "And he backed down." The following week Young printed "A Correction" and acknowledged in print that the *Guide* was "in error."[61]

Young's liberalism and lack of journalistic objectivity once evoked the wrath of H. L. Mencken, editor of the *American Mercury*, who speculated that the *Guide* was "fast becoming communist." Young responded that Mencken's thinking was "warped" and referred to Virginius Dabney's book *Liberalism in the South*, which called the *Guide* "balanced and sane."[62]

However, despite the journalistic success of the *Guide*, former employees alleged that Young took advantage of the economic dislocation generated by the Depression to keep their salaries low and to squelch union activities. Addison King earned only $3.50 per week in 1933 although he worked twelve hours a day. Former managing editor Southall Bass and religious editor Thomas Dabney earned $12.00 per week when they were first employed during the 1930s. Because of low wages, long hours, poor working conditions, and what one observer called "outright jealousy," incipient union activities began during this period, but they were quickly extinguished by Mr. P. B. According to Bass, editor John Jordan, and black pharmacist David Schwertz, Young's tight-fistedness was in part the result of his supposed personal bankruptcy in 1929 and the fall of the black Metropolitan Bank and Tidewater Bank shortly thereafter.

By the end of the decade, the *Guide*, like its publisher, had emerged as one of the most outspoken black organs in the South for civil rights and social justice. Just how difficult that was, in the face of the hard times and some of the racial crises they engendered, becomes apparent when one examines closely the *Guide's* response to some of the decade's most important cases involving racial justice.

∎ 7 ∎

Race in a Time of Crisis

Side by side on the pages of the *Journal and Guide* Young ran campaigns for equality under the law and news reports and features designed to advance interracial goodwill. He likened himself to an ambassador, and indeed he was viewed by many prominent white southerners as "an able and safe Negro leader."[1] Likewise, black leaders hailed "Mr. P. B." as a race man and considered his views on race relations to be sound. To blacks like C. C. Spaulding, J. M. Gandy, and J. E. Shepard, in the absence of the ideal solution of integration, racial harmony within the South's segregated system was an important goal.

Black and white leaders alike acknowledged that the greatest need of the South was improved education for blacks. Until that could be achieved, the Negro would need the assistance of whites. The fact that prominent whites were condemning lynching and attending interracial forums seemed proof to Young that race relations in the South were improving. Jim Crowism persisted and the Depression worsened the plight of blacks in the South, but nevertheless there was this small cadre of liberal thinkers who pleaded for what the *Guide* called "quickened social justice." Thus was laid the foundation, Young believed, for remedial legislation.[2]

Leaders of both the black and the white communities belonged to the Commission on Interracial Cooperation (CIC). Formed in 1919 by whites and blacks who feared that returning black soldiers might provoke massacres all over the land, the commission worked intelligently, efficiently, and so quietly that what everyone in 1919 discussed as an impending social crisis had passed out of the national consciousness by 1930. The commission had two goals during its twenty-five years of operation; one, to correct injustices and inequalities wherever possible, and the other, to improve southern attitudes on matters of race. The commission was headed by Will Alexander, affectionately called "Dr. Will." Young frequently corresponded with "Dr. Will," Frank Graham, James E. Shepard, L. R. Reynolds, and other members of the CIC, and also attended many CIC annual conventions. In 1935 he served on the board of directors, along with Mary McLeod Bethune and black educator John Hope of Morehouse.[3]

The strategy of the CIC was to secure the support of people, both black and white, but mainly white, throughout the South, who would spread the gospel of racial tolerance and goodwill. They would talk about the "best things" about the South, interpret the races to each other, prevent violence, and gradually improve racial attitudes and social conditions. The idea was that the best people of both races understood best the problems of the South and thus were the best qualified to draft a solution. The CIC regularly mailed press releases to more than 2,000 newspapers throughout the country. It sent supporters to observe court procedures in felony cases involving blacks. Members quietly disrupted impending lynchings, investigated the Georgia chain gangs, championed Negro traveling libraries, fought for "black principals for black schools," and lectured on black college campuses. They attempted to teach the white South not only how to "treat" the educated Negro but how to "educate him as well."[4]

Virginia's governor Harry Flood Byrd, Sr., was a solid supporter of the CIC. Once he mailed over one thousand letters to his supporters, encouraging them to become members. His support of the CIC was continued by John Garland Pollard upon his ascendance to the governor's office in 1931. At a meeting of the North Carolina CIC in Chapel Hill on June 2, 1933, Young read what UNC president Frank Graham termed an "excellent paper" on the Negro press.[5]

However, despite the willingness of white and black leaders to support one another and the CIC on the behalf of better race relations, these were troubled times, and race was still a bitter social issue. After the Chapel Hill meeting, Young, C. C. Spaulding, Charlotte Hawkins Brown, J. W. Seabrook (president of the Fayetteville State College for Negroes), and others met in Spaulding's Durham home to discuss the increased social proscription of blacks in the South and the seeming ineffectiveness of the CIC. They complained of lethargic whites; of Louis Austin's *Carolina Times*, which advocated the disbanding of the CIC; and of specific injustices experienced by some among their number. Young repeated his belief that the Depression and Jim Crowism were sapping the spirit of blacks, leaving them "bruised and bleeding."[6] But these were worries expressed in private.

A few weeks later Young presented a different perspective to a large white audience on the campus of Atlantic Christian College in Wilson, North Carolina. Young predicted improved race relations and punctuated his speech with descriptions of "tangible steps" that would close the economic gap. He asserted that the "Rape Magic" had lost its "charm" and attributed the decline of mob violence to "stricter law enforcement," an awakened social consciousness, the spread of education, and a more liberal white press. He praised the Raleigh *News and Observer* and the Greensboro *Daily News* as "outstanding exponents of justice and fair play." One observer commented that race leaders in the South like Young, Shepard, and Charlotte Hawkins Brown always carried two speeches—one for white audiences and another for black.[7]

Young's assessment of race relations in North Carolina was benign—and inaccurate. In September 1933, a few weeks after Young's Wilson speech, Howard Odum, L. R. Reynolds, Frank Graham, and other liberal whites met to discuss the critical situation in North Carolina. And in November the NAACP organized a mass meeting of 2,500 blacks in Raleigh to protest mob violence and increased discrimination.[8] A similar meeting was organized in Durham. In both instances, the NAACP organizers were also prominent members of the CIC. The protests reflected the impact of depression and the increased social proscription on black teachers, businessmen, and religious leaders. The organizers hoped to placate the militant blacks who sought change and, at the same time, to restore confidence in the conservative methods of education, diplomacy, and the ballot.

The dilemma of black leaders was best expressed by C. C. Spaulding: "I am besieged on all sides." Spaulding said that members of the CIC needed to debate topics "with our gloves off." And, in fact, Spaulding, Young, Shepard, W. G. Pearson, and others once clashed head-on in Durham's White Rock Baptist Church with Louis Austin; W. O. Saunders, editor of Elizabeth City, North Carolina's (black) *Independent;* and black educators R. L. McDougold and E. R. Merrick, who argued that the CIC was of "no value and ought to be disbanded."[9] At this point, late 1933 and early 1934, Young's philosophy was clearly antithetical to that of the progressive black leaders in the South. He was extremely cautious and content to follow established southern racial etiquette and to acquiesce to the white power structure's lead. Young published an angry editorial in the *Guide.* "The CIC is not an armor-clad sword fighting organization," he asserted. "If the Carolina *Times* wants a more vocal, militant, sword wielding, bomb throwing leadership," perhaps Austin should form his own organization. Young implied that Austin and other blacks in North Carolina were jealous of "outside leadership." [10]

As the Depression devastated the South's "Forgotten Man," CIC leaders, both black and white, failed to take an enlightened attitude toward the black community. They were overwhelmingly concerned with interracial cooperation, even as economic dislocation and political disfranchisement ate away at their every effort. Despite blacks' deteriorating situation, in 1935 at the joint Virginia–North Carolina CIC meeting C. C. Spaulding read a paper entitled "Some Indications of Progress Made by Negro People," while Guy Johnson and Gordon Hancock discussed "How the Negro Has Come through the Depression." President Gandy of the Virginia State College for Negroes delivered a major address entitled "Areas in Which Negro People Need the Assistance of Their White Friends." [11] He argued that the Negro's greatest need was not economic assistance, enfranchisement, or relief from violence but education. He urged whites to inspire blacks through "kindness and cordial treatment." Undoubtedly, the conferees left the meeting convinced that blacks were successfully negotiating their way through the Depression and that "great improvements" in what the *Guide* called "legal justice" were occurring. The black delegates chastised black dissenters and blamed themselves for their lack of economic progress in the belief that whites no longer feared, in the words of the *Guide*, "qualified Negroes" like themselves. They probably agreed with Young, who asserted that "there is no real race issue in Virginia politics; . . . there is no agitation on the question of franchise." [12] Meanwhile, blacks were excluded from jury duty in Virginia and circumscribed legally throughout the South, as the Scottsboro case had made all too clear.

Two weeks later the Negro Organization Society met in annual convention in Southampton County. The main speaker was Howard's president Mordecai Johnson, who envisioned a New South, a South without racial prejudice. Following his optimistic remarks, one delegate lightly remarked that he felt like a member of the Elect. Young, who was seated on the platform, presumably agreed with another speaker, J. M. Gandy, who apologetically characterized Alice Jackson's attempt to desegregate the University of Virginia as symbolic of "the growing pains among our people." [13] Young, Gandy, and other conservative blacks worried that her efforts might disrupt interracial goodwill and erode white support of black schools, thus endangering the reputations of race men like themselves.

Conservative blacks like Young, Spaulding, Gandy, and Shepard held interlocking membership in the CIC, the NAACP, the Negro Organization Society, and other organizations. In addition, Young, Shepard, and William O. Walker also met during regional and state meetings of the Black Elks (IBPOE), and Spaulding, Young, and Mordecai Johnson caucused during meetings of Howard University's board of trustees. Young was, in the words of *Guide* managing editor Southall Bass, "a man with a mission" during the 1930s. "He was always on the road," he remarked. "He was always going somewhere to speak."[14] For all their caution, men like Young, Spaulding, Gandy, and Shepard were not just men of probity and humility; they were dreamers and prophets, too. They envisioned themselves as equals of their white counterparts, albeit in a separate and segregated society. The social contacts and interracial goodwill they fostered with whites would emerge later as important ingredients in black efforts to desegregate the South.

Young shouldered tremendous personal tragedy during the 1930s. His sister Mary died in July 1932; his brother Winfield S., in August 1933. His mother, Sallie, who resided with his brother H. C. in Portsmouth, died on September 5, 1935. In addition, the marriage of his younger son Thomas to Aileen Diggs, the beautiful daughter of his best friend, Norfolk attorney J. Eugene Diggs, was slowly dissolving into a divorce. Moreover, Young himself was ill during the mid-1930s and missed meetings of the CIC and important conferences on black graduate education at Duke University and the University of North Carolina. In each instance he sent his favorite son, P. B., Jr., whom he proudly described to Frank Graham, organizer of the conference, as "a professional newspaper man."[15]

Outwardly, P. B. Young was unaffected by the personal tragedies that befell him during the 1930s. His contemporaries described him as an "iron man . . . a cold man" who seldom demonstrated emotions. He was the exact opposite of his wife Eleanor and brother H. C. Young, both of whom were warm, caring, and compassionate. Young's unemotional response to personal tragedies reflected the internal conflicts in his life. Externally very individualistic and tough but internally a man consumed with the social welfare of his "proscribed people," Young seemed to take his aggression out on the ever-present unlighted cigar in his mouth.

It was more than Young's health, though, that discouraged him from attending the organizational meeting of the Southern Conference for Human Welfare (SCHW) in Birmingham, Alabama, in November 1938. The conference was organized in part by the Alabama Policy Commission and a group of liberal white southerners after the Roosevelt administration issued a controversial report, with statistical evidence, that characterized the South as the nation's number-one economic problem. The 1,300 delegates, of which over 300 were black, represented thirteen states and formed a "Who's Who" of Southern liberals. National leaders attending included Mary McLeod Bethune, F. D. Patterson, Benjamin Mays, Frank Graham, George Mitchell, Charles Johnson, and Horace Mann Bond. Young probably declined to attend because of its purported radicalism. He and cautious whites like Howard Odum, Wilson Gee, and Virginius Dabney viewed the SCHW as temporary and stayed away, avoiding the appearance of endorsing it. Young declined because "the SCHW was a little ahead of the political South." He expected nothing but the usual resolutions "praying for social justice." He also believed that the SCHW was a Communist front but observed that the organization's membership included enough "high class, substantial southerners" to generate a balance.[16]

During the stormy conference the delegates passed resolutions demanding freedom for the Scottsboro boys, equal pay for equal work, abolition of the poll tax, and the passage of a federal antilynching bill.[17] The New York *Times* characterized the resolutions as "fair words and bold announcements." The white South was stunned. White Alabama newspapers denounced the conference; the response in the upper South was also unfavorable. "Unfortunate," observed the Raleigh *News and Observer*, Newport News *Times-Herald*, and Norfolk *Ledger-Dispatch*. Norfolk's *Virginian-Pilot* said the resolutions were tantamount "to turning a bull loose in the South's race relations china shop."[18]

Although the *Guide's* response was less than enthusiastic, Young soundly rejected the *Times-Herald's* charge of "outside interference." He agreed with *Opportunity* magazine, which observed that the SCHW conference signaled that the "South was on the move," and with black sociologist Charles Johnson, who characterized the conference as "the first bold emergence of the liberal South as a self-conscious group." The SCHW was the first attempt by southern liberals to utilize political power. In Young's view, their views were typical of southern liberalism as later defined by Gunnar Myrdal, who was present at the conference.[19]

Although the SCHW functioned until 1948, there is no evidence that Young was active in it or regularly attended its conventions. He was aware that Howard Odum and other liberal whites were quietly designing an organization to replace the CIC,[20] but at the moment he believed that the CIC represented "the true spirit of the South" and was in greater harmony with southern liberalism.

Young's interaction with Frank Graham, Guy Johnson, L. R. Reynolds, and other liberal whites within the CIC and his personal friendship with C. C. Spaulding, Charles S. Johnson, Walter White, Mary McLeod Bethune, and other prominent blacks helped bolster his optimism about race relations in the South. He sincerely believed that whites and blacks in the South shared "a common destiny" and were "going forward together." In an editorial entitled "The Changing South" in December 1938, he predicted "interracial unity in the South." He saw the "forces of liberalism" on the march, tolerance reborn, mental attitudes adjusted, and social consciousness asserting itself. Like Frank Graham, he saw the South as the battleground for American democracy.[21]

Young's political realism was based in part on his relationship with high state officials in Virginia, men like Senator Harry Byrd, Sr., and Governor James H. Price. Young frequently quoted Governor Price, who regularly cited the *Guide* as a reflection of black opinion. White CIC members in Virginia subscribed to the *Guide* and other southern black newspapers, exchanging newspaper clippings that depicted incidents of interracial cooperation and violence. They encouraged black editors to speak out on specific issues; then, armed with evidence of backing from the black community, white CIC members would approach the governor. They could do so "without pressure" because they knew that he rejected the long-established custom of "keeping the Negro down" in the belief that it "keeps us all down together." For example, in the summer of 1939, after Young wrote a two-column editorial supporting black management of black institutions such as the Piedmont Tuberculosis Sanitarium, the State Insane Hospital at Petersburg, and the State Hospital for Children at Petersburg, L. R. Reynolds, director of the Virginia CIC, and other white CIC members encouraged the governor to initiate the proposed suggestions because "times have changed." Reynolds pointed to North Carolina, which had derived "great benefit" from black management, and to the "excellent record" of J. M. Gandy at Virginia State College as "substantial proof" of black managerial skills. The governor accepted the suggestions because "colored people have made good wherever they have been given the opportunity."[22] The Norfolk *Ledger-Dispatch* and the Norfolk *Virginian-Pilot* called the proposed changes "fair, just and enlightened state policy."[23]

Young occasionally reversed the CIC strategy and urged friendly whites to encourage influential whites in the other states to investigate or to speak out on a sensitive racial issue. In August 1939 Young asked L. R. Reynolds to urge Jonathan Daniels, editor of the Raleigh *News and Observer*, to write an editorial critical of New Jersey governor Harry Moore's announced intentions to curtail the seasonal migration of black farm workers to the potato fields of New Jersey. In another instance, Young sought Reynolds's help to prevent the displacement of 500 black female tobacco workers by white females in Kinston, North Carolina, in August

1939. Reynolds promptly dispatched letters to both Daniels and Frank Barfield, secretary of Kinston's Chamber of Commerce, "to see if something might be done locally to appease this situation."[24]

A few days later, a tall, fair-skinned man in a pinstriped suit, with pocket watch and gold chain, and sporting an unlighted cigar, strolled into the office of Frank Barfield in Kinston and introduced himself—he was P. B. Young of Norfolk. As it turned out, Young's trip was unnecessary. Barfield said the press had been "misinformed." "No Negroes were displaced," he explained; in fact, "white women were hired because of a shortage of black labor." Young characterized Barfield's attitude as "friendly" and reported to Reynolds that the unemployment situation had been grossly exaggerated. In an editorial entitled "Problems in Employment," Young reminded the white community that "a prosperous Negro community is essential to a prosperous white community." Reynolds asked Barfield to issue a press release "to clear up" the misunderstanding.[25]

Apparently Young, Shepard, Spaulding, Seabrook, and others enjoyed their privileged relationship with whites. They regarded themselves as progressive leaders who had the confidence and support of the white South. They were, in the words of black Norfolk attorney J. Hugo Madison, "pure southern gentlemen." They counseled "reason" and believed that the South would eventually remove the color bar and do the "right thing" in response to growing public sentiment. Young, Spaulding, and Shepard agreed with L. R. Reynolds, who called A. Philip Randolph's proposed march on Washington in 1941 to protest discrimination in the defense industry "badly conceived."[26] Young and Spaulding quietly attempted to erode public support for the proposed march on Washington in the upper south and thwarted efforts to organize a similar march on Richmond.

It must be pointed out, though, that Young exploited his relationship with elite whites to his own personal advantage, selling advertising space to white-owned businesses. The Cavalier Hotel, Norfolk and Western Railroad, Virginia Electric and Power Company, Schwartz Department Stores, Conoco Oil, and Norfolk's own "Southern Beer" took out full-page ads. John Belden, former circulation manager, recalled that "these were accounts other black newspapers only dreamed about." Also, owing to Young's prominence as a race man, he captured printing jobs he could not otherwise have expected to have. His plant secretly printed church bulletins and wedding announcements for prominent local whites, in addition to ethnic-related printing jobs for white newspapers, hospitals, and merchants throughout the South.[27]

Although local white advertisers were attracted to the *Guide* because of Young's interracial activities, the national advertisers such as Goodrich, Ford, and Pillsbury probably purchased full-page ads in the *Guide* because they recognized the advertising potential of the black press. The *Guide's* $3.50 national subscriptions numbered well over 50,000 by 1940, and according to Young, the paper reached 100,000 homes every week. "On more than one occasion," recalled former editor John Jordan, "when our presses were inoperative, local white presses ran our copy and white unionized workers exhibited indifference. Had Young been a different type of person, and the *Guide* a militant tabloid like the Chicago *Defender* or Pittsburgh *Courier*, we would have missed our publication date on several occasions."[28]

Despite his optimism, as a race man and a successful businessman, Young knew well, as did any black southerner, that justice in the South was touchy, even volatile, and unpredictable. Economic hardship only made the problems worse. The well-known cases of Scottsboro, Angelo Herndon, and Claude Neal attest to the failure of the southern legal system, but there is another side of southern legal history, represented by several less well known cases from the early 1930s, that proves that the South did not always use the law as an instrument of white supremacy. The decade saw the worst economic oppression of free blacks in American history and the political and legal subjugation that accompanied it propelled the southern legal system into what Young called "Justice in Crisis."

Throughout the decade the *Guide* prominently featured articles on so-called Negro-did-it crimes. Feature articles on the scapegoating carried such titles as "'Negro-Did-It-Crime' Brings White to Bar"; "'Negro-Did-It-Crime' Spiked by Police"; and "'Negro-Did-It' Slayer Gets Second Trial." They were typical of what Young later called "Echoes of William Harper."[29] In August 1927 the *Guide* featured an article by Asa T. Spaulding entitled "How Negroes Are Made Scapegoats in Crime." One striking example of the mentality Young was attacking occurred in January 1933. Following a robbery at the Richmond airport, police arrested a white man who had blackened his face and hands with shoe polish and carried false identification papers. In another, a white farmer was acquitted of murder after he killed an alleged "Negro rapist" in an attempt to cover up the murder of his own wife and child.[30]

The Scottsboro case became a cause célèbre during the 1930s. It inflamed the passions of blacks throughout the South and united black Norfolkians in their support for the International Labor Defense (ILD) and the *Journal and Guide*. The *Guide* sarcastically referred to the case as

"Alabama's Harper" and "Scottsboro's Skaggs." The case arose after nine young black men were arrested and charged with the rape of two white females aboard a freight train.[31] Despite overwhelming evidence against their case, Alabama officials vigorously prosecuted it. The NAACP, believing that because of adverse publicity it could not win, initially declined to defend the nine. Samuel Leibowitz, an attorney for the Communist ILD, took up the defense of the "Scottsboro boys" and presented a brilliant argument on their behalf. The "boys," however, were found guilty and sentenced to death. Numerous appeals followed, all without success.

Young sent P. B. Young, Jr., to Decatur, Alabama, to cover the trial. He used the editorial columns of the *Guide* to spearhead a financial drive for the defense and also to scrutinize the ILD. P. B., Jr.'s car was impounded shortly after he arrived in Alabama, and he was later arrested for walking across the courthouse lawn. Undeterred, he wrote weekly reports from inside the courtroom that aroused Norfolkians' empathy and anger. He vividly described courtroom scenes, the spectators' mannerisms, the judge's decorum, and the contradictory testimony of plaintiffs Ruby Bates and Victoria Price. He castigated the white Alabama media for lack of professionalism, and he alluded to the apathy and fear in Scottsboro's black community. His father emphasized the *Guide's* "on the scene coverage" with pictures and with captions such as "Inside the Courtroom," "Direct from Scottsboro," "Hot off the Wire," and "Exclusive Interview." The *Guide* and the Baltimore *Afro-American* were the black community's only sources of information from inside the courtroom. Because the white press only summarized the testimony and ignored the embarrassing aspects of the trial, the *Guide's* readers were among the best-informed people in America about the Scottsboro trial.

Young used the church and mass meetings to enlist support for the Scottsboro defendants and to excoriate the Hoover administration for its lack of concern. The *Guide* carried headlines that kept the case and its issues before its readers week after week.[32] After the "boys" were convicted, Young responded with the longest editorial in the history of the paper.[33] During the four years of appeals, reverses, and new trials, Norfolkians were in the forefront of blacks throughout the South who shouted, "The Scottsboro Boys Shall Not Die!" The *Guide* maintained that Scottsboro was not an ordinary criminal case but a struggle to offer competent counsel, an unbiased jury, and an impartial trial to blacks in the South. Young charged that Hoover had succumbed to political pressure and an inflamed public opinion. In this instance, Young was closely aligned with publisher Robert Vann of the Pittsburgh *Courier*, who was vehemently anti-Communist and pro-NAACP. More typical of the black newspapermen's attitudes were those of William ("Kid") Kelley of Harlem's *Amsterdam News*. He asked, "why should the black man not look favorably on communism? Capitalism had given him little or nothing."[34] The Chicago *Defender* and the Baltimore *Afro-American* expressed similar views.

Young was suspicious of the ILD and believed that its involvement in the Scottsboro case would do more harm than good. He appealed to blacks to reject the organization's "Blood and Thunder" approach. "For the sake of the unfortunate boys," he wrote, "support the NAACP." In Young's view the case was complicated by the issue of race, the nature of the crime, and the involvement of the ILD. He called the Communist campaign slogans "sophomoric" and cautioned that their militant tactics were likely to boomerang and hasten the defendants' date with the electric chair.[35] Young was echoed by a prominent NAACP official, who charged that the ILD's "sledgehammer methods" in the Scottsboro case had aroused bitterness, hatred, and increased violence against blacks in the South.[36]

"The Communists have overlooked two important points," Young asserted, that "the mass of American workers are not proletarian" and that "blacks are not only a minority in America, but economically dependent as well." On the other hand, he counseled, the "orderly watchdog" approach of the NAACP was the best strategy to maintain "Our Eternal Vigilance." The *Guide* angrily rejected charges by the ILD and the Baltimore *Afro-American* that the NAACP was "less militant," "flabby," "laying down on the job," and more concerned with "pink tea and caviar" than black civil rights.[37]

The Scottsboro case provoked considerable comment within the Norfolk branch of the NAACP. Again, Young found himself and his newspaper on the defensive. In October 1932 approximately 350 Norfolkians, both black and white, attended a meeting in Liberty Hall about the Scottsboro case. The main speakers were white activist Fred Allen of the Communist party and Rufus Beaverbrook of the ILD. Allen challenged whites and blacks to stand together and to defend the Scottsboro boys by "armed defense if necessary." He shouted, "Death to lynchers is our motto."[38] Thomas Dabney, former religious editor of the *Guide*, noted that the crowd was "jubilant" and unanimously voted to send a telegram to Chief Justice Charles Evans Hughes to demand immediate release of the Scottsboro boys.

A short time later during a Sunday evening forum at the Workers Center on Church Street, Alexander Wright, a local ILD representative, unleashed a barrage of criticism against the Norfolk NAACP. He characterized it as "The National Association for the Advancement of CERTAIN People." He criticized the reformism of the NAACP and castigated the Norfolk branch for refusing to join a community effort to free Robert Lee Johnson, a black man who had been sentenced to life imprisonment for killing a white police officer. On another occasion, Max Bedacht, a national chairman of the International Workers, a Socialist organization, addressed a capacity crowd at an open-air meeting in Portsmouth. He too criticized the Norfolk NAACP and the *Guide*.[39] Although all of the ILD-sponsored meetings attracted several hundred spectators, Young buried their activities on the inside pages of his paper.

The Scottsboro case spawned what the *Guide* called a "War in Alabama." Young called the case a "smoke screen" to hide the persecution of innocent blacks. As the "eyes of the world" focused on Alabama, Young worried about the possible harm to the social fabric of the American South. What if Alabama officials lost control? What if blacks responded violently? Daily reports "hot off the wire" from his son confirmed his fears. After a Decatur jury recommended the death penalty for Haywood Patterson, one of the Scottsboro boys, the *Guide* published a Scottsboro extra on Sunday, April 9, 1933, a day before local white dailies hit the streets.[40]

The *Guide's* bold, dramatic coverage during the Scottsboro trials significantly enhanced its circulation. Young could be confident that he could sensationalize the Scottsboro trials without offending liberal white publishers. Owing to the *Guide's* treatment of the Scottsboro case and of the similar cases of William Harper and George Crawford, its circulation jumped to approximately 35,000 by 1935.

At times Young was too optimistic about the influence of liberal whites in the South. Although liberal white southern newspapers such as the Richmond *News-Leader*, the Raleigh *News and Observer*, and the Norfolk *Virginian-Pilot* condemned the verdict at Decatur and demanded a new trial by a black jury, their calls did not generate an organized movement among liberal whites to free the Scottsboro boys.[41] Young's optimism was prompted more by such individual acts of liberalism as a condemnation of the Decatur decision by Judge A. M. Stack of the Greensboro (North Carolina) Superior Court.

The Scottsboro controversy and the nationwide publicity that accompanied the arrest of six alleged ILD insurrectionists in Atlanta provoked considerable controversy within the national NAACP and the Norfolk branch. Walter White favored cooperating financially with the ILD, and elements of the Norfolk branch supported ILD efforts to raise $5,000 for the defense fund. But Young sided with conservative elements and may have supported Will Alexander, CIC director, who rejected the ILD because its officials were more interested in "propaganda" than justice.[42] The *Guide* ignored the controversy that arose after the arrest of the six ILD associates in Atlanta.

However, one issue it could not ignore was the case in 1933 of Russell Gordon, aged thirteen, who allegedly raped a young white woman in Norfolk County. The Gordon case, which received less publicity than other cases, raised the issue of the exclusion of blacks from the jury. The ILD spearheaded Gordon's defense and, as in Scottsboro, used the case as a platform for publicizing it grievances. It also attacked the Norfolk NAACP. Blacks were excluded from the jury, and the courtroom was cleared when the victim was called to testify. As a large crowd milled about the courtyard, P. B. Young, Jr., was knocked to the ground and his camera smashed as he attempted to photograph the alleged victim. Gordon was convicted and sentenced to prison. The Scottsboro and Gordon cases, however, were not the only cases in the 1930s that made Virginians realize that "something had to be done about the Southern jury system."[43]

The Harper case began on January 6, 1931, when Dorothy Skaggs, a young white resident of Portsmouth, Virginia, claimed that she was sexually assaulted and robbed in the vicinity of Upton Lane by William Harper, a Negro. Harper was arrested the following day on an unrelated misdemeanor but confessed to the crime on January 8, 1931, at 12:30 A.M. Harper acknowledged that he waited in Upton Lane for Skaggs, "hit her in the stomach," and started "messing with her." He also admitted that he took $1.50 from her pocketbook. At the time, Norfolk police described Harper's crime to a reporter from the Norfolk *Virginian-Pilot*, who was present during Harper's interrogation, as one of "the most daring and brutal acts" in Norfolk's history. Meanwhile, the *Virginian-Pilot* reported that Skaggs was "hysterical" and confined to bed with a badly bruised body.[44]

Harper's family hired W. H. Land, a black Norfolk attorney, to represent him on the assult charge. Land noted that Harper was "not of normal mentality" and asked the court for time to investigate, but after Harper's confession and indictment, Land withdrew from the case and the court appointed a white attorney, William H. Starkey, to represent Harper. Starkey later emgerged as one of Harper's strongest defenders; however, at this time, he indicated that he was "not anxious" to defend a Negro and that he would not oppose Harper's trial date of January 15, 1931.

Harper was declared sane by three court-appointed physicians on January 12, 1931. When his trial finally began on Wednesday, January 28, spectators were prohibited. Thus, the *Guide* was the black community's only source of information. The judge instructed the jury to find Harper guilty if they determined that he possessed the capacity to distinguish right and wrong and understood the character and consequences of his act. He also explained that where the state establishes a prima facie case and the defendant offers an alibi, the defense must prove its innocence "not beyond a reasonable doubt, nor by a preponderance of evidence, but by such evidence." The jury found Harper guilty on Thursday, January 29, and fixed his punishment at death.[45] This case might have slipped into obscurity had it not been for the efforts undertaken on Harper's behalf by his white attorney, William H. Starkey, and by P. B. Young, Sr. They made the Harper-Skaggs case one of the most celebrated in tidewater Virginia.

Starkey immediately introduced a motion for a new trial on the basis of "after discovered evidence." He presented affidavits from Rex W. Rodgers and his wife, Virginia Rodgers, who maintained that they were knowledgeable of Skaggs's "habits" and "customs" and that it was impossible for her to have been in Norfolk between 6:30 and 6:45 P.M. on the night of January 6, 1931. The affidavits called Skaggs's testimony "false," "perjured," "without foundation," and "wholly and completely designed" to injure Harper. Judge Allan R. Hanckel set aside Harper's conviction and ordered a new trial.[46]

Although the Harper case was not that unusual—many a black man "without friends or funds" had faced a sexual assault charge by a white woman in southern port cities—most whites in the city were skeptical about the charge. And after Harper was found guilty by an all-white jury, the white citizens of Portsmouth, in the words of Young, "revolted at the prospect of a legal lynching."[47] They were concerned because an innocent man was being railroaded to the electric chair. Editor John Jordan, a Portsmouth native, recalled that in an unusual display of interracial cooperation, both whites and blacks labeled Harper's case "a frame-up" and supported the *Guide's* call for "a careful inquiry" and a new trial.

New evidence was introduced at the second trial on March 5, 1931. First, the defense proved that at the time of the alleged rape Skaggs was with her lover in a dance hall in Elizabeth City, North Carolina. Second, white citizens in the vicinity of Upton Lane neither saw nor heard an attack during the hours Skaggs claimed to have been assaulted. A strong point for the defense was testimony by the police, which noted that on the night in question Upton Lane was patrolled three times between 6:30 and 11:00 P.M., and "no victim was laying there." Third, it was proved that Skaggs had a questionable reputation. Nine white witnesses said that she was in North Carolina during the time the alleged attack took place. Even her lover contradicted her story. According to the *Guide*, a restaurant owner testified that he accompanied her to Caroon's Dance Hall in Elizabeth City on the night of January 6 and returned early the following day. And her landlord, Rodgers, testified that she briefly listened to Lowell Thomas on the radio on the evening of January 6 and then left his home, which was approximately twenty-five minutes from the Norfolk-Portsmouth ferry, after 6:45 P.M.; therefore, he asserted, it was "utterly impossible" for her to have been in Norfolk before 7:15 P.M. He noted that Skaggs "suffered from delusions," once claiming that she was "drugged" and, on another occasion, "kidnapped." Virginia Rodgers sustained her husband's testimony. Dr. D. K. Howard, a white physician, testified that he found "no bruises" or other evidence that Skaggs had been "attacked or roughly handled." It was also noted that she waited until the afternoon of the following day to report the alleged rape. Throughout the bitterly fought trial, more than one hundred defense witnesses came forward to shatter the prosecution's case and to establish Harper's innocence. On the other hand, the prosecution characterized Mrs. Skaggs, who during the trial sat beside her husband and frequently dabbed tears from her eyes with a handkerchief, as an example of fine southern womanhood who had been wantonly attacked by an imbecilic black brute. Spectators were barred from the courtroom when she took the stand to describe how Harper, who was 5 feet 6 inches tall, had raped her.[48]

Following the closing testimony, Judge Hanckel reminded the jury that they were not bound to consider the evidence as "equally balanced." Moreover, the credibility of a witness was "exclusively" the duty of a jury, and a jury had the right to determine from the appearance of witnesses "their candor and fairness." Perhaps, more importantly, Judge Hanckel explained that Harper was presumed to be innocent and that the burden of proof was upon the state. Also, if "reasonable doubt" existed, then Harper must be acquitted. "Reasonable doubt," he observed, must not only be based upon evidence, or evolve from evidence or the lack of evidence, but also must be "serious and substantial" and based upon "material fact." It must not be an "arbitrary doubt" and "without evidence." He also asked the jury to take into account Harper's mental capacity, the embarrassment occasioned by his arrest and confinement, the menace of death, if any, and a term of imprisonment.[49]

The jury began its deliberations on Thursday, March 5, and after only thirty-four minutes found Harper not guilty. The *Guide*, which maintained reporters inside the courtroom throughout both trials, called the judge "absolutely fair" and Harper's acquittal "Justice Vindicated."[50] Harper was released, and his attorney was later paid twenty-five dollars from Norfolk's treasury for defending his indigent client.

Had the Harper scenario ended at this point, the case would have been only an anomaly in southern justice. However, it did not, and within a few weeks, it had evolved into one of the most interesting cases in Norfolk's judicial history. A few weeks after the trial a grand jury indicted Skaggs for perjury. And in another case the grand jury indicted Harper on a robbery charge. In both instances, however, the charges were later dropped.

Throughout the controversy, the *Guide* kept up its support for Harper. Although scores of white reporters from throughout the state covered the trial, the *Guide* was the only black newspaper with reporters inside the courtroom. Because spectators had been barred from the first trial and at various intervals in the second trial, and inasmuch as the white press ignored sensitive and embarrassing aspects of the trial, it turned out that the *Guide* was the only source of detailed accounts of the proceedings. It was also the first newspaper to publish Skaggs's name and photograph.[51] The *Guide* interviewed Harper's attorney and individual witnesses and also served as a conduit for information flowing among Starkey, the national NAACP, and its local branch. The case, indeed, made its mark on the local NAACP chapter.

As the case wore on, the Norfolk NAACP and the *Guide* organized a defense fund for Harper. The national NAACP saw the case as an opportunity to resurrect its Norfolk chapter and to increase black Virginians' support of the organization, which had been lackadaisical.[52] The chapter, reorganized in 1925 by P. B. Young, had again become inactive in 1930 because of internal bickering and dissatisfaction with Young's leadership. The Harper case presented a unique chance to unite a divided black community. Once again Young and his newspaper were leading the fight.

Although not an active member of the NAACP, Young cooperated with prominent black Norfolkians in arranging a mass meeting to be addressed by Walter White, Robert Bagnall, and other national NAACP leaders. Young, who sat on the podium alongside Harper, observed that "Norfolk has set a salutary example for the rest of the country. . . . No talk of violence following Harper's acquittal." Also, he said, "the Norfolk police is on notice" that Norfolkians disapprove of confessions obtained by police in "Secret Chambers." Later, when Harper himself spoke, he waved the March 14, 1931, edition of the *Guide* that headlined in bold type: "Out of the Shadow of Death . . . William Harper's Own Story."[53]

The white press responded favorably to Harper's acquittal. The conservative Petersburg *Progress-Index* editorialized that "Virginia narrowly escaped committing judicial murder"; the Roanoke *World-News* noted that the reputation of the courts in Virginia was at stake. Similar opinions were expressed by the *Virginian-Pilot* and the Richmond *Times-Dispatch*.[54]

The Harper case was closed in April 1931 after Judge William Sargeant granted prosecutor James G. Martin's request for nolle prosequi. Martin called the indictment for robbery "unfair and immoral."[55] Skaggs was sentenced to five years in prison on the perjury charge. Young editorialized that the case was the first instance in which "a white woman has been found guilty of perjury, for placing the life of a colored man in jeopardy. If the defendant never serves a day," he reasoned, "justice has been vindicated." The verdict, Young predicted, would signal an end to the time when white women could cry "rape" "to cover up their nefarious acts and . . . ulterior motives."[56] The case opened a new chapter in the administration of southern justice and helped make Virginians sensitive to what the *Guide* called "Negro-Did-It" crimes.

The Crawford case was another story altogether. It involved not only sex and violence but money, mystery, and power. It had all of the ingredients of a soap opera, complete with a surprise ending. It began in January 1932 when a wealthy Middleburg, Virginia, woman, Mrs. Agnes B. Ilsey, and her maid were allegedly murdered by George Crawford, an indigent black caretaker. In fear for his life, Crawford fled to Boston. The national NAACP and the *Guide* sent Helen Boardman, a white woman investigator, to Middleburg to look into the case. A few weeks later the *Guide* headlined: "Virginia Fugitive Believed Goat." The investigator concluded that Crawford was being used by a wealthy relative of Mrs. Ilsey to cover up the crime of someone else. As in the Scottsboro and Harper cases, it is difficult to separate facts from opinions in many reports in the *Guide*, for Young wrote opinions in feature articles and used friendly witnesses to corroborate his assessments. It is unclear who created the portrayal of Crawford as a "goat," but the supposed plot was widely publicized by the *Guide*. Although the governor of Massachusetts, Joseph B. Ely, initially refused to extradite Crawford because of insufficient evidence, he later changed his mind only to be overruled by a federal judge, who noted that "no Negro has ever served on a jury in Loudoun County."[57]

As the evidence mounted, Crawford's guilt or innocence became less and less important. The most pressing issue was who could best represent him, the NAACP or the ILD. Other issues were the exclusion of blacks from grand juries in Virginia and the integrity of the state's legal system.

The case assumed added importance after the U.S. Supreme Court declined to hear Crawford's appeal, thus clearing the way for his extradition to Virginia. The NAACP's strategy shifted from fighting extradition to fighting for Crawford's civil rights. The case gave the NAACP an important opportunity to recapture the spotlight and to regain its self-esteem and momentum after Scottsboro. It quickly rejected legal assistance from the ILD. In turn, the ILD praised the NAACP for its earlier decision to stay out of the Scottsboro case and pointed out that its own militant tactics in that case had forced many southern states to accord blacks representation on juries.[58]

Throughout the controversy, the NAACP, the ILD, and the *Guide* kept up their support for Crawford. An NAACP press release announced a mass meeting at the Salem AME Church in New York City "to lay before the public the real truth about the Crawford Case." An organizational meeting of the Newport News NAACP was disrupted by militant ILD representatives. Walter White advised the organizer of the group, Mrs. Marian Poe, "to organize an entirely new branch" and to invite P. B. Young to speak.[59]

Eugene West, president of the Norfolk branch, complained to White that the Norfolk ILD had used the Crawford controversy to recruit former NAACP members. West asserted that he could not work with the ILD because "they believe force is our only solution." White responded sympathetically and a few days later advised West to avoid future altercations with William Patterson, secretary of the ILD. "I have stated time and time again," White observed, "that the chief purpose of the ILD . . . is to destroy the NAACP." White characterized as "pure lies" Patterson's assertion that the NAACP was a "do-nothing organization that had failed the American Negro for twenty-two years."[60]

In response to the growing controversy and the obvious pressures from the ILD, prominent NAACP officials made several trips to Norfolk and the tidewater area during late spring 1933. At a mass rally in June, White shouted, "We are in the Crawford Case to stay." He called Crawford a scapegoat and condemned the militant tactics of the ILD.[61] Meanwhile, a headline in the *Guide* read, "Crawford and Scottsboro Cases in Spotlight."

To assure Virginians that the NAACP was the best choice to represent Crawford, Young and national executive director White sent newspaper clippings to Douglas Southall Freeman of the Richmond *News-Leader* and Virginius Dabney of the Richmond *Times-Dispatch*. The clippings depicted ILD members as revolutionaries "trying to overthrow the American government." The NAACP said it was "fighting for justice" and an "absolutely fair trial" for Crawford in order to insure that "the Communist may not again have ammunition with which to attack America." Dabney, Freeman, and other prominent white Virginians "sounded out local sentiment" and encouraged the national NAACP to appoint Charles Houston, a respected black attorney, to defend Crawford.[62]

However, planning NAACP strategy was temporarily less pressing than dealing with mundane matters such as food and lodging. In rural Virginia, as in other rural sections of the South, a black attorney had to employ a white attorney in order to represent a black client in court. This quasi-legal practice posed a dilemma for the all-black Crawford defense team. Whites in Leesburg and Loudon County allegedly threatened White because they assumed that he was a Caucasian who was "dealing on terms of equality with Negroes." Freeman cleared the misunderstanding when he revealed that Walter White had "colored blood." The absence of a black hotel and the unwillingness of local residents to house Houston posed a serious problem; daily round-trips from Washington, D.C., would have been prohibitive for both the defense team and black reporters. White complained to Freeman that there was "considerable reluctance on the part of colored people to house us." In the end, P. B. Young and his son Thomas W., who was an attorney and who covered the trial for the *Guide*, arranged for the defense lawyers to reside with local residents. Governor John Pollard, as well as Freeman, Dabney, and the presiding judge, J. L. McLemore, helped to assuage white fears about Charles Houston and to thwart what Freeman called "passion and prejudice."[63]

Houston confided to the *Guide* that he approached the trial with "fear and trepidation." Despite his brilliant defense, Crawford was found guilty and sentenced to life imprisonment, but he did escape the death penalty. The *Guide* and black intellectual Kelly Miller characterized the verdict as a "vindication of Virginia justice" and editorialized that Crawford received "a rare quality of justice." Unlike Scottsboro, the atmosphere at this trial was cordial, and Houston won the "genuine admiration" of whites in Loudoun County. The governor of Virginia later invited him and White to his official residence.[64]

A few weeks after the trial the *Guide* headlines read: "George Crawford Talks." In an exclusive interview Crawford "voluntarily confessed" to the murder of Mrs. Ilsey. Houston was stunned. Mr. P. B., according to John Jordan, "turned as red as a beet" when informed of Crawford's confession but was quickly consoled by his wife Eleanor. Young editorialized, "May he spend his remaining days in repentance, trying as best he knows how to purge his soul of some of the lies he has told."[65]

Several years later the *Guide* sent a questionnaire to every black lawyer in Virginia and North Carolina to inquire whether a white man had ever been convicted of rape involving a black woman. All responded negatively.[66] The paper probably wanted to protect the gains of the Harper case and to extend the principles of the Crawford case to white-on-black crime. The survey would be useful in the development of future legal strategy.

In late 1933, probably in response to political pressure and the controversy surrounding the Harper and Crawford cases, the cities of Richmond and Norfolk began to add the names of blacks to their grand jury lists. The national NAACP regarded this action as "direct and tangible evidence" of Houston's brilliance in the Crawford case and a "vindication" of NAACP methods.[67] But in Norfolk blacks felt differently. They talked about the "great victory" the ILD had won by having blacks serve on juries. "They forgot," retorted Eugene West, president of the local NAACP chapter, "that we won decisions before the Supreme Court before the ILD was heard of."[68]

The Harper, Scottsboro, and Crawford cases were alike in many ways. All three involved interracial sex, violence, and the constitutional rights of blacks to serve on juries. The Harper case publicized the issue; the Crawford case, in the words of Virginius Dabney, convinced Virginians "that something had to be done." The defendants, except Crawford, were represented by white lawyers.

A fair trial was impossible for the Scottsboro defendants, but according to the *Guide,* "there was not a hint of racial prejudice at Crawford's trial." In each case, the NAACP and the ILD were contenders. A black lawyer probably could not have succeeded in Decatur; a white attorney could not have done better in Loudoun County.

In each instance, beliefs about the innocence or guilt of the individuals initially divided along racial lines. Also, owing to the sensational publicity generated by each case, the question of the innocence or guilt of the accused was soon subordinated to legal and public issues. Although the *Guide* kept up a steady barrage of reports and conducted exclusive interviews with all of the key participants in each case, its impact on the outcome of the cases is subject to varying interpretations. It was the only source of information during Harper's trial, and its revelation of the name of the alleged victim generated support for a new trial and ultimately Harper's freedom. On the other hand, it was so obsessed with Crawford's innocence that it overlooked contradictions and fallacies in the case that hard investigative reporting would have uncovered.

The activities of P. B. Young and the *Guide* in response to all these cases intensified the quest by blacks to serve on juries in Virginia and, at the same time, helped to lay the legal challenges to *Plessy* v. *Ferguson*. The *Guide's* "hot off the wire" coverage not only increased its circulation but also enhanced Young's image as a successful businessman. He was a strong believer in the American economic dream and undoubtedly took great pride in achieving success as both an entrepreneur and a civic activist. He remained essentially a conservative, supporting the NAACP's approach while networking with liberal whites in the community to invalidate the strategy and objectives of the Communists in the black community. His public efforts as an ambassador for interracial harmony expressed only one aspect of his fervent desire for racial justice. His involvements with Scottsboro, Harper, and Crawford cases reveal how effectively he could make the *Guide* serve both his own and his community's needs.

▪ 8 ▪

The War Years

The Second World War permanently changed American life. The changes for black Americans were cataclysmic. The exigencies of war prompted legislation aimed at reducing or eliminating racial discrimination. Writing during the war, Gunnar Myrdal predicted that "there is bound to be a redefinition of the black man's status in America as a result of the war." Historians later concluded that the war indeed had changed the intellectual atmosphere and marked the point where blacks were no longer willing to accept discrimination in employment and housing without protest.[1]

Americans were emotionally involved in the wars abroad many years before they were committed officially to waging war themselves. While white Americans awaited news from the battlefields of Europe during the 1930s, black Americans focused their attention farther south, in the Mediterranean and Africa. The watershed event in the American black press was the Italo-Ethiopian conflict of 1934–36. One observer wrote that he knew of "no event in recent times that stirred the rank-and-file of Negroes more than the Italo-Ethiopian War." Another commented that the conflict in Ethiopia "did more to unite" black interest in Africa than any previous event.[2] Throughout the crisis, the *Journal and Guide* exalted the "Glory of Ethiopia" and apocalyptically predicted the realignment of European powers before World War II.

The Ethiopian crisis began on December 5, 1934, when 600 colonial troops from Italian Somaliland clashed with 1,500 Ethiopian soldiers at Wal-Wal, in Ethiopia's arid southeastern triangle. Fascist Italy under Benito Mussolini seized this opportunity to increase its armed forces and its empire. The *Guide* reported the clash at Wal-Wal and the subsequent bombing of Ethiopia by Italy, and it dismissed Italy's expressed desire to avenge its defeat at Adowa and blamed the war on the alleged "riches" of "King Solomon's Mines" in Ethiopia. The *Guide* asked the State Department to intervene diplomatically. But the United States and its allies England and France were watching Hitler's Germany, not Haile Selassie's Ethiopia. The United States, in Young's view, "evaded" Ethiopia's appeal for assistance.[3]

In an editorial entitled "Onward Christian Soldiers," the *Guide* urged the Ethiopians "to fight man-to-man, rifle-to-rifle, and sword-to-sword." It equated Haile Selassie with Hannibal and praised him as a man imbued with the same fiery spirit of liberty and independence that motivated Patrick Henry to declare "Give me liberty or give me death." It carried pictures of "Abyssinian warriors," the royal family, and Emperor Haile Selassie proudly displaying a modern machine gun. The Ethiopian army was pictured in modern uniforms alongside what the *Guide* called "the latest instruments of warfare."[4] Young's coverage implies that he was optimistic that Ethiopia could somehow stave off an Italian invasion.

During the summer of 1935, as tension mounted in both Europe and Africa, war, in the words of the *Guide,* seemed "nearer and nearer." Young accurately predicted that a war in Africa between Ethiopia and Italy would bring about a realignment of European powers and "another world war." At the time, there was considerable discussion about America's role in foreign affairs. The central issue was how best to guarantee America's security, and how much responsibility the United States had for maintaining world peace. Isolationists such as Gerald P. Nye of North Dakota, William E. Borah of Idaho and George W. Norris of Nebraska favored reduced American participation.[5] But black internationalists like Young, W. E. B. Du Bois, Carl Murphy, and Robert Vann of the *Courier* argued that the United States had emerged from World War I as a strong and wealthy world power; accordingly, in their view, America could not escape the effects of world problems and should therefore cooperate with foreign nations.[6] The internationalists favored a limited embargo and a League of Nations blockade against Italy.

As the crisis worsened during the late summer and early fall of 1935, the black media in America pressed Ethiopia's claim with the League of Nations and dismissed Italy's charges of Ethiopian aggression as a "fascist fabrication." Black newspapers such as the *Guide,* the *Courier,* the *Afro-American,* and the Chicago *Defender* overflowed with news, special features, editorials, letters to the editor, and photographs of the conflict. The *Crisis,* the official organ of the NAACP, saw the conflict as "a sad spectacle of white civilization." Interestingly, few American blacks realized that the proud Amharas, who ruled Ethiopia, considered themselves Caucasians and in recent times held black slaves themselves.[7]

Italy invaded Ethiopia on October 3, 1935. The Roosevelt administration imposed an arms embargo in the region, but the League of Nations failed to impose an oil embargo against Italy or to close the Suez Canal, helping Mussolini to achieve a quick military victory. The *Guide* criticized the League's diplomacy as a scheme to protect England's colonial possessions in Africa and India, and Young reprimanded England and France for "ganging up" to preserve white domination. He predicted that the war would unite the darker peoples of the world.[8]

The Italian invasion of Ethiopia provoked a storm of protest in black America and spawned a strong sense of racial solidarity, promoting the cause of pan-Africanism. Black newspapers like the *Guide*, the Baltimore *Afro-American*, the Cleveland *Gazette*, the New York *Age*, the New York *Amsterdam News*, the Los Angeles *Eagle*, and the Philadelphia *Tribune* published a multitude of articles, columns, and editorials relating to the war. To many blacks the name of Ethiopia implied a proud and dignified Africa. Black clergymen preached pro-Ethiopian sermons, and many black churches petitioned the pope to mediate the conflict. On October 4, 1935, the day after Italian troops invaded, enraged and frustrated blacks in the United States retaliated with physical attacks against Italian street vendors and called for a national black boycott of Italian-American stores.[9]

Despite the patriotic sentiments the black press, black organizations, and black leaders knew that Ethiopia's defeat was inevitable. Although Young termed Ethiopia's eventual defeat "inevitable," he remained hopeful that the United States and the major powers would intervene. However, Ethiopia collapsed in May 1936.

Young disagreed with columnist Walter Lippmann, who observed in August 1938 that "the danger of a European war had passed." As the German army marched triumphantly into Austria, the *Guide* characterized England and France as "helpless" and called England's appeasement "a dangerous precedent." Young reasoned that England's policy was designed to protect its "vital interest" in Africa and India. He charged that England "sold China, Austria, and Ethiopia down the river." Therefore, "as a last resort, small sovereign nations and minority groups" must "close ranks," he wrote.[10]

Young was consistent in his support of American foreign policy. He believed that America should take a leading role in foreign affairs because of its "abundant resources." He termed American neutrality "a mirage" and urged blacks to support FDR's foreign policy, because a "blundering Democracy" was preferable to the barbarism of Fascism.[11]

During the war the *Guide* reached new heights of influence, not only locally but nationally as well. P. B. Young received recognition and awards rarely accorded any editor, black or white, in the South. The White House staff as well as Mrs. Roosevelt were regular readers of the *Guide*. Young was a member of a Hampton Roads Peninsula interracial delegation that met privately with Mrs. Roosevelt after her address at the seventy-fifth anniversary of Hampton Institute. The New York *Times*, the New York *Herald-Tribune*, and the Richmond *Times-Dispatch*, and other newspapers throughout the nation frequently quoted him as a "liberal southern statesman." As he became more involved at the national level, he received calls from the national executive office concerning his views on race relations, on the Fair Employment Practices Commission, or on Jim Crowism in the military. The *Guide* was one of four southern newspapers commended by the Office of War Information for investigating and exposing false rumors of impending racial conflict in southern communities. Blacks, too, throughout the South regarded the editor-in-chief as a source of information and favors. Young's mail for a typical day might include a request to pray for a husband, a request from a mother in a distant city for Young to visit her son in a local hospital (she didn't know which one) and report to her, a request to become a sponsor for a prison inmate, a proposal of marriage, and a request from a youth to help him join the navy.[12]

The war years were exciting times for the *Guide*. According to John Jordan, the *Guide* operated three shifts daily. Its circulation jumped to a phenomenal 85,000. Like other black newspapers, the *Guide* kept the black community informed of individual acts of heroism by black soldiers fighting in Europe, Australia, and the Pacific. Its "exclusive" war coverage was designed to inculcate its black readers with a feeling of patriotism and pride. The *Guide* enthusiastically supported FDR's call to arms after Japan attacked Pearl Harbor.[13] "We want to defend our country in whatever manner it needs to be defended, and wherever we are called upon to go." Speaking directly to the more militant blacks who raised the issue of Japan's nonwhite ethnicity, Young asserted that Japan had forfeited its right to such consideration by its uncivilized manner of declaring war and by joining in an unholy alliance with Hitler and Mussolini.

Joe Louis, the "Brown Bomber," in Young's view symbolized the initial black response to the war and gave America a new slogan. Appearing on the Eddie Cantor radio program a few weeks after the attack, Louis was reminded that he had defeated the Baer brothers, Max and Buddy. "Now that I've taken care of the Baers," Joe replied, "I'm going after the snakes." The studio audience gave him a thunderous ovation. Young proudly remarked that Joe Louis had done more for blacks than any man since Booker T. Washington. He called Louis "a great fighter, a modest gentleman, a good citizen, and now, the proudest title of all—'Soldier of the U.S.A.'"[14]

When it became obvious that the United States would indeed enter World War II, Young, now a "militant Democrat," adopted a new tone. As the crisis in Europe worsened and America hastily cranked up its war machinery, the *Guide* reported that blacks were finding that jobs in the armed forces and defense work in the civilian sector were closed to them. In response, the Committee on Participation of Negroes in the National Defense Program (CPNND), founded in Washington in May 1938, stepped up its program to desegregate the armed forces. A CPNND conference in Hampton, Virginia, in November 1940 passed a resolution calling on the Defense Department "to end discriminatory practices." They pledged their support of the Burke-Wadsworth bill which provided for a military draft. Although the bill contained no provisions against segregation, Young, who attended the conference, expressed optimism because it reflected the Defense Department's drive to make equal opportunity in the armed forces a reality. Indeed, Young endorsed Roosevelt for a third term in 1940 in part because of his support of the bill. In a letter to Claude Barnett, Young noted that FDR's election would have a stabilizing effect upon business, industry, and agriculture.[15]

Although Young opposed the use of frontal attack as a matter of principle, he occasionally employed it. In early 1941 he initiated a bold campaign to end discrimination in the defense industries in the tidewater area. The *Guide* waged a vigorous drive to place qualified black carpenters on the Norfolk Naval Base and at forts Eustis and Lee near Petersburg. But when scores of blacks answered an emergency radio appeal for 1,500 carpenters in January 1941, they were rejected. The contractor explained, "You must be unionized," and "we cannot mix the races."[16] Young called their rejections un-Christian and undemocratic. He complained that defense-related industries were refusing to comply with an order from the Federal Works Administration, which banned discrimination against black skilled and semiskilled workers.

Each week the *Guide* chronicled employers' reprisals and subterfuges that were revealed to Young by job applicants, black contractors, and local officials of the Virginia State Employment Commission. When the Newport News *Daily Press* equated black demands for employment with a desire for social equality, Young angrily asserted that it had "missed the point." He urged black workers to join the American Federation of Labor and the shipbuilding and boilermaker trade unions. Democratic congressman Arthur W. Mitchell of Illinois and Mrs. Roosevelt voiced similar themes during separate visits to tidewater Virginia.[17]

Many black leaders were, like Young, gravely concerned about the employment problem in the spring of 1941. To dramatize the black man's economic plight, A. Philip Randolph, a longtime racial activist and president of the Brotherhood of Sleeping Car Porters, began organizing a march on Washington in February. Randolph, Kelly Miller, Robert L. Vann of the Pittsburgh *Courier*, and other northern black leaders had already adopted a strategy of protest at the height of the defense mobilization in 1940 in an attempt to extract concessions from the White House. They viewed blacks' "close ranks" strategy during World War I to have been a mistake because, as Kelly Miller said, "if the Negro forgets his grievances while the war is on, the American people will ignore them when the war is over." Randolph's march was set for July 1, 1941, and 50,000 participants were planned for. Young and black Norfolkians responded cautiously. Young saw nothing un-American in the march; nevertheless, he wondered how the demonstrations would be viewed "in the heat of our present perilous crisis." Young's concern was shared by C. C. Spaulding and black congressman Arthur W. Mitchell who, like Young, asked, "Lord! What will they think in Berlin?"[18]

On June 25, 1941, the president issued Executive Order No. 8802 prohibiting discrimination in defense industries and establishing the Fair Employment Practices Committee (later Commission) to investigate complaints of discrimination and to redress valid grievances. Randolph promptly canceled the march. The order had an immediate effect. A black plumbing firm and a black electrical firm were awarded contracts to work on houses for defense families in Warwick County (Newport News). For the first time in its history the Newport News Building and Trade Council accepted blacks on its executive board. Union and nonunion contractors employed black carpenters, painters, plasterers, bricklayers, and cement finishers in larger numbers than before. Young applauded FDR's order and predicted that failure to comply with it would bring more affirmative protest.[19]

Despite the fact that the war and the pressures it brought to bear on American citizens exacerbated racial tensions in tidewater Virginia, and indeed throughout the nation, Young continued to believe that whites and blacks could live together amicably in the South. He used his influence to organize a meeting on October 20, 1942, of a group of influential southern blacks in Durham, North Carolina. They issued the so-called Durham Manifesto.[20]

Although the leaders who met in Durham achieved no consensus on segregation or southern black strategy, they projected the changing black mood in the wartime South. They were not prepared to challenge segregation directly; instead, they set out in plain but courteous language to explain "what the Negro wants." Benjamin Mays, president of Morehouse College, and Gordon Hancock favored integration of the armed forces and a more aggressive political and legal challenge to the separate-but-equal doctrine. Young, Spaulding, and Shepard assumed moderate positions: they argued for an expanded role for blacks within the existing defense structure and warned that having integration as a goal would undermine their positions of leadership in the South. Moreover, Young warned of a white backlash if whites perceived the conference as a platform "to press for racial equality." The exigencies of the war demanded racial unity and personal sacrifice.[21]

Shortly after the Durham conference, Young received "firm assurances" of support from Jessie Daniel Ames, Ralph McGill, editor of the Atlanta *Constitution*, and other influential white southern leaders. However, optimism and confidence began to evaporate after the Durham statement failed to receive what Young called "ready and open support" in the South. White southerners feared "personal losses and embarrassment" and initially declined to meet with blacks to discuss the conference. Young, somewhat peeved, in a letter to Jessie Ames criticized southern whites for their lack of commitment and concluded, "we are in a bad fix." Young worried that the lack of a formal reponse from white southerners would be interpreted as a repudiation of the Durham statement. Another concern was the response of white syndicated newspaper columnist Paul Mallon and other moderate whites, who publicly expressed "personal disappointment" with the Durham meeting. Mallon called the Durham statement "fine" but disagreed with blacks who defined the "Negro problem" in America as political and legal rather than social and economic. "If the poll tax, compulsory segregation, and lynching were abolished immediately by a stroke of the pen, the condition of the Negro would not improve one whit," he argued. Mallon characterized the Durham conference as "nothing more than resentful water on the wheel of Negro radicals."[22]

Time magazine and *Reader's Digest* decided not to publish a preconference interview with Young because, he thought, of Mallon's "astonishing statement." However, later Young thought that both periodicals were controlled by northern reactionary groups who were in coalition with southern reactionary groups to liquidate the social legislation of the Roosevelt administration. In Young's view the Durham declaration was suppressed by both periodicals because it was "too strong."[23]

Trouble, however, did not come just from the white community. Black educator James E. Shepard insisted upon organizing a fact-finding conference before liberal whites had caucused and formally responded to the Durham statement. Young and Gordon Hancock were furious; Virginius Dabney was "puzzled"; and Jessie Ames, "worried." The Shepard-Young controversy polarized southern black leadership and threatened for a time to derail the Durham conference. The source of the controversy was what Shepard called a "misunderstanding." On the eve of the adjournment of the Durham conference, a motion allegedly was passed to meet and to cooperate with Shepard's fact-finding conference as a regular organization with a "distinct mission," although it had not functioned since 1929. Although Shepard had endorsed the Durham statement, he believed that the October 1942 Durham conference "failed to meet the needs of the people" and that the purpose of the fact-finding conference would be "to cover these omissions." Shepard, along with Spaulding and J. W. Seabrook, believed that the Negro's main problems were educational and economic, and not political. Shepard's views were extended by Roscoe Dunjee, editor of the Oklahoma City *Dispatch*, and by Maynard Jackson, a prominent religious and civic leader in Dallas. They assailed the all-black conference and denounced the conferees' failure to condemn segregation.[24]

Shepard's recalcitrant behavior in 1942 forced Young to abandon his gentlemanly approach temporarily. He even traveled to Durham and confronted Shepard on the campus of North Carolina College. The meeting was both tense and short. Shepard complained that although the Durham conference had been held on his campus, it had relegated him to a secondary role. He believed that as one of the leading black educators in the South, he was more familiar with the needs of all blacks than was a newspaper editor from the tidewater. Besides, he was better known and respected by whites in the South than was Young.[25]

An angry and dejected Young returned to Norfolk, according to one observer, determined to show Shepard that he, Young, was the rooster, while Shepard was still a baby chick. He promptly set about to isolate Shepard politically. Virginius Dabney, Jessie Daniel Ames, Will Alexander, and other influential whites prevailed upon Shepard to postpone his planned April 1943 conference. Jessie Ames wondered "who and what is back of Dr. Shepard's persistence?" Dabney, in an angry letter to Jessie Ames, called the conference "unwise" because Shepard had invited "radical northern Negroes."[26] Gordon Blaine Hancock worked closely with Young to "line up" the press and the pulpit. Meanwhile, Young drafted letters to President H. L. McCrorey of Johnson C. Smith University in Charlotte, President Horace Mann Bond of Fort Valley State College in Georgia, historian Luther P. Jackson, Fisk University's Charles Johnson, and other blacks to prevail upon "our mutual friend" to postpone his fact-finding conference until after southern whites had formally responded to the Durham statement. As Young's offensive gathered momentum, Hancock proudly noted to Jessie Ames: "Our opposers are on the defensive." Hancock, in an obvious reference to Shepard, called him a "traducer . . . lying in wait."[27]

In Young's view, Shepard's calling a new conference was tantamount to a repudiation of the Durham conference. "Is that your intent?" Young asked. "If so, you will stir up a lot of resentment" in both the black and white communities. He angrily asked, "Exactly what are your plans?" "Unless we get together on this," Young asserted, "you will jeopardize both conferences and race relations in the South as well." Young urged Shepard to invite Spaulding and "anyone else you wish" and meet with himself and Hancock.[28]

Southern white opposition and Young's strategy of isolation forced Shepard to capitulate. He postponed his conference until October 1943. Shepard, somewhat apologetically, wrote to Young that "there is no reason for conflict or confusion; I am perfectly willing to cooperate." Shepard also sought "to clarify" the incident with historian Luther P. Jackson, Sr., and Horace Mann Bond, because "I shall have to rely upon you" in order to make the October meeting a success.[29]

Meanwhile, the Conference of White Southerners on Race Relations met in Atlanta, Georgia, on April 8, 1943. Jessie Ames was understandably nervous and observed that the outcome was in the "lap of God." She had deliberately organized an all-white conference because many whites were "a little skittish" about coming to an interracial meeting. She also clamped a lid on preconference publicity to prevent public controversy. Young called her strategy "no doubt the best," and like Hancock, he approved of an all-white conference in the belief that whites needed "to huddle" alone for greater understanding.[30]

The Atlanta conference "accepted in principle" the Durham Manifesto and issued a statement of its own that, in the main, was not very different. The *Guide* called the Atlanta conference "a significant forward step." Young regarded both conferences as an "evolutionary" approach rather than a revolutionary, frontal attack on segregation. The Chicago *Defender* called the conference "news of the first magnitude," but the Pittsburgh

Courier and the New York *Amsterdam News and Star* attached no importance to it. The *News and Star* characterized both the conferences as
"Double Talk." The southern white press was uniformly sympathetic to
the Atlanta conference. The Atlanta *Journal* declared it "notable"; the
Richmond *Times-Dispatch* called it a "sanely conservative . . . way to
progress," and the *Virginian-Pilot* was "struck at the amplitude of the
common ground."[31]

The response of a few southern liberals who were unable to attend the
conference but who willingly signed its statement was typified by S. Y.
Austin of Sylacauga, Alabama. He characterized it as "weak" and observed that he would have preferred to sign a more definite, "to-the-point
statement." It was written with "crossed fingers" by a body of men who
believed that it was better "to wade in cold water ankle deep than waist
deep or knee deep," he wrote.[32]

On June 16, 1943, collaboration committees from both the Durham
and Atlanta conferences met in Richmond "to work out methods and
practical means" of interracial cooperation. Young caucused with Ralph
McGill and Jessie Ames before the conference and later chaired the
Richmond meeting. Although Young, Hancock, and others accepted ac-
colades for the Durham conference, "this noble thing," Hancock wrote,
"was born in the heart and mind of a southern white woman"—Jessie
Daniel Ames.[33]

Schism and conflict followed the Richmond meeting. Blacks felt "let
down," discouraged, and depressed; whites expressed disillusionment
with black leadership. A new name for the Commission on Interracial
Cooperation was debated because, to many blacks, "interracial" meant
"Uncle Tomism," and to whites, it conjured up images of "social inter-
mingling." In January 1944 a new organization, the Southern Regional
Council (SRC), was chartered as a corporation by the state of Georgia. At
the charter meeting the CIC met and formally merged its programs and
assets with those of the council. The SRC was headed by one of Young's
closest personal friends, Guy B. Johnson, whom he characterized as "courageous" and "well known."[34] Like the CIC, the SRC quietly investigated
acts of racial violence in the South and proselytized among southern
whites to improve race relations. Young and other moderates prevailed
for several years as the SRC trod the path of caution, avoiding direct
attacks on segregation.

Little wonder that during the war blacks and liberal whites in the South
found it easy to agree on principle but difficult to come to terms when
tactics had to be decided. The delicate balance of southern race relations
was thrown askew by the social dislocations caused by the war. For ex-

ample, large-scale black migration from throughout Virginia and eastern North Carolina into the Hampton Roads industrial centers increased the economic competition between blacks and whites for employment. The frequent result was friction and conflict.

Norfolk experienced shortages of everything and became what one author called a "conscripted city." Jammed buses, crowded restaurants and schools, and long lines at movie houses exacerbated racial tensions. In Newport News streetcars and buses carrying white workers to their homes traveled through the black community, making contact unavoidable. Blacks usually waited for whites to get on first and then pushed through standing whites to enter or exit. Clashes erupted on streetcars over transfers and the use of front seats. The situation was aggravated by long working hours, impatient drivers, and the greasy clothing of the shipyard workers. Women frequently complained of clothes dirtied by "Negro shipyard workers" as they pushed to the rear of the bus. Inevitable conflicts resulted when black male passengers, unable to find seats in the rear, sat next to white female passengers. At the time, Virginius Dabney described race relations in Virginia and the South as a "crisis" and warned blacks that "insistence upon complete equality in the South would result in a racial war in which blacks were bound to be losers."[35] P. B. Young agreed.

The crisis in race relations in Norfolk was heightened by what the *Guide* called "a desperate housing situation" and the attending afflictions of poor health and crime. The *Guide* reported that one eleven-room house was home for twenty-one persons. It had one bath and a toilet that emptied through a pipe into buckets on the lower floor. Each occupant paid $7 per week for the privilege of living in the heated 55-year-old unit. "Hot beds" were "yours for twelve hours and someone else's for twelve hours," at $2.50 per shift in tenement districts. It was not uncommon for seven or eight persons to call "home" a room containing two small beds. The "sublet racket" took thousands of dollars from war workers. Young complained that mandatory rent ceilings were easy to evade, given the shortage of inspectors. The cost of a small room jumped from $9 to $22.50 per week in three months. Through shrewd subletting, one landlord earned more than $350 a week from 161 persons living in six houses. Tenants who complained were threatened with eviction.[36]

It was in response to these abuses that the Norfolk Housing Authority and later the Norfolk Redevelopment and Housing Authority were created. Indeed, Norfolk became one of the earliest American cities to clear its slums and rebuild. Norfolk's slums were, according to Nathan Straus, a federal housing administrator, "the worst in the nation."[37] On July 30,

1940, slum clearance in Norfolk began when the city council unanimously adopted a resolution "Declaring the Need for a Housing Authority in the City of Norfolk, Virginia." Organized opposition to slum clearance was led by the Real Estate Board, but the YWCA, the Business and Professional Women's Club, the Norfolk County Medical Society, the *Virginian-Pilot*, and the *Guide* supported the establishment of a local housing authority.

Rear Admiral Joseph K. Taussig, commandant of the Fifth Naval District, contended that 1,000 low housing units were needed immediately to forestall "extreme hardship" to navy personnel.[38] The *Virginian-Pilot*, in a July 28, 1940, editorial, described defense housing as "incidental to the principle mission . . . slum clearance." City Manager Charles B. Borland and "Mr. P. B." complained to the city council that the housing shortage was frustrating military authorities. After the national flag was wrapped around the housing issue, the city established the Norfolk Redevelopment and Housing Authority (NRHA).

Shortly after the housing authority was created, the Norfolk Negro Advisory Committee (NAC) surveyed approximately forty housing agencies in various cities throughout the South to ascertain if black housing projects were managed or supervised by blacks. Ninety-five percent responded affirmatively. One exception was Savannah, Georgia, which had concluded "that the Negro is not suitable for executive work, certainly not on a larger project." Young asked W. H. Stillwell, executive director in Savannah, "not to hold to the conclusion" and "count out the entire race" because one black person failed to measure up to his expectations. Although the editor-in-chief declared his intentions not to interfere in local affairs, he nevertheless forwarded to Stillwell the responses of seventeen housing authorities who successfully employed blacks.[39] The employment of blacks as managers, supervisors, and staff personnel in defense housing, and later in public housing, was a nonnegotiable demand of the NAC.

Young's power in civic affairs by the time of the war is revealed in one incident involving the housing authority. A bitter feud erupted in September 1942 between the NAC and W. T. Mason, a black project manager. Young provoked the feud because he was "disappointed" with Mason's hiring policies. A power struggle quickly developed between Young and Mason, and the Norfolk Housing Authority was caught in the middle. When Young threatened to resign from the NAC, the housing authority's executive director, Lawrence Cox, hastily organized a meeting with Young and members of the Norfolk Committee on Negro Affairs (NCNA), on which Young also served as chairman. Cox instructed Mason not to make personal appointments that were unsatisfactory to the NAC and "to secure" its "approval" on administrative procedures.[40] Young was victorious not only because he could reach the public through the *Guide* but also because he served as chairman of the NCNA, which represented a cross section of black leadership. When Young met with city officials and appeared before the city council, he was speaking for the black community. Black tenants and city officials alike accepted his leadership. When delinquent tenants had their gas turned off, they called P. B. Young for help. When rowdyism disrupted the tranquillity of Roberts Park, the tenants called him. City officials consulted him about the type of coal and paint for tenant projects, and Liberty Park tenants asked him to secure a commercial center for their district.[41]

Segregated housing aggravated the poor social conditions in wartime Norfolk. Norfolk and Norfolk County became known as America's worst center of venereal disease. Prostitution, gambling, liquor law violations, rapes, petty thefts, public drunkenness, and aggravated assaults became a major problem for law enforcement agencies, as approximately 12,000 sailors, 2,000 of them black, came to town every night. The *Guide* initiated a campaign to suppress illegal activities. In the meantime, black sailors were "totally neglected," in Young's view. They were banned from the navy "Y" and the dives on East Main Street; the only entertainment available to them was that little provided by the civilian black community. Few whites realized it, but the same friction between sailors and civilians prevailed in the black section of the city as in the white section. Black sailors, like white sailors, got drunk and brawled with civilians. Black nightclubs experienced so much difficulty that they refused to admit uniformed patrons unless civilians vouched for them. Young and Louis Jaffe of the *Virginian-Pilot* initiated a campaign to provide entertainment for the area's black servicemen. Their efforts made it possible for Saturday night dances to be held in the Booker Washington High School.[42]

Even before World War II, Norfolk had a higher crime rate than most cities in Virginia. Despite the crime statistics, Young had always praised the Norfolk police, but during the war he believed that area police had become corrupt and inefficient; the county jail allegedly served as a speakeasy and brothel. Several assaults by local blacks upon white sailors prompted the navy commander, "who feared racial friction and riots," to place the black community off-limits to white sailors. When a black citizen of "good reputation" was beaten up by two whites, a marine and a sailor, a city policeman from whom he requested help told him, "Sorry, I'm off-duty."[43]

To introduce reform and eliminate incompetence and corruption, both the Norfolk *Virginian-Pilot* and the *Guide* called for the appointment of black policemen. "We want police officers," screamed an April 10, 1943, editorial in the *Guide*. In bold type a feature article exclaimed: "We Want Negro Officers on Tense 25th and Jefferson Avenue." City Manager Borland received "a flood of letters" from the white ministerial alliance.

In April 1943, the *Guide* claimed that 1,300 black officers were employed in sixteen southern cities, and by January 1945 the Southern Regional Council alleged that twenty-four cities in eight southern states had "experimented" successfully with black policemen.[44] Young and Jaffe challenged whites to dismiss fears of "social equality" as "silly" and "irrelevant." The purpose of a police force is to prevent crime and to apprehend criminals. Nevertheless, all discussions of black policemen turned inevitably to the question: "Will Negro policemen arrest white people?"

It was not until November 1945 that Norfolk appointed two black male police officers. City Manager Borland said, as he swore them into service, "The eyes of both races are upon you." He admonished them to "be calm and deliberate" in the exercise of authority. "You are pioneers," he asserted, "and pioneers cannot afford to make mistakes." The *Virginian-Pilot* called Borland's words "good advice for any city"; the *Guide* referred to the appointments as "A Notable Step Forward for Racial Unity." The Newport News *Daily Press* expressed confidence and urged cities on the peninsula to get in step with the modern trend. A black minister echoed the feeling of the black community when he hummed, "My soul has been lifted."[45]

Young's energetic pursuit of blacks' rights in employment and housing on the local level, coupled with his spreading reputation via the *Guide*, inevitably caught the eyes of national officials in Washington. Perhaps remembering Young's strong support of the executive order instituting the Fair Employment Practices Committee in 1941, President Roosevelt appointed him to the FEPC in June 1943.[46] He served as an industry representative alongside John Brophy of the CIO, Milton P. Webster of the Brotherhood of Sleeping Car Porters, Boris Skishkin of the AFL, and the Right Reverend Monsignor Francis J. Haas, who served as chairman of the FEPC during Young's tenure.

Although the FEPC lacked enforcement powers, its designation as the president's committee enhanced its work. Nonetheless, its authority was openly challenged and its directives were ignored by private groups and congressional committees. In January 1944 Young and other members of the committee petitioned the president for a meeting to discuss, among other things, the status of the committee as well as discrimination against Mexican-Americans in the Southwest.[47]

Though appointed in June, Young did not attend an FEPC board meeting until October 18, 1943, because of ill health. He consequently had missed the important railroad hearings conducted by the FEPC during September 1943 in Washington, D.C. He also missed meetings in September and October that involved discussions of FEPC policy, seniority rules, hiring policy, race relations, and discriminatory employment practices at a Western Electric facility in Baltimore. From July 1, 1943, to April 30, 1944, the FEPC held eleven public hearings, investigated twenty-five work stoppages, and handled 4,435 complaints. At the time of Young's appointment in 1943 the FEPC had 1,016 cases pending, and it had docketed another 1,930 before January 1, 1944.[48]

Young attended only three public meetings during his tenure. All of the hearings involved charges of racial discrimination, but Young was most vocal at a December 10, 1943, hearing held in Norfolk. The complainant was a black named Rone Sidney and the respondent was Robert H. Holt, postmaster of Newport News. Sidney protested that he was denied appointment to a clerical position in the Newport News post office in favor of white men who had not taken the Civil Service Examination. When other blacks inquired at the post office, they were allegedly told, "We don't appoint colored clerks." Holt rejected Sidney's allegations. He testified that the Newport News post office employed 21 white clerks and 21 black carriers at the time of his appointment in 1936 and that the staff in 1943 included 110 white clerks and 31 black carriers. Although black applicants had passed the Civil Service Examination, Holt noted that he selected "the best qualified" clerks. Concerning his refusal to employ Sidney, Holt said, "I didn't like his manner . . . and his general attitude."[49]

Holt's practices were consistent with unofficial but established employment practices in many southern communities. The taboo against black mail clerks was motivated largely by a desire to restrict contact between black men and white women. Unlike teaching and preaching, which were the main sources of middle-class employment for black men, the "elite" post office jobs paved the way to economic security and upward mobility. White postal officials hired only blacks—mulatto blacks—who came highly recommended, and then only those who were graduates of good black schools such as Hampton Institute, Fisk University, and Tuskegee Institute. Young, in fact, frequently had been asked to recommend prospective black employees to postal authorities (there is no evidence, however, that he was acquainted with either Sidney or Holt).

The *Guide*'s coverage of FEPC hearings was limited. Despite their front-page banner headlines, the articles on the FEPC lacked substance and were extracted from the Associated Negro Press or extrapolated from published FEPC directives and statements. On the editorial page, however, Young occasionally reviewed various discriminatory cases and condemned what he called "the vicious congressional . . . southern bloc."[50]

Congressional opposition to the FEPC was led by senators Theodore Bilbo and John Eastland of Mississippi, who labeled the FEPC "a mongrel . . . communist bunch." When President Harry Truman recommended a permanent commission in 1945, congressional critics and the white press responded angrily. But Young and the *Guide* escaped harassment from Bilbo and congressional critics. Perhaps Young's reticence during his brief tenure in the FEPC was a conscious attempt to avoid national criticism. He was incensed by Bilbo's demagoguery, but there is no evidence that he complained to either the president or to other FEPC members. Unlike militant northern black newspaper editors, Young shied away from responding to vituperation in the white press. He described the FEPC as a tool to advance blacks economically and to improve race relations in the South, and he approached the controversy much as he had approached others—cautiously, temperately. He resigned from the FEPC in February 1944 because of poor health and a manpower shortage at the *Guide*. FDR thanked Young for his "wisdom and judgment" and his "splendid service in a difficult and important assignment."[51]

The strain of the war and perhaps encroaching age momentarily seemed to have caught up with P. B. Young, Sr. In November 1943, at the age of fifty-nine, he stepped down as editor-in-chief because of declining health. His younger son, Thomas W. Young, was made president as well as business manager of the *Guide* although he was overseas at the time. His elder son, forty-two-year-old P. B. Young, Jr., affectionately called "Junior," became editor-in-chief. He had served as a war correspondent during the early part of the war, and later, in October 1944, he would travel to Accra, Ghana (West Africa), as a representative of the State Department. The war over, he would cover the Bikini atomic tests as well as the founding conference of the United Nations at San Francisco. But for now, he stepped in for his father and stayed at home.

Strikingly different in temperament and appearance, the Young brothers made a good team. The abilities of each complimented the other's. The elder son was quiet and retiring and concentrated his efforts on the editorial side. The younger son concentrated on the business end of the paper, with rare excursions into reporting during the war. Like his father and brother, Tom took an active role in civic affairs. He served as a member of the board of trustees of the Norfolk Community Hospital for eight years. He was the first secretary-treasurer of the National Negro Newspapers Association, until his resignation in 1943 to go overseas as a war correspondent. Just before his departure for Africa with the 99th Fighter Squadron, he married Marguerite J. Chisholm, a graduate of Cheyney (Pa.) State College and Overbrook High School in Philadelphia. The ceremony was performed by one of his father's closest friends, the Reverend Richard H. Bowling, at his residence. A daughter, Millicent, was born on August 9, 1944.

Even as editor emeritus the senior Young remained the *Guide's* chief editorial writer. He visited his office daily to keep an eye on the newspaper's operation. He sternly repeated the *Guide's* philosophy on race relations to his sons: "I am definitely opposed to the frontal attack. I believe in negotiation, arbitration, conciliation and persuasion. If that does not work, then I resort to the courts." By 1945 Young's health had improved, and he returned to full-time duty as editor-in-chief.

As America tooled up for war, the army readied the nation's first black fighter squadron, the 99th, for combat. It was committed to combat on June 1, 1943, and flew over the Sicilian island of Pontelleria daily until it was occupied by American forces on June 11, 1943. The 99th also escorted bombers.[52] Thomas W. Young accompanied the 99th as a *Guide* war correspondent and remained with the unit as it advanced through Tunisia and invaded Sicily. An aerial dogfight between pilots of the 99th and a German Messerschmitt or the shooting down of a German Focke-Wulf made exciting news. Every week Tom Young described in detail how individual black airmen such as Melvin T. Jackson of Warrenton, Virginia, and Wendell Pruitt of St. Louis, Missouri, blasted "Jerry from the skies." A typical account read: "Jerries passed under me, I rolled over, shoved everything forward, dove, and closed in at 475 miles per hour."[53]

Tom Young's exclusive and sensational reporting from "Somewhere in North Africa—Censored—Delayed—Reproduction Prohibited" electrified the black community. Family members are said to have wept as they read his narrations of the personal reminiscences of the "Black Eagles," the handshakes from generals James Doolittle and Dwight Eisenhower, and individual airmen's places of birth, schools they attended, and wives' names.[54]

In February 1944 the *Guide* headlined in bold type: "Hall Downs Two More Nazis" and "Army Air Force Chiefs Laud 99th Pilots." The first reference was to Captain Charles Hall of Brazile, Indiana, the first 99th fighter pilot to shoot down a Nazi plane; and the second to Willie Ashley, Robert Deiz, Leon Roberts, Howard Baugh, and Edward Toppin, who allegedly shot down twelve Nazi planes in two days.[55] The *Guide's* war correspondent personally inducted the men into the *Journal and Guide's*

"All-American Flight of Negro Pilots" list and later interviewed each flier and forwarded personal messages to their families through the *Guide's* Norfolk office.

In Tom Young's view, the 99th epitomized the best tradition of the army. He thanked the army for its logistical support and, more importantly, its unhesitating encouragement. The "splendid achievement" of the 99th refuted *Time* magazine's charges that it was withheld from combat or rendered ineffective by the use of outdated equipment. Thomas Young characterized the allegations as "sheer folly," and his father explained that "you can't shoot the enemy down, if he refuses to come up and fight." Tom Young asserted that the 99th received its "fair share of missions." Both father and son believed that the allegations were an attempt to embarrass the 99th and to downgrade the role of black aviators in the war. Criticism continued, even though Eisenhower and Doolittle heaped praise upon the "Fighting 99th." On September 18, 1943, the *Guide* headlined: "Black Fighters Share Victory As Italy Quits." Tom Young was then reassigned to England. P. B. Young dryly predicted that Hitler's propagandists would explain that the successful 99th was a squadron of "sun-tanned nordics." [56]

In February 1944 Fletcher Martin began to cable exclusive stories to the *Guide* from Guadalcanal and from an "Advanced South Pacific Base." Martin accompanied marines on patrol in Guadalcanal, interviewed a black ordinance unit on Bougainville in the Solomon Islands, and wrote of life on the battlefront. The heroism of the 93d Division on Bougainville was recounted by the *Guide* in stories of individual soldiers accompanied by photographs. Both black and white soldiers were pictured reading the *Guide*. [57]

In February 1944, a month after Tom Young returned home, the *Guide* sent its assistant city editor, Lem Graves, overseas. Shortly after his arrival at an Allied air base "Somewhere in Italy," Graves was given a tour of the secret facility by black general Benjamin O. Davis of the 99th. He was later the guest of Captain Hugh Mulzac aboard the USS *Booker T. Washington,* which was anchored in an Italian harbor. A Liberty ship, the *Booker T. Washington* was an experiment, and Graves found a "marvelous spirit of cooperation" among its interracial crew. Graves spent several days aboard and observed a "constant stream" of high-ranking officers who were anxious to view the interracial crew. The *Guide* published a long interview with Captain Mulzac and listed the names and hometowns of black officers with the ship. When the ship returned to America, its white chief engineer, J. O. Garrett, and several crew members visited the *Guide's* Olney Street headquarters. [58]

A few weeks later Graves hitched a ride aboard an army tank and reached the burning Italian city of Gaeta six hours after its capture by Allied forces. The stench of the dead was "overpowering," he wrote. He recorded the activities of a black tank unit; the *Guide* showed a black combat crew poised for action. In July 1944 Graves cabled P. B. Young, "this is 'Thirty' for me in Italy." He recorded the impact of Nazi robot bombs on London before he was replaced by John Jordan, the former manager of the *Guide*'s Portsmouth office, who was overseas from June 1944 until March 1945.[59]

A few weeks later the *Guide* headlined: "Jordan Eyewitness Invasion Story; with Airborne Troops over Southern France Beachhead on D-Day." Jordan claimed that he flew over southern France in a C-47 Dakota a few hours before the first assault wave of Allied troops and that "this *Guide* correspondent" had advance knowledge of the invasion. He said that General Tristam T. Tupper had briefed war correspondents and pledged them to secrecy two weeks before the invasion.[60]

Jordan punctuated his reports with descriptions of the weather and France's topography and colorful accounts of his experiences. Jordan was caught in a crossfire in Toulon between the Free French Forces and German snipers, and, in his words, he was "almost kilt." When the French encircled a town with armor, explained Jordan, they considered it captured, neglecting often to mention pockets of German resistance. And so, when Jordan and colleague John Smith of the *Herald-Tribune* raced into the "captured" city of Toulon, they were fired upon.[61]

Jordan was also briefly assigned to the black 92d Division in the Italian towns of Viareggio and Forte dei Marmi. Wade McCree, at the time an officer with the 92d and later solicitor general of the United States, remembered Jordan as a correspondent attached to his unit. He was always out front, recalled McCree; "he always insisted upon going where the story was."[62]

McCree declined to discuss and Jordan neglected to cover the stormy controversy that engulfed the 92d during the fall and winter of 1944. The black troops were charged with "mass hysteria and panic," "straggling," and a lack of aggressiveness. They reportedly questioned the wisdom of the fighting and holding a hill, when there were only more hills and more Germans. In response, the army sent a black civilian, Truman K. Gibson of the War Department, to Italy to investigate. Gibson's "candid" appraisal of the situation and the heavy emphasis of the white press on his analysis of low literacy and on the so-called melting away of black troops invoked the wrath of the black press, although Gibson's appraisal had cited racial discrimination as a factor.[63] "Somebody's Gotta Go!" screamed an editorial in the Chicago *Defender*, which characterized Gibson as an "Uncle Tom" and noted that blacks had fought bravely and valiantly in all American wars. The Michigan *Chronicle* characterized Gibson's statement as the "Gibson Folly," and to Congressman Adam Powell's New York *People's Voice*, it was a "smear."[64]

The *Guide* and the Baltimore *Afro-American*, who had their own correspondents in Italy, responded more philosophically. "The term [melting away] may prick us painfully," observed P. B. Young, "but Mr. Gibson might not have been as wrong as some would like to believe that he was." Young noted that white units frequently "melted away" before enemy pressure, but army news releases would call their withdrawal a strategic retreat. The *Afro-American* observed that Gibson's statement was "not new" and commented that its correspondents had reported similar incidents before Gibson's arrival.[65]

The *Guide* received news from the front from others besides its professional correspondents. Sergeant James Hugo Madison cabled to the *Guide* exclusive stories of a black barrage balloon unit, the only black combat unit in the Allied assault on France and Italy. While dug into foxholes along the shore, the unit manned the cables erected along the coast to hold barrage balloons aloft. Their mission was "to keep the balloons flying" to circumvent enemy aerial attacks. The men who tended the balloons could not change clothes and had no access to sanitary facilities, but despite these discomforts and bleeding hands, the men of the unit "worked hard."[66]

In August 1944 the *Guide* headlines announced another scoop. Tom Young was the only reporter aboard the destroyer escort USS *Mason*, which was manned by a predominantly black crew, on its maiden combat voyage. The *Guide* characterized the "Tan Yanks in Navy Blue" as the first blacks to man a fighting ship. During his two months at sea Tom Young forwarded vivid stories, along with pictures and personal information, about the men aboard the *Mason*. "Every man's a fighter," he wrote.[67]

Meanwhile, his brother P. B., Jr., or Bernard, made plans to visit West Africa and French Equatorial Africa as a member of a Roosevelt commission on African affairs. The other members of the commission included James B. Coshin of the Chicago *Defender* and Vincent Tubbs of the *Afro-American*. Bernard Young characterized the people in Accra as "dignified and friendly" and reported that "serious discussions of the Durham, Atlanta, and Richmond Conferences had preceded him to Africa via England."[68]

To keep the *Guide*'s subscribers abreast of "life and news" in West Africa, Bernard Young asked Henry B. Cole, assistant editor of the *African*

Morning Post, at the time West Africa's oldest and most influential daily newspaper, to write a bimonthly column for the *Guide*. Cole agreed, and throughout the winter of 1944, the *Guide* published his columns.[69] His first "Newsletter" detailed "two sensational trials" in West Africa.

Bernard Young claimed that he was the first black American to visit Lake Bosomtri in Sierra Leone. He interviewed missionaries and local leaders and wrote long descriptive articles in the *Guide* on life and culture in Freetown, Sierra Leone. He met Thomas Dosumu Johnson, a black missionary, who alleged that he was briefly held in a German concentration camp after the Germans torpedoed the SS *Zamzam*, en route to Liberia in April 1941. Young also claimed that he was the first black American to address the Liberian Congress. Following an audience with Liberia's president W. V. S. Tubman, the Roosevelt commission journeyed to Lagos, Nigeria, where they were presented a gift of elephant tusks for FDR.[70] Bernard forwarded a list of military personnel from Virginia who were serving with the Allied forces in West Africa to the *Guide*. After a tour of Brazzaville, French Equatorial Africa, members of the commission returned to America in February 1945.

It is difficult to ascertain the impact on the black community of the reports filed by black war correspondents. The headlines and articles seemed to be designed not only to invest the black community with a sense of pride but also to convince skeptics that America was fighting a just war and would win. The correspondents fought to change the image of the black soldiers and to correct the allegations of those in the white press who belittled the black soldier's bravery and endurance.

P. B. Young's response to a black who complained about the paucity of hard news from the war zone best described the problems of black war correspondents. Their objective was to "seek out the forgotten men." Young pointed out that black combat units were assigned "less spectacular things" like driving trucks, building and repairing roads, guard duty, unloading ships, and civil engineering. Thus, the black correspondents often had to report news when there was none. Moreover, they were excluded from the major wire services. Because their accounts were based upon individuals' accounts and the reports of friendly white correspondents, they rarely debated tactics or strategy or attempted to evaluate the outcome of a battle. They were an "experiment," and it was their duty to report on the activities of segregated units. The weekly headlines, pictures, and personal messages in the *Guide* enhanced America's image of a united front. The "forgotten men," ignored by the white media, were resurrected by men who, like them, were segregated at home and abroad.

The black soldiers fought bravely, and the black reporters doggedly sought the news to report home. [71]

Even though a total of twenty-seven black war correspondents covered World War II for every major black newspaper, many whites still asked, "Are Negroes fighting in this war?" A typical inquiry came from Charles C. Berkeley, a prominent white attorney in Newport News, who asked in a letter to the Richmond *Times-Dispatch*, "What has happened to our Negro Troops?" Berkeley expressed concern about their lack of recognition. Young responded editorially. He blamed biased coverage about blacks in the white press and charged that the unavailability of information about blacks in the white community was "part and parcel of the whole interracial problem." [72]

After the war the *Guide* continued its overseas press coverage. Bernard Young himself covered what was perhaps the most significant event of the postwar years, the explosion in 1946 of the atomic bomb on Bikini. He was one of two black reporters selected by the White House to watch the historic event. Bernard initially hoped for the last vacancy aboard the B-29 press plane in order to watch the scheduled dropping of the bomb on July 1, 1946. He was instead assigned to the aircraft carrier *Shangri-La*. The *Guide* gave the events in Bikini full-page accounts with photographs. In his coverage Bernard highlighted the "Tan Yanks" on the island of Kwajalein, a preparatory site, along with their names and home addresses. Of the explosion itself, he said that he was "awed by the Inspiring Sight." "I feel Pygmy," he wrote; "the story is too colossal to write, and words too inadequate to transmit." The temptation to look at the blast overpowered him, and he looked seconds before the announced safety period. However, "the risk," in his words, was "distinctly worth the reward." When the *Shangri-La* moved closer, Bernard described the damage he saw as "terrible to behold." A battleship which received a direct hit had vaporized. Like his father, he asserted that "there is no defense against this weapon except peace." [73] He solemnly prayed that the American people—in fact, any people—would never be subjected to another war in which the atomic bomb was used.

Norfolk's blacks energetically, even bravely, supported the war effort, but their enthusiasm was tempered by the problems posed by crime, job discrimination, and poor housing. World War II changed the social and intellectual atmosphere in Norfolk; its blacks now were unwilling to accept discrimination in housing and employment without protest. Black migration to the tidewater industrial centers during the war altered family patterns as well as political and social alignments, and it sowed the seed of discontent that erupted in the early 1950s. As in years past, the *Guide* attempted to acquaint newcomers with the complexities of urban living and at the same time to explain and direct public opinion. As before, the *Guide* was an advocate, crusader, and mirror of Norfolk's black community during the war years. But the war added a new edge to its criticism, a new militance to the activism of its publisher and editor. The large influx of migrants and Young's expanding social and political activities made the *Guide's* circulation jump to approximately 80,000. Greater changes were on the horizon: the postwar years would see a resurgence of black political activity, a heightened sense of racial consciousness, schism and conflict within the *Guide*, and increased competition from the white press. All would challenge Young as never before. Coming was a time when the *Journal and Guide* would no longer seem invincible.

▪ 9 ▪

Postwar Politics

A s World War II came to a close, P. B. Young wondered what the future of blacks in America would be. Following Roosevelt's death in April 1945, he observed that blacks were ambivalent toward Truman. He knew that Truman would have to prove himelf to black Americans to garner their support in future elections. In the postwar decade Young visualized the seemingly impregnable walls of racial prejudice coming down—not tumbling, but crumbling. Moreover, he predicted that this period would be more fruitful politically for blacks in Virginia than any other since 1900. Although he was to remain a "militant" Democrat, whenever civil rights was the issue the *Journal and Guide* supported local candidates of either party who gave a "proscribed people" hope.

In January 1946 Young lost his wife of forty years and the *Guide* lost "the brains . . . the It" behind its success with the death of Eleanor White Young. She had been director-treasurer of the *Guide* since 1914, and her work accounted for its early financial stability. Her daughter-in-law Undine Young described her as "outgoing, warm, affectionate," with a keen interest in the rearing of her sons Thomas and P. B., Jr. Eleanor Young was most remembered for her dissenting voice. For example, she had consistently opposed the *Guide*'s sending war correspondents overseas during World War II. As editor John Jordan was leaving to go overseas in June 1944, she admonished him "not to venture into dangerous areas unless he absolutely had to." Like her husband, she was active in civic affairs and was a lifetime member of the Grace Episcopal Church. A month after her death, her brother Dykins ("Peaches") White, Catcher for the Norfolk Red Stockings and the Baltimore Black Socks, also died.

P. B. Young, Sr., became Norfolk's most eligible bachelor during the

139

late 1940s. He fell in love with Josephine Moseley, a beautiful Norfolk schoolteacher, but initially he demurred expressing his feelings because he had learned that one of his best friends, Lyman Brooks, the future president of Norfolk State College, was her suitor. One night while visiting Buckroe Beach, Hampton, with his son Thomas and black historian Luther P. Jackson, Young remarked, "I'm tired of this." Jackson proclaimed Josephine Moseley "a good choice." Later that same evening, "Plummer," as Josephine called him, proposed marriage while they were waltzing to "Let Me Call You Sweetheart." However, according to Josephine Young, the night before their marriage on February 11, 1950, Plummer declared, "I don't know if I can make it." He incessantly puffed cigars as Father Richard Martin, rector of Grace Episcopal Church; Mary Drake, Young's housekeeper; and John Givens, his physician, attempted to allay his fears. Eventually, they were able to calm him down.[1]

Meanwhile, competition from white dailies led the *Guide's* circulation to fluctuate between 67,000 and 75,000 during 1945 and 1946. In 1949 Thomas Young, at the time president and general manager, acknowledged that the paper's circulation had dropped to 65,000 and was principally circulated in Virginia and North Carolina. Nevertheless, it still ranked fourth in the Negro press, right behind the Pittsburgh *Courier*, the Chicago *Defender*, and the Baltimore *Afro-American*.[2]

Whether from choice or necessity, the *Guide* tried to avoid what editor John Jordan called the stigma of "radicalism" during the immediate postwar years. Young, always a conservative, still carefully operated within boundaries dictated by the white community. The *Guide's* declining circulation now meant that he needed increased financial support from both the black and white business communities. But his conservatism continued to reap benefits. The Young approach, among other things, got Gloucester County to float a $750,000 bond issue to improve conditions in black schools. After a series of *Guide* stories highlighted the intolerable conditions of black schools in Princess Anne County, a state investigation was conducted and sweeping improvements were recommended. For this, the *Journal and Guide* was awarded the highest honor in black journalism, the Wendell Willkie Journalism Award, in 1946, the first time it was given. The bronze plaque read: "For the best example during 1946 of public service which contributed to the greater enjoyment of the democratic way of life."[3]

The first Wendell L. Willkie Awards for Distinguished Writing by Negro Journalists ceremony was held on March 1, 1946, in Washington, D.C. P. B. Young, Sr., delivered the main address, "The Negro Press in a Changing World," and the speech was carried live, nationwide, by NBC radio. The main task of the black press, Young asserted, was to tell the truth about race relations in America. Black journalists should point out injustices in the administration of law and publicize the lack of equality of opportunity. The proud father then watched as the first honorees were awarded their plaques: P. B. Young, Jr., *Journal and Guide*; Robert L. Vann, Pittsburgh *Courier*; Olive Diggs, Chicago *Bee*; Algers Adams, *Amsterdam News*; and Alex Barnes, *Carolina Times*. After the ceremony, Young and the recipients visited with President Truman at the White House.[4]

When the *Guide* captured a disproportionate number of the Wendell Willkie awards for Virginia in 1947, black reporters and editors, according to John Jordan and Thomas Dabney, understandably cried "foul." The Region 4 nominating committee, which included Virginia, consisted of Virginius Dabney, who was the liberal editor of the Richmond *Times-Dispatch* and a personal friend of both Young and P. B., Jr. Moreover, Young and board chairman Douglas Southall Freeman, who regularly corresponded with each other, had discussed the Willkie awards before the winners were announced. Young sent Freeman a copy of *Headline and Pictures*, a magazine that exalted the Young family and the *Guide* because of their "splendid service" and "interest" in the awards. Freeman responded that he was "mighty proud of the Youngs" and "proud to have you distinguished in this manner." Apparently, the Wendell Willkie awards leaned toward the conservative black press and were designed to solidify black support for the Democratic party.[5]

During the postwar years the upper South's black leadership—Young, J. E. Shepard, and Gordon Hancock—attempted to avoid what John Jordan and Benjamin E. Mays called the "stigma of radicalism." They were optimistic that blacks' loyalty and patriotism during the war would be rewarded by a reappraisal of their economic and social conditions. They thought they could see what a May 1946 editorial in the *Guide* characterized as "a general improvement in race relations." "The millennium has not arrived," Young noted, but "the proscribing, the restrictive, the discriminating and the depressing" were greatly outnumbered by what the *Guide* called "constructive events," such as the appointment of Charles W. Anderson as a black public prosecutor in Kentucky and the decision by the United Automobile Workers and the Bendix Corporation to end discriminatory employment. Despite what Young called "untoward incidents," he maintained that race relations in Norfolk were steadily improving. The establishment of the Norfolk Division of Virginia State College, the promise of a new black elementary school, and the candidacy of a black man in the local council elections he viewed as proof of racial progress.[6]

During the early months of 1946 black historian Luther P. Jackson of Virginia State College in Petersburg devised a plan to advance black suffrage in Virginia and to exact more patronage and respect from the Democrats. According to Jackson, "organized" white opposition to black suffrage no longer existed because the solid South had been disrupted by the powerful forces of organized labor (AFL-CIO). Accordingly, Jackson reasoned, the postwar years were a "very propitious time" for a campaign to increase the number of registered black voters, up to 100,000 statewide. He proposed the slogan "Double or Nothing." Jackson explained that white public sentiment, as expressed in the Richmond *Times-Dispatch*, Richmond *News-Leader*, Newport News *Daily Press*, Petersburg *Progress-Index*, and Portsmouth *Star*, favored increased black enfranchisement and repeal of the poll tax. Jackson's positon was sustained by Virginia's governor Colgate Darden, Jr., who asserted that "in a free society, the ballot should rest in the hands of all persons."[7]

As 1946 came to a close, Shepard, Hancock, and Jackson agreed with Young and Howard University's president Mordecai Johnson that race relations constituted the South's principal problem. Their strategy was to pursue slow, steady, unannounced progress. In their view, the best formula for racial progress in the South was for every black person to align himself or herself with an organization whose objective was black advancement. They rejected migration to the North as illogical because such action merely transferred the problem to future generations. Their aim was to eliminate segregation rather than to flee. The undemocratic thinking of Theodore Bilbo, Herman Talmadge, and Strom Thurmond certainly dominated many regions of the South, but the influence and liberalism of such southern whites as Virginius Dabney, Frank Graham, Howard Odum, and Louis Jaffe challenged their segregationist philosophy.[8]

But southern black leaders did not unanimously agree. Benjamin E. Mays, Louis Austin, and Miles Mark Fisher retorted that white liberals had indeed helped blacks to achieve genuine advances in education, health, and economic well-being during the war, but that the liberals' insistence upon moral persuasion and their wartime stand against black militancy—especially in the case of Dabney—tarnished their reputation. Although Mays and others conceded at the time that liberal whites, to some extent, determined black economic and political advancement, Mays nevertheless remained opposed to a separate but equal South. In response Young wrote, "Let there be no faltering step among us," for "we do have tomorrow, bright before us like a flame."[9]

Young believed that segregation and the poll tax were responsible for the paucity of registered voters in the black community. Virginia's black adult population had numbered 365,717 in the 1940 census; yet only 11.3 percent of them qualified to vote in 1944 and still just 12.0 percent in 1945. In other words, 88 percent were disqualified, in Young's view, by the notorious "blank sheet" voter registration system and by the poll tax requirement. Jackson argued that racial discrimination was "corroborative," but the main problem was black apathy, which had been engendered by years of disfranchisement rather than the poll tax. Black Democrats assumed that their vote was unwanted and therefore unnecessary. Black Republicans believed that their ballot was futile because it would not tip the balance toward a Republican candidate.[10] However, the "indifference vs. discrimination" argument was short-lived. The main issue, according to Jackson, was not the structure of the southern judicial system or the effects of racial discrimination on black suffrage but the absence of blacks from public office.

Young lamented the dilemma of black politicians in the postwar South. On the one hand, a frontal attack on segregation was political suicide and invited personal violence from white segregationists. On the other hand, a moderate campaign invited charges of having "sold out." In either instance, the black candidate risked, in Young's view, "being sold down the river" by the "ole colored man." Nevertheless, he angrily challenged blacks to stop complaining and to take advantage of the postwar economic opportunities. "We are undergoing the severest test in our history," he remarked. In short, "we are on trial." Young and Jackson believed that blacks in the new South risked permanent repudiation as leaders and workers if they failed to take advantage of the new economic and political opportunities. Young stated firmly: "Our future . . . is now."[11]

Although Young and Jackson conceded that such debilitating factors as crime, alcoholism, gambling, disease, and apathy hampered black creativity and limited blacks' access to "rights and liberties" earned during the war, an equally limiting factor was the disruption caused by factionalism and the personal jealousies between the black leaders of the upper South—Hancock, Jackson, and Young—and those of the urban North—Carl Murphy, Carter G. Woodson, Alaine Locke, and Rayford Logan. Young and Robert Vann had once conferred at the Teresa Hotel in New York, according to Jordan, over the direction and character of leadership for black America. On other occasions, Young and Murphy feuded at the

Whitlaw Hotel and later at the Dunbar in Washington, D.C., over Young's support of President Mordecai Johnson of Howard and his involvement with the Southern Regional Council. Later, Young's widow noted that many northern urban blacks "never forgave Plummer" for excluding them from the Durham conference, and others were jealous of his popularity with whites and his position as chairman of Howard's board of trustees. Carter G. Woodson, director of the Association for the Study of Negro Life and History, referred to Young, Hancock, J. M. Gandy, and other organizers of the Durham conference as "Uncle Tom Leaders" and "unprincipled politicians." Woodson seemingly resented southern black leaders who posed as spokesmen for all blacks but who, at the same time, refused to include all blacks in their plans. Even though Woodson had not included Jackson on his "Uncle Tom Leaders" list, he nevertheless admonished Jackson to stay away from "bad company." Woodson characterized Young, Hancock, Gandy, and others as simply "tools," influenced by the "preachment" of such white liberals as Virginius Dabney, Jessie Daniel Ames, and John Graves. A contemporary confidential source explained that Woodson, Murphy, Vann, and others rejected Young's claim that interracial cooperation was increasing. They ridiculed the southern black Virginians' desire to lead, to set the "forward trend" in race relations. They charged that southern white liberalism was a facade meant to project the image of harmonious race relations, to stave off black political activity, to threaten the Byrd machine indirectly, and to shield the liberals themselves from blacks' economic and social grievances. The liberals were contemptuous of the southern blacks' social mannerisms and their lack of political sophistication as well.[12]

According to the *Guide*, a recurrent problem in the black community was the "ole" Negro "who sold Negroes down the river." The "ole" Negro told whites what they wanted to hear and injected malicious gossip and extraneous issues into the discussion of legitimate grievances. After Young led a delegation before the Norfolk City Council to protest street conditions and a black man entered Norfolk's 1946 councilmanic campaign, the "ole colored man," according to Young, was consulted by whites as never before. Nevertheless, he challenged blacks to "stop griping." In one editorial he called protest "useless" for a voteless people.[13] Black Norfolkians, in Young's view, like other blacks in the South, relied too heavily upon verbal protest. Politicians are realistic; they count votes, not heads, he explained. He challenged Norfolkians to face reality; he felt that apathetic blacks had only themselves to blame for the intolerable conditions under which they lived.

Problems like intolerable streets and unemployment combined with what was perceived as a "forward trend" in race relations convinced the Norfolk Committee on Negro Affairs (NCNA), of which Young served as chairman, that despite voter apathy a local black, Victor Ashe, could win a seat on the Norfolk City Council. The NCNA was composed of black leaders in Norfolk from "every walk of life." Young, along with R. H. Bowling, J. Eugene Diggs, Winston Douglass, P. B., Jr., John Belden, D. W. Byrd, and other members of the NCNA, caucused in the offices of the *Guide,* church basements, and private homes to listen intently to Luther P. Jackson and the NAACP regional officials—who sometimes included Thurgood Marshall, the NAACP's chief legal officer—outline the so-called single-shot strategy, which Young and Marshall opposed. "Single-shot" voting was the practice of casting a ballot for a black and leaving the remainder of the ballot unmarked. Occasionally, liberal whites who were disenchanted with local politicians or embarrassed at the absence of blacks in elective office surreptitiously stopped by to offer encouragement and support.[14]

Attorney Victor Ashe waged a vigorous campaign through the press, radio, and personal appearances. Full-page advertisements appeared in the *Guide.* A typical one depicted Ashe inspecting city slums and included his pledge to rehabilitate urban dwellings. Despite an ambitious campaign, Ashe lost, as did black council candidates Bernard A. Coles in Charlottsville, C. K. Coleman in Danville, and C. V. Wilson in Lynchburg. "Negroes lambasted Mr. P. B. unfairly," observed Jordan. The *Guide* had to wait until "the last minute" to endorse candidates running on the "single-shot strategy" because white fear of being labeled a friend of the Negro still lingered in Virginia. In a letter dated May 4, 1946, Ashe thanked Louis Jaffe and the *Virginian-Pilot* for that paper's impartial coverage during the campaign.[15]

Young called Ashe's defeat "a great victory" because of the attention it generated. He then turned his attention to the impending candidacy of black Richmond attorney Oliver W. Hill for a seat in the Virginia legislature. Hill was a veteran of World War II and hoped to win the Democratic nomination by campaigning on a biracial platform. He called for the equalization of teachers' salaries, the establishment of a state department of race relations, increased appropriations for hospitals and public health; and abolition of the poll tax as a prerequisite for voting.[16] Losing by a mere 191 votes, Hill generated political excitement throughout the Commonwealth.

Luther P. Jackson termed Hill's candidacy "the most significant advancement in the citizenship aspiration of southern Negroes . . . in the past half-century." Jackson did not blame white opposition for Hill's defeat but instead attributed it to blacks' failure to organize effectively and to meet the voting requirements. Jackson noted that blacks had to pay the cumbersome poll tax, register to vote, and then transport themselves to the polls on election day, a "herculean task" because it involved employment sacrifices, money, and a vast number of volunteer workers. Although Nansemond County for the first time since Reconstruction elected a black man, William Lawrence, to public office as a county supervisor, Jackson seemed angered and dejected. On the other hand, a somewhat more optimistic Richmond *Times-Dispatch* counseled Virginians to prepare for the inevitable: a black in the General Assembly. In addition, the *Times-Dispatch* dismissed a protest against "single-shot" voting as inconsequential.[17]

Civil rights were a major issue in the 1948 presidential campaign. The *Guide* and the Richmond *Afro-American* were ambivalent toward Harry Truman, the Democratic nominee, because of his lack of enthusiasm on civil rights and his failure to condemn openly the segregationist Dixiecrat party headed by J. Strom Thurmond of South Carolina. On the other hand, the *Guide* praised Henry Wallace, the Progressive party's nominee, for his vigorous support of civil rights, though it also characterized his abandonment of the two major parties as "just plain short-sighted." As he had with both Marcus Garvey and the lily-black movement of the 1920s, Young reasoned that a third party would render blacks impotent and politically isolated. He encouraged blacks to remain within the traditional two-party system and to align themselves with liberal whites. Blacks apparently did remain in the Democratic camp, unwilling to forget the benefits of the New Deal. Truman carried Virginia with 200,786 votes to Dewey's 172,070, Thurmond's 43,393, and Wallace's 1,863.[18]

In a detailed editorial after the election Young reflected on the politics of the 1940s and offered suggestions for the upcoming decade. "The time is ripe," he asserted, for a New Deal in black Democratic political leadership. "Those who have been at the helm for the past decade," he wrote, had accumulated what he termed "impediments" that prevented them from inspiring confidence. Although candidates had been "bright and earnest," Young explained that they lacked experience, maturity, and qualifications that matched those of opposition candidates.[19]

As the struggle for black political and civil rights shifted to the Southwest, with the admission of Heman Sweatt and Ada Sipuel to law and graduate schools, respectively, in Texas and Oklahoma, Young predicted an end to segregated schools in the South. But at the moment, he believed, working for equalization and accommodation was more advantageous than campaigning for integration. He challenged Virginians in high places, especially Governor William M. Tuck, to revamp their thinking, because youthful white southerners were not enslaved to white supremacy. Young concluded that the "Forces of Right" would not remain silenced.[20]

In the late 1940s, however, Young and his sons were more concerned with the political right and its militant Communists-in-government propaganda. The titular head of the movement was an ultraconservative New Jersey Republican, J. Parnell Thomas, chairman of the House Un-American Activities Committee (HUAC) during 1947 and 1948. Communists in government were not an issue in the 1948 presidential campaign because the Republicans were confident of victory. However, after Truman's victory and the Republicans' fifth consecutive defeat in a presidential election, conservative Republicans seized control of the party's machinery and used their influence with chairman Thomas and the HUAC to initiate "a second red scare."[21] The HUAC blatantly publicized its investigations not only of alleged Communists in government but also in labor unions, industry, and the scientific community. Of greatest concern to blacks, however, was the right-wing attack on minority organizations.

In July 1949 the HUAC opened its hearings on the supposed Communist infiltration of minority groups. The investigation was prompted in part by a statement by black artist Paul Robeson, who had asserted that it was "unthinkable" for American blacks to fight against Russia in the event of a war. Such prominent blacks as Mary McLeod Bethune, Jackie Robinson, and President Charles Johnson of Fisk University promptly denounced Robeson. Thomas W. Young, now president and general manager of the Guide Publishing Company, was one in a parade of witnesses who condemned Robeson's statement before the committee. He testified on July 13, 1949, repudiating Robeson and labeling his call for black disloyalty a great disservice to the race. He characterized Robeson as a "false prophet" who had "shamelessly deserted" his own people. Thomas Young, Mary Bethune, Charles Johnson, and other black leaders insisted that Robeson had betrayed the black masses, adding the burden of being "red" to that of being black.[22]

P. B., Sr., was initially invited to testify before the HUAC, but he declined because of ill health. These years were a time of difficulty for the aging publisher. He had what he termed "a tedious double operation" in New York in November 1945 and later was a patient of Dr. John Eve in the Pythian Bath House and Hotel in Hot Springs, Arkansas, in February 1947 and again in November 1952. Although he retained the title of "publisher" and continued to write editorials, he conceded that he was "only half-way active" and "slowly recuperating." Young's sons handled the management and the day-to-day operation of the paper.[23] Ill health may not have been the sole reason Young did not testify before the HUAC. Other possible factors may have been the schism and conflict within the various departments of the *Guide* and incipient union activity among its employees. In October 1946 Young conceded to Virginia Beecher, executive secretary of the Southern Conference for Human Welfare, that he was engaged in what he termed "a life and death struggle" with the American Newspaper Guild, an affiliate of the CIO. Young was convinced that the guild, with the CIO, was "bent" upon the destruction of the *Guide*. He characterized the guild's wage demands as "revolutionary" and inconsistent with the usual demands of the average labor union. He charged that it was demanding an immediate 40 to 90 percent wage increase.[24]

Young claimed that the *Guide's* wages and salaries were 25 to 30 percent higher than those paid the average black or white employee in the printing and newspaper industry in tidewater. Young's assertions were somewhat exaggerated. Young's total salary in 1942 had been $7,500; his wife, Eleanor Young, had received $3,600; and his sons, $4,200 each. The next highest salaries went to advertising manager John Belden ($2,184.09) and circulation manager E. F. Corbitt ($2,107). Long-term employees such as John Jordan, J. A. James, Southall Bass, W. M. Hubbard, Lem Graves, and Al Hinton each earned less than $2,000 per year. Scores of permanent employees such as Clifton Williams, E. D. Gee, Vermit White, A. A. Morisey, Emma S. Rowe, and H. C. Downing earned only a few hundred dollars a year; and dozens of part-time employees received quarterly wages of less than $100. The *Guide's* total payroll budget for 1942 was $81,505.88. When Thomas Dabney began work at the *Guide* in 1945, his beginning weekly salary was $12, and other former employees indicated that their salaries were less than $30 a week in 1949. Juanita Yeates Moore, who worked as an accountant and as secretary to Thomas Young, recalled that her highest annual bonus from 1948 to 1962 was $25, although she worked from ten to twelve hours per day, as did several other *Guide* employees. Employees complained of favoritism, hazardous working conditions, and a lack of job security in addition to low wages. They also described Thomas W. Young as a "hard but fair taskmaster." Employees griped about slow promotions and the *Guide's* alleged proclivity for fair-skinned black women.[25]

Negotiations between the American Newspaper Guild and the Guide Publishing Company reached a deadlock in March 1947. Edna Burger, the niece of future Supreme Court Justice Warren Burger, represented the American Newspaper Guild; Thomas Young and P. B. Young, Jr., vice president and secretary, respectively, represented the company. Tension mounted on both sides and reached a peak during the summer of 1947. *Guide* employee William Hoge was fired for alleged inefficiency, and P. B. Young, Jr., forwarded written reprimands to Addison King, Southall Bass, and Thomas Dabney for "unauthorized and improper use of working time." As the controversy intensified, *Guide* employees were pitted against one another, while J. Eugene Diggs, Victor Ashe, Richard Bowling, S. F. Coppage, and other local black community leaders tried unsuccessfully to negotiate an end to the crisis. Finally, after a federal arbiter was called in to settle the dispute, the *Guide* employees voted 42 to 17 for the union, Local 201, on November 15, 1947.[26]

Even though the union was popular and it succeeded in ameliorating local grievances, it expired in 1952 because union organizers made no plans or strategy after November 1947. Also, by 1952 Young's health had improved, and he again assumed full control of the paper. "Ole man Young," as he was now affectionately called, promptly crushed the union.

Young saw the union as a threat to his authority. Although incorporated, the *Journal and Guide* was a family business. He mumbled words about the Unemployed Council of the 1930s; moreover, he wondered why his employees needed a labor union. He regarded himself as a paternalistic employer. He made personal loans to his employees to help purchase automobiles, to pay college tuition, and to alleviate personal financial crises. Although salaries were less than competitive and upward mobility was limited within this small family business, he assumed that his employees loved him.

Instead, in many instances, they feared him. Young had what Addison King called "a disoriented personnel policy." "We had no rights," she asserted. King and other career employees blamed Young's "high-handed methods" for the union activities. King and others noted later that Young ran the paper like "a captain ran a ship" and threatened to close the plant and to cancel their group life insurance. Other employees were reprimanded for talking about the union during working hours.[27]

Another major controversy during the late 1940s arose over black educator S. J. Phillips's plan to establish the Booker T. Washington Birthplace Memorial. The most controversial aspects of the plan called for an industrial training center at the birthplace of Booker T. Washington in Franklin County, Virginia. Phillips hoped to purchase the 216-acre farm where Washington was born and there to erect a replica of Booker T. Washington's birthplace. Phillips's plan to purchase livestock, poultry, and farm machinery and to establish courses in auto mechanics, bricklaying, carpentry, and home economics provoked reactions ranging from laughter to organized resistance. In response, Phillips claimed that 6,000 ambitious blacks, mainly ex-GIs, were eager to enroll.[28]

Phillips met with President Truman in March 1946 and with Governor Tuck the following month. Tuck characterized Phillips as "being all right" but nevertheless declined to serve on the memorial's board of directors. The governor did, however, meet with Phillips, Young, and Hancock to discuss the selection of a prominent white person. Governor Tuck favored Virginius Dabney, but Dabney declined because, in Phillips's words, he was "prejudiced" against accepting black Richmond attorney Jackson Davis and Young as fellow board members.[29] Despite Tuck's reservations, he and other high state officials attended the ground-breaking ceremonies in April 1946 and stood alongside Phillips, President Luther H. Foster of Virginia State College, and other blacks to honor the first public celebration of the birthday of Booker T. Washington. Shortly thereafter, on May 23, 1946, the U.S. Congress authorized the coinage of five million Booker T. Washington memorial half-dollars. Congress also marked November 14, 1946, as the first annual observance of National Booker T. Washington Memorial Week. According to Phillips, after the U.S. Mint report a net profit of $1,619,394 on the silver used in minting the memorial half-dollars, Phillips began to publicize the need for a veteran's hospital on the memorial site. Dabney, in identical letters to Young and Foster, asked, "Do you think this is a good place to erect such a hospital?" Young replied, "I do not think Booker T. Washington's name should be exploited for this purpose."[30]

As the plan for the memorial slowly unfolded, more and more whites characterized it as a "patriotic expenditure of money." A typical observation was made by J. D. Eggleston, president of Hampden-Sydney College, who called the proposed school "an asset to race, community, state, and nation." Malcolm Griffin, owner of Hunting Creek Apple Orchards in Big Island, Virginia, wrote that he was "obsessed" with the idea. Griffin's obsession angered Dabney, who responded that Davis, Young, and Foster opposed the project because they feared what Davis called "a Stone Mountain Fiasco" in which controversy had halted the construction of a memorial to the confederacy in Georgia. Because thirty-five black institutions in Virginia had barely extracted $1,500 from the legislature, Dabney agreed with black leaders who favored increased financial support for Hampton and Tuskegee instead of yet another ill-equipped and underfunded black school. Dabney, who was a close friend of F. D. Patterson, president of Tuskegee Institute, observed that Phillips had been fired from Tuskegee and was now attempting to use the memorial project as a scheme to embarrass Patterson. Griffin retorted that blacks in Franklin, Henry, Roanoke, Bedford, and Lynchburg needed the school. "What is the source of opposition?" he demanded. "Be free and frank."[31] The source of opposition had been Young, Foster, and the late Jackson Davis.

Despite the opposition, Phillips successfully negotiated the purchase of 564 acres in Franklin County in 1949, and in January 1950 the first students enrolled in the school. Phillips was a frequent visitor to the offices of the *Guide* during the early 1950s. He unsuccessfully lobbied Thomas W. Young to cosponsor a series of nationwide consumer institutes. He also attempted to persuade P. B. Young, Sr., to deliver the Washington Memorial's Roanoke Trade School commencement address on May 8, 1951. Young declined because he remained convinced of Phillips's "illusions" and insincerity. However, he did invite Phillips to Norfolk for "a long talk."[32]

A few weeks later, at Young's Norfolk office, bitter exchanges occurred among Young, Phillips, Thomas Young, and representatives from the NCNA and the Richmond Civic Council (black), an umbrella organization. Phillips was questioned sharply about the new George Washington Carver–Booker T. Washington half-dollar, which had been authorized by Congress to help fight the spread of Communism. Everyone agreed that a commemorative coin was a sound investment; however, Phillips's radio and newspaper advertisements were characterized as "dangerous." A typical radio announcement asked, "Do you want to see Communism among Negroes banished from our shores? Would you like to see a more staunch spirit of Americanism installed in the colored race?" Listeners could help by buying a Carver-Washington half-dollar.

Young and other blacks asserted that they, too, "detested" Communism; however, Phillips's advertisements and his Carver-Washington Americanism Commission created the erroneous opinion that the American black community was so infested with Communism that a commission and the profit from the sale of commemorative half-dollars were necessary to stamp it out. James P. Spencer reported that Richmond blacks were so angered by the sale of the half-dollars that the Richmond Civic Council appointed a committee, of which he was chairman, to investigate.[33] Like Richmond blacks who had debated the issue earlier, participants at the Saturday morning caucus inside Young's office urged Phillips to "cease and desist" from further sale of the coins. They questioned the wisdom of a predominantly white board of governors and demanded to see the business records and a list of employees.

The increased criticism of Phillips's Americanism Commission prompted confidential letters of inquiry to Young from prominent whites throughout Virginia. Blacks like Young's son Thomas wondered why William Sanger,

president of the Medical College of Virginia in Richmond, who functioned as chairman of Phillips's commission, did not show comparable
interest in the training of black physicians, who were more critically
needed than carpenters and tailors.[34] Blacks criticized the relationship
between Phillips and a white professional fund-raiser in Richmond and
questioned the alleged disappearance since 1946 of thousands and perhaps millions of dollars from Phillips's sale of coins and other memorabilia.
In response to the continuing controversy, President Sanger, Sue Slaughter, chairman of the Norfolk Interracial Commission, and other distinguished whites urged Young to "get a group of able, reputable nationally
known people to delve into the whole matter."[35] There is no evidence
that Young honored Slaughter's suggestion.

In February 1954 a New York public relations man, Jesse Gordan, was
denied a claim against the birthplace memorial for $5,150 in U.S. District
Court in Roanoke, Virginia. Several additional suits were later brought
against Phillips and the Memorial Foundation in conjunction with the
promotion and sale of the Washington-Carver half-dollars. Later that
year, in November, the Richmond *Times-Dispatch* indicated that the memorial was a "bright dream bogged down in a muck of uncertain finances." A few months later—in January 1955—the Booker T. Washington Memorial Foundation closed. Phillips blamed black leaders for their
lack of support. Black spokesmen in Roanoke were "stunned." A move to
have the federal government appropriate $200,000 to provide for the es-
tablishment of a Washington monument and park was rejected by Interior
Secretary Wesley D'Eulart in February 1956.[36]

The Memorial Foundation proved how gullible whites were to black
entrepreneurs in postwar America. The project was supported almost en-
itrely by whites; and, according to the *Guide,* less than 3 percent of the
2.2 million memorial coins were purchased by blacks. Phillips lacked the
skills necessary to create a "Tuskegee in Virginia." Virginia's black leadership was unwilling to give the project a chance. In fact, their gossip,
criticism, and sundry "investigations" hampered it. The foundation operated a trade school in Roanoke for five years and made possible the
coinage of the Washington-Carver half-dollar. But its impact on Virginia
education and politics was negligible, and little tangible evidence remains
to perpetuate its memory.

Concurrent with the memorial fiasco, the uproar over Communists in
government, and the conflict within the *Guide* offices was the case of the
"Martinsville Seven." It was, in many ways, analogous to the celebrated
case of the Scottsboro boys during the 1930s. In May 1949 seven black

men were convicted of raping a pregnant Lynchburg housewife. In January 1951 final hope for a retrial vanished when the U.S. Supreme Court refused for a second time to hear the men's case. The Virginia Supreme Court had affirmed their conviction, but Governor John Battle stayed their execution pending their appeal to the U.S. Supreme Court. Governor Battle's refusal to grant executive clemency angered Young. He called conviction a "tragedy" and observed that "justice would be served if the men's lives were spared." The men were not spared. They were executed February 1951.[37]

From the date of their first conviction in May 1949 until their execution, the *Guide* and the Virginia NAACP waged a persistent campaign to enlist public sympathy and support. The tactics employed were similar to those used in the Alabama cause célèbre. The Virginia NAACP periodically proclaimed "Martinsville Seven Week"; the *Guide* initiated a defense fund; and the mothers, wives, and children of the doomed men made pathetic pleas to the public and the press.[38] Unlike the Scottsboro case, however, in this case the innocence or guilt of the men was never the issue. In earlier unsuccessful Supreme Court appeals the men argued that the trial was held in the locality of the crime and that their case was compromised by an "atmosphere of prejudice and hostility." Young's anger was more a reflection of his feelings of powerlessness and frustration over the severity of the sentence imposed than it was disagreement with the legal processes. He believed that the death sentence for rape in Virginia was reserved solely for blacks.

Throughout this period and for the remainder of his career, Young supported the reforms initiated by FDR's New Deal. He believed that the Democratic party was the best instrument to extend and to perpetuate black civil and political rights. Although such obstacles as the poll tax and Klan violence inhibited black voter participation, black apathy engendered by years of disfranchisement and de facto segregation constituted an equally serious problem. When Luther P. Jackson asserted that "it's time to separate the sheep from the goats," Young agreed. On the other hand, he disagreed with Jackson's scheme to highlight delinquent poll-tax payers in the *Guide*.

As America entered the 1950s, Young recognized that World War II had unleashed a new political consciousness in the black community. He had founded Norfolk's first NAACP chapter in 1917, but by 1950 his political conservatism was inconsistent with the activism of the present generation. He disliked criticism, and according to Josephine Young, he expressed private contempt for the NAACP's national leadership. At times, he felt unappreciated. He feared for the future of blacks in America and worried that activitist politicians were insensitive to the nuances of local politics and would exacerbate poor race relations.

As an elder statesman and publisher of the *Guide* he was still respected by the white community, and, to some degree, feared by the black community. Young's concerns during his twilight years were not only of race relations and politics but also of his beloved Norfolk and the future of the *Journal and Guide*. These same years would see one fundamental issue— the educational rights of blacks—come to a head. Like no other civil rights issue, this one captured the essence of both Young's political savvy and his limitations. No grasp of his career is possible without coming to terms with his views about separate but equal education.

■ 10 ■

Educational Reform

Wh+hen P. B. and Eleanor Young came to Norfolk in 1907, the young parents joined a community whose schools still bore the scars of the Civil War and Reconstruction, of social disruption and racial injustice. The first free black schools in the city had been opened by order of the Federal occupying forces in 1863; after Reconstruction, the city's public schools overwhelmingly favored white children. Education for Norfolk's black youngsters beyond the grade school level was sponsored privately, in large part by white church groups—early on by the American Missionary Society, later by the United Presbyterian Church. It was a pattern repeated in city after city in the South. In 1883 the Presbyterians opened Norfolk Mission College, which served as both a prepatory school and a junior college. As America entered the twentieth century, Norfolk was still devoid of a public high school for black youth, though it did provide seven black elementary schools—the Barboursville Bell, Cumberland Street, Wide Street, Lambert's Point No. 1, Atlantic City, South Norfolk, and Huntersville schools.[1]

Because of Norfolk's proximity to Hampton Institute, the education of its black children during the first two decades of this century bore the stamp of Booker T. Washington's educational philosophy. The Hampton-Tuskegee idea of Negro education emphasized Washington's concept of "Education for Life," which consistently drew support from whites who agreed with President Theodore Roosevelt when in 1906 he asserted, "Vocational work is 'best' for the average person of color." However, W. E. B. Du Bois of Atlanta University most decidedly did not agree. In 1906 he attacked the Hampton-Tuskegee idea, calling instead for a mastery by Negroes of the humanities, mathematics, and economics. "The

155

race must have thinkers," he argued.[2] Hamptonians were outraged, and the debate was still simmering when Young and his wife arrived in Norfolk the next year. Thoroughly imbued by his father with the Washingtonian philosophy, Young thought Du Bois's ideas were impractical.

During Washington's visits to tidewater Virginia between 1907 and 1914, he made it a point to meet with the faculty and students of Norfolk Mission College, as well as Norfolk's only black high school, John T. West, opened in 1911.[3] His visits, Norfolk's proximity to Hampton Institute, and Young's own proclivities all helped to solidify his educational ideas into political doctrine. The black high school was renamed Booker T. Washington High School and opened as a unit of the Norfolk public school system in the main building of the old Norfolk Mission College, which had closed in 1916. During the opening ceremonies in March 1917 black educators J. R. Dungee and R. A. Tucker, as well as P. B. Young, lauded the progress of blacks in Norfolk. They also praised Norfolk's white superintendent of schools, A. R. Dobie, for giving black youngsters "a fair chance."

By World War I, Booker T. Washington High School was one of the best black academic high schools in the South. It offered four years of Latin, English, history, science, and three and a half years of mathematics. Soon, its graduates were appearing on the campuses of Howard University, Hampton Institute, Fisk University, Tuskegee Institute, and other leading black institutions of higher education in the South. Norfolk's black educators also attracted the praise of Du Bois, who called the city's teachers "well qualified, enthusiastic, and efficient workers."[4] Other black educators journeyed to Norfolk to study and later to emulate their methods.

During the 1920s, the influx of migrants from southside Virginia and eastern North Carolina overwhelmed Norfolk's black public schools. In fact, black schools throughout the tidewater were overcrowded. Finally, in 1935 Norfolk's superintendent, C. W. Mason, converted Chapel Street School (formerly Henry Clay) into a school for blacks. The building was not new, but it was, according to the *Guide,* "one of the most imposing and substantial structures housing our pupils." The *Guide* termed Chapel Street School "a blessing" and editorialized that the fourteenth black public school was "much needed." "It won't do away with the severe overcrowding," Young observed, "but it will help to relieve it."[5]

The Chapel Street School was an important acquisition, and in the view of many blacks, it deserved more than a name derived from its location. Young, attorney J. Eugene Diggs, Dr. G. Hamilton Francis, and the Reverend B. W. Harris of the Grace Episcopal Church favored changing the name from Chapel Street to honor Richard B. Harrison, popularly known as "De Lawd," the character he portrayed in Marc Connelly's 1930 production of *The Green Pastures,* a fable of a Negro's conception of the Old Testament. With its long run in New York and on the road, the play convinced many Americans that there was a place for blacks on the legitimate stage. Undoubtedly, the artistic and social atmosphere generated by the Harlem Renaissance touched Norfolk's black intelligentsia. The name, in their view, would not only honor the memory of a great individual, it would highlight black culture and tradition, promote interracial cooperation, and bestow upon blacks a sense of dignity and pride. Unwittingly, editor P. B. Young editorialized, "We Started Something."[6]

The "something" Young started was a raging controversy that engulfed Norfolk's black community. "Harrison is not an educator," one prominent Norfolkian complained. Another said that Harrison was not from Norfolk and did not symbolize the struggle and aspirations of black Virginians. Young, in the face of overwhelming opposition, withdrew Harrison's name from consideration. The controversy gradually abated after the school was renamed in honor of Mrs. Laura Titus, a local black teacher and civic leader.

Also during the mid-1930s a movement was under way to establish a black junior college in Norfolk to educate well-qualified black high school graduates who were financially unable to attend college elsewhere. The movement was led by Winston Douglass, the principal of Booker T. Washington High School, and was supported by A. H. Foreman, chairman of the Norfolk School Board; City Manager Thomas P. Thompson; and Louis Jaffe, editor of the Norfolk *Virginian-Pilot.* Young, predictably, numbered among the civic leaders who also backed the plan.

Thompson conducted a survey to determine if city land was available, and Louis Jaffe predicted that the junior college "may reasonably hope to become an established local institution." Jaffe noted that the overwhelming acceptance of the Norfolk Division of the College of William and Mary showed that many ambitious local students were denied the privilege of a college education because of the expense of living away from home. He praised Virginia Union University for its efforts to establish the "first Negro Extension College of the state."[7]

Young often reflected upon the "cultural asset" that would be provided by a black junior college. Like Jaffe, he praised Virginia Union for its confidence in Norfolk and predicted that the proposed junior college would greatly benefit black education in Norfolk, and in Virginia as well. At mass meetings held throughout the city Young and other leaders solicited support for the college. They received pledges of loans and equipment. Ebenezer Baptist, First Calvary, and Shiloh Baptist churches awarded scholarships and enrolled interested members of their congregations in July 1935, a few months before the college opened and several weeks before it published a cirriculum, hired an administrator, or agreed on a location.[8]

As the junior college movement gained momentum, the *Guide* predicted that Norfolk would become a "center of learning" and "a haven for youth thirsty for knowledge."[9] On Friday, October 11, 1935, the Norfolk branch of Virginia Union University formally opened with seventy students and four faculty members (two part-time). The event marked the beginning of black higher education in Norfolk.

The Norfolk branch of Virginia Union operated until 1942, when it was renamed Norfolk Polytechnic Institute, to be administered in part by the city. Two years later the Norfolk Polytechnic was completely taken over by the state, and its students and administration were merged with Virginia State College for Negroes in Petersburg. The Norfolk branch of Virginia State College later became Norfolk State University, an independent institution.

Together, Norfolk Mission College, Booker T. Washington High School, and the Norfolk Division of Virginia Union University laid the foundation for black secondary and higher education in Norfolk. Their alumni served the Norfolk community with distinction, as teachers, ministers, physicians, lawyers, and municipal employees. But, as blacks' struggle for the equalization of facilities and for pay parity intensified during the early 1930s, the action shifted from tidewater to southside Virginia. Here, too, Young was a participant, helping to publicize the cause.

A movement for equal teachers' salaries in Virginia was inaugurated in Buckingham County in 1930. After an appeal for pay equal to that of white teachers was rejected by Governor John Garland Pollard, black petitioners extended their passive protest throughout the tidewater counties. Within a few months 571 teachers and approximately 1,500 black supporters had signed a petition of protest.[10]

In 1930 the movement was led by Thomas Dabney, then the president of the Buckingham County Teachers Association, and black educator Charles Allen. Young and the *Guide* supported their activities, calling unequal pay a "fundamental injustice." For years, Young noted, the *Guide* had vigorously attacked "with accurate facts and statistics" unequal pay, discriminatory school appropriations, and inadequate facilities, and he praised Dabney for his effort. The Buckingham County fight against salary inequities was supported by more than 600 black teachers at a regional meeting on the campus of Hampton Institute in 1931 and later by the 44th annual convention of the predominantly black Virginia Teachers Association. In both instances the black conferees signed petitions and unanimously passed resolutions that asked state authorities to establish and enforce a minimum salary scale for teachers.[11]

Dabney, Allen, and Young also protested what the *Guide* called "glaring discrimination" in the disbursement of the State Equalization Fund. For example, in Accomack County white schools received 40.86 percent and black schools 24.71 percent of the money. In Northampton County white schools received 71.74 percent but black schools only 36.43 percent. Although black constituted one-fourth of the state's population in 1930, only one-twelfth of the Commonwealth's high schools were designated as black, and only 19 of 100 counties had accredited four-year black high schools. Young editorialized that the difference represented "quantitative discrimination" as well as blatant "qualitative discrimination."[12]

Dabney complained that the largest and most effective black organization, the Negro Organization Society (NOS), was too busy with "the head and the heart" to get involved. Dabney said that on one occasion President J. M. Gandy of NOS demanded to know where he had obtained information about Buckingham County schools, as if to question their accuracy. Dabney also alleged that the silence of conservative blacks and dissension between rural and urban black teachers weakened the initial protest against unequal pay and discriminatory disbursement of the State Equalization Fund.

After Governor Pollard and the Norfolk City Council announced a reduction of all government salaries because of the Depression, a reduction that would hit all the public school teachers, Young, at a mass meeting of black teachers, urged them to "voice objections" and called separate-but-equal education a "shibboleth and a mockery." "Black teachers have no margin above daily need," he asserted.[13] The unequal pay movement in Buckingham County dissipated after Dabney was fired, and the protests over pay reductions soon fizzled in the hard times of the Depression. In addition, what the *Guide* called an "educational dilemma" temporarily deflected attention away from the unequal pay controversy.

The "dilemma" arose in August 1935 when Alice C. Jackson, a black 1934 honor graduate of Virginia Union University, applied to the prestigious University of Virginia for admission as a graduate student. The *Guide* and white newspapers such as the Richmond *Times-Dispatch*, the Norfolk *Ledger-Dispatch,* and the Portsmouth *Daily Star* sympathized with Jackson but worried that the case might "stir up ill will" between the races. The main issue was whether the state should provide equal but separate higher educational facilities for blacks. The issue was prophetically stated by the *Ledger-Dispatch:* "We [the state] must either provide facilities or Federal Courts will." The court in Charlottesville upheld the University of Virginia's denial of admission to Alice Jackson. Shortly thereafter, Virginia expanded educational programs at predominantly black Virginia State College in Petersburg and established a special scholarship fund which paid the tuition and fees for blacks to pursue graduate degrees outside the state.[14]

The unequal pay dispute and the Jackson case attracted the attention of the national NAACP, which at the time was searching for an issue to resurrect dormant local NAACP chapters in Virginia. In 1934 Daisy E. Lampkin, regional field secretary of the NAACP, had recruited 800 black Norfolkians, and she enrolled another 600 in 1935. The national NAACP regarded Norfolk as "the best bet" when it decided to accelerate its activities and to test the constitutionality of discriminatory pay. In October 1938 Thurgood Marshall, NAACP assistant special counsel, in a personal and confidential letter asked Young to encourage Melvin Alston, a Booker T. Washington teacher, to become a plaintiff in an equalization of teachers' salaries case. "Keep the matter strictly confidential," wrote Marshall. "Talk to this man . . . encourage him to take this step." Young personally interviewed Alston and reported that he was "determined to go through with the test case." However, after Alston's decision, his colleague Aline Black also agreed to become a plaintiff and was determined by the NAACP to be "the better qualified" of the two. Young selected Alston because he was a male and emotionally stronger than Black. Meanwhile, the NAACP reaffirmed to Young its hope that the case would revive the Norfolk branch.[15]

Tension gripped Norfolk during the late spring and summer of 1939, as the pay parity issue intensified. After the Norfolk School Board decided not to renew Aline Black's contract, the *Guide* and the Norfolk NAACP helped to organize a protest meeting. The *Virginian-Pilot* characterized this meeting as "the most formidable protest by Norfolk Negroes in modern history." The *Pilot* condemned the state's use of Norfolk as a "cat's paw" and urged the school board to reconsider. The powerful Richmond *Times-Dispatch* called parity "inevitable," while both the Virginia *Journal of Education* and the Virginia *Teachers Bulletin* indicated that their members favored a single salary scale.[16]

As the case slowly moved through the judicial system, tension developed between the national NAACP and city officials in Norfolk, on one hand, and the NAACP and black Norfolk teachers on the other. But what is almost incomprehensible at this juncture is the action of P. B. Young, who personally attempted to negotiate an end to the teacher salary case.

In so doing, he compromised the case, according to Thurgood Marshall. It was a political blunder that was not characteristic of Young.

During the initial stages of the case Marshall praised Young and his two sons for their "splendid cooperation." Marshall had asked NAACP attorneys Leo Ransom and Charles Houston to consult with the Youngs concerning the case. The NAACP leaked confidential information about the case to Young and withheld press releases from white dailies until Thursdays, the *Guide*'s publication day. In turn, the *Guide* promised to write editorials and "to do everything within its power" to help the cause. "In the years to come," Marshall wrote Young in 1939, "Negroes in Virginia will fully realize the part that the *Journal and Guide* played in the struggle to equalize teachers salaries."[17] Not long thereafter the relationship between the two men soured. One observer described the source of the conflict humorously: "The NAACP met with the judge during the day, Mr. P. B. met with white folks at night, unraveled the agreement, and rewrote it to his own satisfaction."[18]

The conflict arose after the U.S. Circuit Court of Appeals (4th District) on June 18, 1940, reversed the decision of the lower court and remanded Alston's case back to the lower court for a hearing on its merits. Soon after the decision NAACP attorneys Leo Ransom and Oliver Hill conferred with the Norfolk city attorney on the possibility of an "amicable settlement of the Alston case." The city attorney promised a written offer; instead, he applied to the U.S. Supreme Court for a writ of certiorari, which was granted on October 28, 1940. Meanwhile, Young allegedly had convinced the plaintiff, Melvin Alston, to settle the case "without the lawyers." In addition, Young, without prior approval or knowledge of the NAACP, contacted City Attorney Alfred Anderson, Mayor J. D. Woods, and City Manager Charles Borland to work out a compromise, "a settlement" in the interest of "good race relations," and the promise of a new black elementary school.[19]

Thurgood Marshall was furious. He immediately organized a mass meeting of Norfolk's black teachers "to protect the reputation of the NAACP." A few days after Young's secret meeting, an angry Marshall confronted Young in his Norfolk office. Young claimed he was "innocent" and explained that the city manager had agreed to call together other city managers and county superintendents in Virginia "to straighten out this problem." Young asked Marshall to be "decent," to accept the offer and, in return, "get many other things accomplished."[20]

After Marshall announced that he was obligated to tell the teachers "exactly what was going on," Young, according to Marshall, "became very red in the face and very excited . . . and stated that I was going to put him on the spot." Expletives were exchanged, and Young, in Marshall's words, "became angrier and less coherent." "The NAACP needs me," shouted Young. Furthermore, "Norfolk teachers accepted my compromise last week." Marshall called Young a "liar."[21]

The cards were stacked against Marshall at a mass meeting of black teachers. L. F. Palmer, president of the State Teachers Association, P. B. Young, and others urged acceptance of the city's offer and emphasized the importance of "good race relations," the benefits of an elementary school, and the city manager's promise to "straighten things out." After many hours of spirited debate, the teachers voted to accept a settlement "almost like the city attorney's offer." Marshall called their action "the most disgraceful termination of any case involving Negroes in recent years." At this point NAACP executive director Walter White and uncompensated lawyers such as Hastie and Ransom debated abandoning all efforts to help Virginia teachers and taking the equalization campaign to another state.[22]

A black church was the scene of a mass meeting a few weeks later, as Marshall "took off the gloves" and made the NAACP's position "perfectly clear." He counseled the teachers to disavow the city attorney's offer and to appoint a committee to negotiate an agreement. P. B. Young, Jr., questioned the utility of a committee because the NAACP had "acted nasty" about his father's earlier committee. Marshall imprudently characterized the previous committee as "backdoor," to which P. B. Young, Jr., shouted "You're a liar." Pandemonium ensued, and Marshall angrily stormed out of the meeting. Marshall later confided to William Hastie, "I am sick about the whole thing."[23] However, in February 1941 Norfolk's black teachers voted 132 to 34 in favor of a settlement prepared by the NAACP.

The teacher salary case left "deep and ugly scars" in Norfolk's black community. Jerry O. Gilliam, president of the Norfolk NAACP, complained that his organization was "pushed to the rear" and "excluded from meetings." He said that he was often misinformed and "not allowed to meet teachers," although city officials allowed P. B. Young to do so. It was "bad and insincere leadership" by city officials, Gilliam observed, rather than disloyalty to the NAACP that caused the dissension among Norfolk's black teachers. "The rank and file of teachers are for us," but, according to Gilliam, "they were kept in the dark." In addition, Gilliam charged that Norfolk's black leadership identified with the ruling white power structure "even to the point of deceiving their own people." Gilliam favored public demonstrations "to put on the heat," but his plans were quickly eliminated by Norfolk's black leadership and the national NAACP.[24]

In fact, the national NAACP and Young and others of Norfolk's black leadership probably contributed equally to Gilliam's ineffectiveness. Marshall, Hastie, and other national NAACP officials often bypassed the Norfolk branch and communicated directly with Young, city officials, and other principals in the case. Gilliam strongly suggested to Walter White that the attorneys "notify us" and "meet with us" during their visits to Norfolk. Norfolk's teachers were often, in Gilliam's words, "contemptuous" of the local NAACP because at strategy meetings "big Negroes" made what he called persuasive arguments while the official agent of the NAACP—the Norfolk branch—was often ill-informed.[26]

The NAACP's ultimate victory in the teacher salary case put the issue of teacher pay inequities into sharper focus and accelerated salary parity in Virginia. Seemingly, the NAACP's strategy was to capitalize upon the increasingly flexible attitude of white southerners and, at the same time, to direct the justifiable aspiration of blacks to the mutual satisfaction of both races. Young's attempts at conciliation did not immediately yield the promised elementary school. In 1945, five years after his "compromise," Norfolk schools were still "notoriously inferior." He responded with an angry front-page editorial entitled "How Long, Oh, Lord, How Long!!"[27] Young's and Marshall's differences over the best strategies would only deepen as time passed.

During this same period the *Guide* also launched a crusade to secure the admission of blacks to previously all-white state colleges and universities. In February 1933 it supported unsuccessful efforts to desegregate the graduate school of the University of North Carolina by Thomas Raymond Hocutt, a graduate of North Carolina College. Hocutt's desire to enroll at the all-white university signaled the beginning of an eighteen-year campaign to desegregate graduate and professional schools in the South. An additional impetus for expanding black higher education came in January 1936, when the Maryland Court of Appeals ruled that a black man, Donald Gaines Murray, must be admitted to the University of Maryland Law School. But the most significant civil rights case of the decade occurred in November 1938, when the Supreme Court ruled that Lionel Gaines should be admitted to the University of Missouri Law School. Moreover, the court held that the policy of remission of tuition for blacks to attend out-of-state graduate and professional schools was inadequate as a substitute for equality. Young agreed with NAACP attorney Charles Houston that "the Gaines decision affected all phases of education" and set a new standard for the separate-but-equal doctrine. In a speech before the Orioles, an elite black male group, Young said the *Gaines* decision was "the most momentous ruling by the high court in the area of civil rights since the Civil War."[28]

The Gaines case sparked considerable debate in the South on how best to educate the Negro. Among others, Young; Mordecai Johnson, president of Howard University; John W. Davis, president of West Virginia State College; Arthur Howe, president of Hampton Institute; J. M. Tinsley, president of the Richmond NAACP; and Louis Jaffe, editor of the *Virginian-Pilot*, favored a graduate and professional program at Virginia State College for Negroes at Petersburg. The black president of Virginia State, J. M. Gandy, and a white sociologist from the University of North Carolina, Guy Johnson, pointed out that the study of medicine, dentistry, and other specialties required heavy financial support for plant, equipment, and staff. They wondered if Virginia would support a separate black graduate program.

Guy Johnson pushed for the establishment of black regional centers of graduate and professional study. His opponents acknowledged the feasibility of such a plan but wondered if it met the Supreme Court's definition of equality any more satisfactorily than did the grant-in-aid plan. As an alternative plan, Johnson's detractors favored the creation of segregated black graduate and professional units at exclusively white campuses. Perhaps the rationale for this plan was best expressed by the *Virginian-Pilot*, which remarked, "it can be discussed only as a solution that the Supreme Court's decision forces the South to face.[29]

Following the *Gaines* decision, the national NAACP escalated its campaign to equalize educational opportunity in the South and, at the same time, to expand its membership and influence. In February 1939 "the largest crowd ever" jammed Norfolk's St. John's AME Church to hear a speech by Walter White, executive director of the NAACP. White patiently reviewed the then-current teacher salary case and explained the significance of the *Gaines* decision. He urged Norfolkians "to fight intelligently, unitedly, and persistently." "Stand up and fight for Democracy," he shouted, as he skillfully linked "Democracy" with the *Gaines* decision and the teacher salary case. Following White's address, 112 Norfolkians either joined or renewed their memberships in the NAACP. The next week, in an editorial entitled "Common Destiny," Young characterized White as an "uncompromising contender for liberty, justice and equality."[30]

Despite the significance of the *Gaines* decision, the constitutionality of separate-but-equal doctrine remained unanswered through the 1940s. Further high court decisions made little headway. Then, on Monday, June 5, 1950, the Supreme Court ordered Heman Marion Sweatt admitted to the University of Texas Law School and G. W. McLaurin admitted to the graduate school of the University of Oklahoma. Although the

Plessy decision of 1896, which established the separate-but-equal doctrine, was not specifically overruled, Thurgood Marshall noted that "its effectiveness in graduate and professional education was destroyed." He prophesied "the complete destruction of all enforced segregation." The *Guide* cautioned blacks that the court did not specifically outlaw the practice of racial segregation. "Something or someone is bound to crack sooner or later," Young wrote, but meanwhile blacks were on what he called "a legal merry-go-round." A similar view was expressed by the *Virginian-Pilot*, whose editor remarked that "a tide is in motion, and it is unlikely that any man or group can stop it." The Atlanta *Constitution* and the Houston *Post* termed the decision "expected," and the *Times-Dispatch* asked the Court not to declare segregation unconstitutional.[31]

As the NAACP prepared for an all-out crusade against segregation in public education, the struggle over black civil rights again focused on Virginia. On November 29, 1949, a black man, Gregory Swanson, applied for admission to the University of Virginia. After several legal skirmishes he eventually won admission, but in the words of former governor Colgate Darden, Swanson was a "poor choice" to test the discriminatory admissions policy at the University of Virginia. "He was incompetent . . . he didn't have the ability," asserted Darden. Although Darden encouraged Young, as the leading black spokesman in Virginia, to "quietly keep up the pressure" in support of Swanson, he wondered why Swanson had been selected to push the issue. What Young probably neglected to tell him was that the NAACP had been searching for a courageous "qualified" black since the Jackson case of the mid-1930s. In April 1939, before the rift between the two men had occurred, Marshall, in a confidential letter to Young, had strongly urged "publicity" in order "to secure a qualified applicant," but Young demurred because he favored private "persuasion" and believed that the use of public pressure might do "more harm than good." Young was supported by W. L. Ransom of Richmond's First Baptist Church, who also urged Marshall not to "advertise" but instead "to work quietly . . . somewhat secretly" in order not to offend educated blacks.[32]

Ironically, at the time he was fighting for university admission beginning in 1949, Swanson off campus was engaged in a bitter feud with the *Guide*. On one occasion, after the *Guide* printed the opinions of various white southern editors on the segregation issue without balancing its coverage with opposing views from the NAACP, Swanson denounced both Young and the *Guide* at a public forum. Later, he unleashed bitter personal criticism of Young to Ellis Corbitt, the *Guide's* circulation manager.[33] Young was furious. The normally pacific editor-in-chief threatened to neutralize Swanson the same way that pugilists Randolph Turpin and

Jersey Joe Walcott had recently defeated Sugar Ray Robinson and Ezzard Charles. Young characterized Swanson as a "laboratory specimen."

Young initially ignored Swanson's allegations. "Never explain," he wrote. "Your enemies will not believe you and your friends need no explanation." But in 1951, as Swanson stepped up his public attack on the *Guide*, his actions generated an angry letter from Young. Young reminded Swanson that he was "a kid in swaddling clothes" when the *Guide* was fighting for civil rights and full citizenship. Young vigorously declared that he had not only established the first NAACP chapter in Virginia but had purchased the first NAACP life membership and would never "surrender" his intellectual integrity or betray the cardinal principles of a free press. "Revenge is a two-edged sword," he wrote. Despite his anger, Young showed no malice toward Swanson, even though he, in Young's opinion, was spitefully "attempting to destroy" the *Guide*.[34]

A few weeks later Young, accompanied by his new bride, Josephine, attended the NAACP's 1951 annual convention in Atlanta, where he arranged an informal meeting with Roy Wilkins, Oliver Hill, Lester Banks (of the NAACP), and the black intellectual Ralph Bunche to discuss the Swanson case. Upon his return to Norfolk, Young characterized Swanson as "in the category of the worst ingrates our race has produced."[35] Swanson was eventually admitted to the University of Virginia but withdrew after one semester.

Later, when the NAACP decided to challenge segregation in schools, Young expressed ambivalence. He feared white abandonment of public education, decreased employment opportunities for black teachers, and future financial instability of black schools. More importantly, perhaps, he feared political and social repercussions should the school desegregation controversy evolve into a campaign issue in future gubernatorial elections. He agreed with Thurgood Marshall that "the complete destruction of all enforced segregation is in sight."[36]

Previously, despite his occasional quarrels with the NAACP, Young's strategy of compromise had been consistent with the NAACP's conservative approach to race relations. But the 1950s ushered in a new breed of attorneys, headed by Marshall, who favored a direct challenge to segregation. Virginia's NAACP officials (Spottswood Robinson, Oliver Hill, Leo Ransom, and others) complained to Marshall about Young's "gentlemen, go slow" approach to race relations. However, a student strike in Prince Edward County, Virginia, on April 25, 1951, forced Young temporarily to abandon his conservatism and launched him on a militant crusade to end segregation.[37]

The black students struck for better school facilities, and the NAACP agreed to represent them in court. Young visited Prince Edward County and met with the dissident students and NAACP officials. He initially supported the strike and used the *Guide* to highlight the inequities of the county school system. Also, he publicly condemned the county's board of education and promised to expose the source of the conflict throughout Virginia and the South, as well.

Young used his political influence to arrange a private meeting with Governor John S. Battle and quickly relayed the governor's sentiments to NAACP attorneys Oliver Hill and Spottswood Robinson. Later, whenever NAACP attorneys met to outline strategy, Young or a reporter from the *Guide* was present. He was, Young once stated, "clearly in the devil's camp on this one."[38] Young's support of the student strike and his tacit approval of the NAACP decision to overturn segregation was probably an attempt to allay charges of "ineffective leadership" from vigorous NAACP state officials. He worried, though, because he believed that the white South was not ready to accept a direct challenge to its biracial system.

On May 17, 1954, the Supreme Court in *Brown v. Board of Education of Topeka* declared segregated public schools unconstitutional. Young advised blacks to accept the decision with "calmness, prudence, and quiet thanksgiving." He agreed with Thurgood Marshall, Roy Wilkins, and other black leaders that the decision symbolized blacks' increasing economic and political power. More importantly, it was a "major turning point" in the quest for civil and political rights. He believed that the great bulk of white Virginians and southerners would "gracefully and calmly" accept desegregation. On the other hand, he feared that the decision might spur a "reshuffling of the population." Nevertheless, he predicted that "segregated public schools will eventually disappear."[39]

After the *Brown* decision the now elderly Young continued to vacillate between the conservative and liberal positions. He was not an inflexible man; over the years he had changed from an ardent Republican to a New Deal Democrat. And yet, even though he had condemned the separate-but-equal doctrine for years, when the court outlawed the practice he wondered if blacks were ready and if they fully understood the political and social implications of the decision. As Congress enacted mild civil rights laws during the 1950s, Young seemed preoccupied with the Cold War, repeatedly referring to the 1954 decision as a turning point in the westward march of Communism.[40]

According to black educators Vivian Mason and Thomas Dabney, Young was not in the forefront of educational reform. He was, in Dabney's words, "as wishy-washy" about education as he was about politics. He championed equalization when he spoke to whites but advocated integration when he met with blacks. Young was liberal at times and conservative at other times. "Privately," a confidential source noted, "Mr. P. B. Young felt that black teachers were unqualified."

The fairest assessment of Young's role in the fight for educational equity for blacks, however, must take into account his larger role in the community.[41] Never the charismatic reformer who epitomized a grand principle in the tradition of Booker T. Washington or Martin Luther King, Jr., Young was instead a leader in the black community by virtue of his accumulated accomplishments as a "solid citizen." As successful businessman, journalist, and family man, he attained the reputation of a "race man"—that is, as one of those all-important people who can act on behalf of a minority because of the recognition and acceptance they have won in the eyes of the majority in power. In the midst of ongoing controversy, the importance of such ambassadors (and, indeed, Young saw himself in just such a role) can be overlooked and even misunderstood. From the vantage of history, though, their function as vital points of contact between estranged communities is clearer. As Young's work in educational reform reveals, his kind of effort was as necessary as was that of activitists like Marshall. Despite their disagreements, the more militant leaders who finally brought segregation down were standing on the foundations built by the likes of P. B. Young, Sr.

Support of Young and the *Guide* extended throughout the upper South during the 1950s. Roy Wilkins, executive director of the NAACP, and Whitney Young, executive director of the National Urban League, visited Young's Norfolk home whenever they were in the tidewater area. Benjamin E. Mays, president of Morehouse College, and Alfonso Elder, president of North Carolina College (now North Carolina Central) often communicated with Young and visited his home. At P. B. Young's dinner table, he and his guests discussed and developed black strategy and ideology in the South.

Young's views on education, school desegregation, and economic development were transmitted by his supporters and his two sons, Thomas and Bernard Young, during regular meeting of the Negro Press Association. His editorials were syndicated throughout the South by the Associated Negro Press and the National Negro Newspapers Association. The white press reprinted his editorials and summarized his speeches to white civic groups in feature articles as reflective of black opinion. Young's views about black education, school desegregation, self-help, and interracial cooperation were consistent with the opinions expressed by the liberal white Southern Regional Council. In turn, Young quoted and serialized the speeches of liberal whites to buttress his own opinions. Additionally,

Young was often the featured speaker at the annual Negro Church Conference in Hampton, Virginia, and at regular meetings of the Negro Farmers Organization in Tuskegee, Alabama. During the 1950s Young and the *Guide* were not always in the forefront of the civil rights movement, but in many instances, the *Guide* functioned as a unifying force which received, synthesized, and generated black strategy and ideology in the South.

▪ 11 ▪

Twilight Years

After Young's marriage to Josephine T. Moseley on February 11, 1950, the couple first settled into a house at 727 Reservoir Avenue and later moved to Beachmont Avenue. Young frequently complained of his health and was, in Josephine's words, "always going to the doctor." Nevertheless, he accompanied her to social functions sponsored by the Colonial Maids, Bugs, Amici, AKA Sorority, and other elite black social organizations. He admired his wife's fine appearance and encouraged her to wear her best dark blue velvet dress, with cowl neckline and matching hat. Josephine felt that the marriage was a happy one. She recalled that during the marriage ceremony, seconds before the minister pronounced them man and wife, Plummer whispered, "Better be glad you're an Episcopalian." "We agreed on everything excepts politics," giggled Josephine, who was an ardent Republican. Her grandfather, William P. Moseley, served in the Virginia General Assembly during Reconstruction, and her father, R. G. Moseley, served one term as a page in the Virginia Senate. Young's pet peeve was disorganized newspapers, which Josephine occasionally and deliberately scattered.[1]

Young bombarded City Manager C. A. Harrell with a variety of complaints throughout the 1950s. An "ugly tree" in front of his residence prompted several letters among Young, Harrell, and D. Paul Decker, director of Parks and Recreation. After the city refused to remove the tree because of its "aesthetic value," Young accused city officials of racial discrimination, but he retracted the statement after the city paved the sidewalk in front of his residence. In another instance, the caricature of a black "Mammy" in front of a West Tazewell Street restaurant angered

Norfolk's black community. The statue prompted not only an exchange of letters between Young and Mayor W. Fred Duckworth but also a personal protest by Young before the Norfolk City Council. He regarded the restaurant's sign as "derogatory" and an affront to "colored women everywhere." An angry "Negro taxpayer and citizen" asked Mayor Duckworth: "Isn't it time to take up arms against some of the evils that lurk in our midst?" Violence was unnecessary, as the advertisement was later removed. A short time later, Young, somewhat "salty," telephoned City Manager H. H. George to complain that the removal of a house on Reservoir Avenue on January 25, 1953, had disrupted his heat, electricity, television, and telephone; he also felt that it damaged trees in his block. A few weeks later, on June 16, 1953, he was annoyed by the "garbage pick-up" and the "appearances" of the street from Chapel Street to East Park Avenue.[2]

Apparently, city officials respected "ole man Young." Their replies to him were generally courteous, and they occasionally invited him to visit their offices to discuss city ordinances. Sometimes lower-level employees would visit Young's home to ascertain the cause of racial incidents in downtown department stores or to explain why black project dwellers were without electricity and sewerage. Young sometimes wrote letters and telephoned city officials on behalf of black tenants. When Esther Roberts experienced "difficulties" in having her windows and plumbing repaired at her residence on the corner of Church and Holt streets, Young telephoned City Manager George, who in turn initiated a prompt investigation and thanked Young for his "civic interest."[3]

After P. B. Young, Jr., paid his water bill "under protest" on December 9, 1953, Young, Sr., drafted a long personal letter to City Manager George detailing the history of water bills at 733 Chapel Street, his former residence. Young again wrote, "I am being discriminated against." The issue was not race but rather what R. W. Fitzgerald, superintendent of the Division of Water, called "an invisible and inaudible leak in the toilet tank." Fitzgerald allowed a 50 percent rebate on the excess consumption of water.[4]

Generally, when blacks complained about municipal services, copies of their letters, along with the particular agency's response, were forwarded to Young. This practice, along with his role as publisher, allowed him to remain knowledgeable about most aspects of life in the black community during his twilight years. In July 1955 Young attached pictures to a letter that detailed violations of city ordinances in the Brambleton area. He later supported his son, P. B., Jr., who complained that "unsightly busses" were parked in a Class A zone residential section near his home. In each case, City Manager George asked the appropriate city agency "to kindly investigate and handle promptly."[5]

In the elite black community a car is an extension of one's personality. In Young's case, his car mirrored both his personality and his political conservatism. He exchanged his late-model Cadillac for a 1953 Bel Air Chevy. He had previously owned a Fleetwood Chevrolet, and during the late 1950s he switched to a Packard. Josephine recalled that a salesman once took Plummer for a ride in a convertible Ford Thunderbird and almost frightened him to death.

Because of Young's position as a member of Howard University's board of trustees, Howard's president Mordecai Johnson was a frequent visitor to Young's home at the start of Young's new marriage. Because Plummer missed many of the board meetings, recalled Josephine, she occasionally overheard things that she would have rather remained ignorant about. Other frequent visitors included John Jordan, John Belden, Southall Bass, Thomas Dabney, Calvin Jacox, and Jordan Kerney, whom she described as "Plummer's right-hand man."[6]

Louis and Phillip Bress, who by 1977 had operated a movie theater on Norfolk's Church Street for sixty-six years, remembered that Young loved Westerns, especially those featuring John Wayne, Randolph Scott, Wild Bill Elliott, and Lash La Rue. He was occasionally accompanied by his granddaughter, Millicent, to see such Westerns as Wayne's *She Wore a Yellow Ribbon* and Scott's *Fort Worth*. Young did not like musicals or movies that highlighted championship fights, but he loved such epics as *Gone with the Wind*, noted Bress. "Old man Young probably saw that movie 20 times," he chuckled.[7]

"Old man Young," as he was now affectionately called in Norfolk, was still a pillar in the community, even though his son Thomas, who ran for the city council in 1952, and other younger blacks represented serious challenges to his leadership. He was still the person to seek out for a job, a speaker who could attract a large audience at a civic function. He was selected to speak for the black community whenever blacks appeared before the city council to voice their grievances. He was regarded by blacks, as well as some whites, as a link to the governor's mansion and to prominent local whites. To the white community Young symbolized "order, stability, interracial goodwill, the best of the Negro race," according to Colgate Darden and other whites. Darden called Young "a calculated accommodationist" like Roy Wilkins, executive director of the NAACP. After the Gray Commission report, which supported limited integration in Virginia during the early 1950s, Young "quietly kept up the pressure,"

Darden observed. "Hell," Darden asserted, "he was more effective than the present crowd of Negro leaders." Whites sought his counsel and read the *Journal and Guide* because, in Darden's view, "It was an intelligent, reliable exposition of the Negro community." As proof of Young's acceptance by what Darden called "the establishment," he pointed to Young's funeral, for which "the whole damn [white] town turned out."[8]

When Young married Josephine in February 1950, Church Street was still the place to see. It was still "always crowded," the center of social and business activity in Norfolk's black community. Blacks from rural communities like Suffolk, Virginia, and Elizabeth City and Ahoskie, North Carolina, still filled Church Street's stores, barber shops, saloons, and restaurants on weekends. Many of the stores and shops were now owned by the descendants of blacks whose parents Young had met when he first arrived in Norfolk in 1907. They considered themselves to be elite. Unlike their parents, the new generation of shopkeepers, lawyers, doctors, dentists, and pharmacists who maintained offices on Church Street were graduates of Howard, Hampton, Fisk, or Meharry Medical College. They owned houses and land and had bank accounts. They shopped out of town and tended to marry fair-skinned mates. They identified with the Links, an elite black female organization, and the Guardsmen, an equally prestigious black male organization, and attended extravagant social functions in Washington, D.C., Philadelphia, New York, and other northern cities. Many maintained elaborate libraries inside their homes and disguised their speech and dress so as to camouflage their southern mannerisms. Friendship with a white family was exalted, and it was fashionable to correspond with "your white neighbor," although you might live on opposite sides of town and meet only once or twice a year.[9]

Although they listened to Fats Domino, Louis Jordan, Ruth Brown, and others, the elite blacks seldom visited the Church Street hotels and dance halls; instead, they arranged private parties at the Plaza Hotel and at Buckroe Beach in Hampton. As in E. Franklin Frazier's *Black Bourgeoisie*, their world was one of make-believe that was punctured by the naked reality of racism whenever they crossed the invisible social boundary. Their fears of failure and rejection were dual factors that sustained their desire to succeed.[10]

Because advanced educational opportunities for blacks were severely restricted in the South, black schoolteachers, principals, and educators in Norfolk and the surrounding areas took full advantage of Virginia's remission of tuition program and enrolled in graduate programs in New York, Indiana, and Ohio that were not available at the Virginia State College for Negroes. Accordingly, many of the black professionals who visited Church Street were well educated.

As they had in 1907, the elite and professional blacks intermingled with large crowds of more lowly folk in front of the Lennox, Regal, and Dunbar theaters. Charles Satchel Morris, Jr., recalled a popular picture of the big six—Willie Mays, Roy Campanella, Hank Thompson, Harry Simpson, Monte Irvin, and Don Newcombe—on the window of the Bon Ton Restaurant. The *Guide* was still "everywhere," according to Morris, as it had been when he first arrived in Norfolk forty years earlier. As in the days before World War I, huge cardboard posters hung on utility poles along the street, some announcing the new—the CIAA Basketball Tournament—and some announcing the old and familiar—the North Carolina State Fair, cultural activities at Hampton, and the medicinal remedy Hadacol.[11]

Chimes from Bute Street's First Baptist Church could still be heard as they announced the beginning of Sunday evening worship services. Richard H. Bowling was still pastor, as he was in 1913, and he still exhorted the value of self-help and condemned Norfolk's slums, race mixing, and love trysts at Lambert's Point. In March 1950 the chimes from Bute Street, along with the bells of other area churches, tolled the death of Louis I. Jaffe, the white editor of the *Virginian-Pilot*. Jaffe had been editor since 1919 and was remembered for what the *Guide* called his "championship of Negro rights when it was not popular to do so." He had vigorously supported a black bathing beach and was the architect of the first antilynching law in the South. On the day of his funeral many of the older Church Street merchants remained closed until after the funeral in homage to "Mr. Jaffe."[12]

During the early 1950s the *Guide's* circulation fluctuated between 45,000 and 50,000. Young was still publisher and chief editorial writer. His son Thomas was still vice president and handled the day-to-day operations of the paper. In response to increased competition from white dailies, the *Guide* subscribed to Hearst's International News Service (INS) in order to increase its appeal to white subscribers. Claude A. Barnett, director of the Associated Negro Press, protested vigorously, terming the INS an "anathema" and the "most biased" of all the news services. He claimed that the INS twisted "straight" news stories. Young countered that the INS was separate and apart from Hearst newspapers. Besides, he noted that his use of the INS was analogous to eating fish: discard the bones and eat the meat. He pointed to the Chicago *Herald-American*, a Hearst newspaper, which had recently not only dropped its policy of "race labeling" but employed a black sports writer who covered both sporting and nonsporting events. Young assured Barnett of his continued support of the ANP, but the *Guide's* affiliation with the INS enabled it, in many instances, "to scoop the Negro press." Barnett responded that the Hearst papers, especially the Chicago *Tribune*, had done blacks "deep and abiding harm."[13] The *Guide* continued to use ANP news releases, though somewhat less frequently.

Young's desire to increase the number of white subscribers to the *Guide* was consistent with his philosophy of interracial goodwill and his continuing search for profit. He still believed that blacks should remain in the South and seek the friendship of whites. From conversations with Oliver Hill, Thurgood Marshall, and Ralph Bunche, he knew that the NAACP would eventually wage an all-out crusade against segregation in public education, from kindergarten to graduate school. Nevertheless, he lamented the slow pace of progress. In a letter to Nannie Helen Burroughs in August 1954, he indicated that "neither side is ready" for integration. He was sensitive to Georgia whites' discussion of massive resistance to circumvent desegregation and to Virginia's support of a so-called regional plan to escape desegregation. Yet, there were indications of a daybreak in southern race relations. The selection of Theodore F. Brickhouse as Norfolk's first black master plumber; the desegregation of Virginia Tech; the personal campaign of C. Lyndon Harrell, president of the Medical College of Virginia, to delete the word "white" as a requirement for membership in the state medical society and the election of blacks to the city council in Lynchburg, Gastonia, and other southern communities not only indicated an improved racial environment in the South but symbolized an end to enforced segregation as well.[14]

The continued entrenchment of segregation in America, particularly the forced separation of races in the South, was a glaring contradiction of American democracy and a repudiation of the U.S. Constitution. In March 1951 Young discussed his ideas about American democracy with black diplomat Ralph Bunche, the Nobel Peace Prize winner in 1950, after Bunche's address to a desegregated audience of approximately 1,500 at the University of Virginia. Like Bunche, he agreed that "America cannot have two brands of Democracy," a pure one for export and an imperfect one for home consumption.[15] America must consider its image abroad.

Young was proud of Bunche, especially because Bunche was a professor at Howard University, where Young had served as chairman of the board of trustees since October 1943. Young regarded Howard as a model of integration and black higher education in America and, indeed, made the university the focus of much of his attention during the 1950s. However, in March 1952 a "great tragedy" occurred that temporarily shook his confidence in Howard University and his friend Mordecai Johnson. Young's friendship with Johnson predated his first appointment to Howard's board of trustees in April 1934; they had met during regular meetings of the NOS and the CIC.[16]

When Young was installed as chairman of Howard's board in 1943, he remarked, "The years ahead will be filled with difficulties." He called for "wise and efficient planning" and challenged the faculty to bring into focus the impact of the repressive forces of high unemployment. In 1949 he resigned as chairman because of ill health but retained his membership on the board. As he approached his sixty-eighth birthday in March 1952, he attempted to resign because in his view, he was "too old." Johnson quickly and "prayerfully" asked Young to reconsider because he himself would reach the mandatory retirement age of sixty-five in 1955 and he needed Young's help to determine his choice of a successor. "No man in America knows better than you the perils through which this university has passed," wrote Johnson. He asked Young to influence the appointment of a president in whom his children and the children of all people could "repose their confidence." Young accepted the responsibility.[17]

Johnson wrote Young again on March 28, 1952, to report "a very great tragedy." Chief custodian Eugene H. Gough, whom Johnson described as "the most trustworthy and highly esteemed of all employees of the university" and for whom he had fought valiantly many years earlier, and Clinton Irvine, James Clinton, and Alfonso M. Smith were killed instantly while moving 420 pounds of sodium chlorate from a storage room in the department of chemistry, where it had rested since 1929. A combined investigative team from the university, the Bureau of Standards, and the Federal Security Agency, which supervised Howard at the time because of its federal appropriation, initiated an immediate inquiry. Several boxes of TNT in a nearby vault were dismissed as unrelated to the explosion. "We are at a loss for an explanation of the disaster," concluded R. Percy Barnes, chairman of the chemistry department. Barnes explained that sodium chlorate will not explode under ordinary conditions; it will not burn, and it can be heated safely to high temperatures. The tragedy occurred at approximately 1:30 P.M. on March 27, 1952. The following day, Johnson included a copy of Barnes's report in his letter to Young. Young responded that "the explosion could have happened at any place where chemicals have been stored over a great length of time." He speculated that friction sparks from the rolling wheels of a hand truck caused the explosion.[18]

Shortly afterwards, Young became involved in the case of G. L. Washington, who alleged that he was forced to resign as business manager of Howard University. Washington forwarded personal and confidential letters between himself and President Johnson to Young, who in turn leaked Washington's strategy to the college president, even though he had promised Washington confidentiality.[19]

The crisis had begun after Washington was appointed business manager, upon the recommendation of Young and C. C. Spaulding. Later, Johnson attempted to fire Washington for insubordination. However, following a heated exchange in Johnson's office, a "gentleman's agreement" was consummated, whereby Johnson agreed to inform Washington of future disagreements with his policies. Washington claimed that Johnson had "trustee phobia" and implied that Johnson was responsible for an alleged appropriation of personal files from his office. On the other hand, Johnson explained that he not only lacked confidence in Washington but also was dissatisfied with his supervision of the campus grounds and janitorial service, his failure to fire a female employee who was involved in a serious domestic dispute, and his retention of a personnel employee whom Johnson disliked. Moreover, Johnson disapproved of Washington's earlier decision to remove Eugene Gough as chief of custodians.[20]

Washington resigned in June 1952, and at the time he complained that Johnson, like other black presidents, insisted upon keeping his hands on "every detail." Washington expressed no ill will toward the university and reasoned that the "blueprint" called for his termination after the business office was organized and "cleaned-up." Young promised to keep Washington's letters confidential; instead, he promptly forwarded them to Johnson.

Faculty members also complained to Young about Johnson's arrogance and intransigent attitude. On January 10, 1955, Emmett E. Dorsey, chairman of the division of social sciences, informed Young that the division had "unanimously adopted" a resolution at a December 21, 1954, meeting that condemned President Johnson's "abrogation . . . of academic freedom." The controversy emanated from a December 14, 1954, meeting called by Charles Thompson, dean of the graduate school, to discuss "the general problem of inaugurating a program for the Ph.D. at Howard." In the ensuing discussion, according to Dorsey, President Johnson characterized historian Rayford Logan as "neither intelligent nor honorable" and not only subjected sociologist E. Franklin Frazier "to unwarranted abuse" but also ordered him "to leave the university." "Johnson's assertion," wrote Dorsey, "destroys mutual confidence and renders impossible the rational, dignified, and democratic consideration of policy." Somewhat later, Logan, in an angry letter to Young, denied that he was opposed to a doctoral program and characterized the allegation as an "unmitigated lie." Young responded that he was unfamiliar with the controversy.[21]

Not only did disgruntled faculty and staff members forward confidential letters and documents to Young, so too did Johnson himself. Often, the correspondents felt the need of an alternate legal opinion from Young's son, Thomas, who was an attorney. On October 28, 1952, upon Johnson's recommendation, the board dismissed Edward L. Jackson, a physical education teacher who had joined the faculty in 1945. The specific charges against Jackson are somewhat unclear, but what is clear, according to the legal brief, is Johnson's violation of Jackson's civil rights. On Saturday, December 6, 1952, Dean J. St. Clair Price asked Jackson to return to the university to open his desk, file cabinet, and office safe. However, when Jackson arrived at his office, he allegedly found President Johnson seated at his desk, surrounded by members of his staff and Dean Price. The desk allegedly had been broken into and the back of Jackson's file cabinet ripped open. President Johnson ordered Jackson to open his office safe but then directed Jackson not to remove documents that outlined his grievances against the university and other personal property, including a tennis racquet. Johnson promised to appoint a committee to determine the "value" of the property. Two months later he had not yet appointed a committee. The legal brief calling Johnson's action "arbitrary" and a deliberate violation of Jackson's civil rights was written by attorney Harry S. Wender of the Washington law firm of Parker and Parker.[22] Young expressed no serious concern about the allegations outlined in the brief, conducted no inquiries, and accepted Johnson's explanation of the incident.

The correspondence between Johnson and Young also reveals how Young attempted to use his position as board member to influence admissions policy. In April 1954 Young wrote to J. L. Johnson, dean of the school of medicine, on behalf of the daughter of a prominent Norfolk physician who had been denied admission to Howard's medical school. Young ordered Dean Johnson "to re-open the matter of her application." He characterized the applicant's father as one of Norfolk's "most respected physicians," who had completed fifty years in the practice of medicine in Norfolk. The doctor wanted to have his daughter succeed him in the field of medicine. Young forwarded copies of his letter to President Johnson and F. D. Wilkinson, registrar. In addition, he "dictated" a letter to Mordecai Johnson that same day from his "sick bed," asking him to resolve the applicant's "immediate problem" because she had already unsuccessfully applied to black Meharry Medical School. After a "careful inquiry," Mordecai Johnson reported to Young that the applicant had been denied admission because she had not completed courses in organic chemistry and physics and was not prepared "to enter any medical school." Johnson indicated a desire to discuss the medical school's decision with Young at the April board meeting. Young responded apologetically, acknowledging that "pertinent facts and information" had been withheld from him. He had assumed that the applicant, who had completed an accredited premedical course at a black female college in the South, had completed courses in organic chemistry and physics. "I am a bit surprised," he wrote, "that the applicant's father had not discovered this." Young missed the April 27, 1954, board meeting, but he and his wife Josephine were the guests of Mordecai Johnson at a special convocation at Howard on Friday, May 28, 1954.[23] In turn, Johnson and his family were guests of the Youngs in July 1954, during the Washington convention of the Frontiers of America, a black service organization.

During a subcommittee meeting of the board in late July 1955, Young and Johnson not only discussed Howard's medical school but also the university's budget of $8,678,000, which had been recently approved by the Department of Health, Education, and Welfare (HEW) and which was $1 million more than the amount originally requested. The budget included $300,000 for salaries and $900,000 for the construction of the law school building and the administration building. Johnson enjoyed the popular support of Congress throughout his presidency, and as a result of the heavy federal subsidy Howard retained its position as "the capstone" of black higher education. Some of the best black minds in America were on Howard's faculty during the early 1950s. Their number included Alaine Locke, Arthur Davis, Sterling Brown, Rayford Logan, E. Franklin Frazier, and Ralph Bunche. During the debate on Howard's budget on June 8, 1954, one congressman remarked, "The Congress has a duty and an obligation to see that Howard becomes a first class university as soon as possible."[24]

Although Johnson reached the mandatory retirement age of sixty-five in 1955, he was reappointed by the trustee board to a five-year postretirement term, and he retired in 1960. He died in 1976. Young's twenty-one years of service on Howard's board terminated in mandatory retirement in April 1955. He was promptly elected an honorary trustee and urged Johnson to call upon him "at any time, for anything . . . in the interest of Howard."[25]

Young's concerns during the twilight years of his life were not only for Howard but also about the current trend in race relations. The NAACP's decision to attack the doctrine of segregation directly still worried him.

He often said to Josephine, "Neither side is ready for integration." He was particularly discouraged by the allegedly irresponsible reporting of *Jet* magazine, which was virtually preaching the funeral of the NAACP. Young was also troubled by *Jet's* claims that black media were exploiting the so-called feud between Roy Wilkins and Martin Luther King and that the NAACP was "using" King as a "propagandist."[26] The dispute between Wilkins and the black press simmered throughout the winter.

As the 1,200 NAACP delegates gathered in Cleveland in July 1958, the burning question was, "Where do we go from here?" According to the Pittsburgh *Courier*, Baltimore *Afro-American*, Philadelphia *Tribune*, and other black newspapers, the delegates complained that the convention was "stagnant," that the workshop was "cut and dried," and that the national NAACP was disorganized and often acted arbitrarily and contrary to the wishes of local chapters. But the most potent criticism was directed toward a newspaper exhibit that displayed only white newspapers. The black press objected vociferously. Also, at a press conference, a black reporter asked the Little Rock Nine: "Since you have managed to pass in Central High School, does this not indicate that you received a good education in all Negro high school?" Wilkins was furious. He regarded the question as an attack by the black press on NAACP desegregation efforts. Meanwhile, conferees whispered about a "head-on collision" between Roy Wilkins, executive secretary, and members of the "top echelon" of the NAACP.[27]

The NAACP's Cleveland convention was later discussed by Louis Latier of the Baltimore *Afro-American* in a syndicated column and by William Nunn of the Pittsburgh *Courier*, who asked, "The NAACP . . . Where Does It Go From Here?" Nunn asserted that it needed a "broader base" and a "blueprint" for local chapters. Wilkins's response was quick and furious. He forwarded a long special-delivery letter to Carl Murphy, editor of the Baltimore *Afro-American*, and copies to Young and other members of the National Negro Press Association (NNPA). Wilkins explained that the NAACP was not a "thing apart" but rather "an enterprise involving the whole race." He angrily noted that black reporters were aiding the "enemy of Negro aspirations" and denounced their readiness "to take a crack at the NAACP." In conclusion, Wilkins unwisely called the *Afro-American* "the hardest hitting paper in the nation, carrying the most news of any weekly."[28]

Wilkins's characterization of the *Afro-American* provoked an angry response from Young; E. Washington Rhodes, editor of the Philadelphia *Tribune*; William Walker, editor of the Cleveland *Call and Post*; and other members of the NNPA. Young, in a telephone conversation with Henry

Moon, NAACP director of public relations, asserted that he was irritated with the NAACP. He was already somewhat distrustful of Wilkins and "that new crowd of radicals in New York." Even though he accepted the view of the NAACP's Washington bureau chief, Clarence Mitchell, that "Negroes have turned the corner," he still favored a "cooling-off" period and a "slowing down." Like publishers Walker and Rhodes, Mitchell agreed that Wilkins's letter was "unwise" and an "affront to his friends." However, he was encouraged by Wilkins's wish to meet with black publishers. Young understood the need for unity but initially rejected Wilkins's explanation that the exhibit of white newspapers had been designed to show the changing pattern of race relations. [29]

Wilkins indicated that he was "greatly distressed" and "greatly disturbed" by the *Guide*'s response. "What really gets to me more than anything else," he wrote in a letter to Young, "was the *Journal and Guide*'s dismissal of my explanation with 'utter condemnation.'" Wilkins said, "This is not like you personally, or like the careful newspaper you have built." Wilkins was hurt by Young's response more than by expressions from other sources because, in his words, the *Guide* not only was the "most perceptive and best edited" black newspaper but could always be counted upon to approach a situation with the "utmost fairness." [30]

Although Wilkins observed that he was not attempting to mollify Murphy, his letter to Young implied otherwise. While the *Guide* was analyzing and debating the issue of segregation, other black weeklies were "wisecracking." Wilkins acknowledged that he had "mis-calculated" and "underestimated the sensitivity" of the black press; besides, the Cleveland incident was "blown-up" by an inexperienced reporter. He requested Young's support in order to clarify the situation. [31]

Young quickly responded and reassured Wilkins of his friendship. He blamed the controversy on the national NAACP's department of public relations, which he characterized as a "liability," and on the NAACP's official magazine, the *Crisis*, which only infrequently quoted the black press but readily responded to and quoted the white press. Young explained that the controversy had been brewing since the early 1950s. He implied that black professionals disrespected the black press, regarding black editors as "dumb" and their newspapers as insignificant and unworthy. When the *Guide* sent its president, Thomas Young, to the 45th annual convention of the NAACP in Dallas in July 1954, the NAACP's director of public relations, Henry Moon, had praised the *Guide* for sending someone "who had some sense." Young was not pleased, for he regarded Moon's letter as an indictment of the black press. The conflict between the black editor and the NAACP worsened shortly after the

May 1954 *Brown* decision. According to Young, Channing Tobias, the NAACP's board chairman, remarked, "Negro leadership has now passed to the NAACP. Any Negro leader who does not fall in line will not be a leader long." At the time Young found Tobias's statement "offensive" because it presumed that all leadership in all fields of endeavor must emanate from the NAACP. He charged that the NAACP branches in the South lost members because of "shenanigans by politicians." Young recalled that Tobias had taken that same attitude toward the Durham conference of 1942.[32]

Young recognized that his conservative, go-slow approach was contrary to the NAACP's more militant philosophy during the late 1950s. Although he had founded Norfolk's first chapter in 1917 and reorganized subsequent chapters in 1925 and again during the 1930s, Young was now subjected to "snubs" and "slights" from blacks whom he characterized as "heaven-anointed leaders." He considered them "publicity hounds" whose objective was a headline in a white daily newspaper.[33]

Since 1927, he wrote, black editors and the black press had "plowed the ground" and "cultivated it," laying the foundation for an end to enforced segregation. Despite this, he complained, the NAACP seemingly discounted the contributions of the black press. His rejection of Wilkins's explanation was not personal but rather an expression of displeasure with the NAACP's haughty attitude. He argued that the NAACP was insensitive to the needs of the South's rural masses and that neither the NAACP nor the black press enjoyed popular support among the South's rural blacks. Like editor William Walker of the *Call and Post*, he noted that both the NAACP and the black press acquired support from the same constituency. He acknowledged that the NAACP had raised the level of black consciousness in the South, but at the same time he agreed with the *Call and Post*, which asserted that the "Negro is hurt enough to cry, but is not mad enough to fight."[34]

The conflict between the black press and the NAACP gradually abated after Wilkins initiated weekly "briefings" for representatives of the black press. The times were "too critical," wrote John Morsell, a NAACP staffer, and the battle was too heavy for misunderstandings between the NAACP and the black press. Wilkins apologized to Young for reacting personally to criticism of the NAACP. He characterized the omission of comments from the black press in the *Crisis* as "no thought-out policy." Wilkins praised the *Guide* for its sharp and frank analysis and thanked Young for including the correspondence between Henry Moon, director of publicity, and Thomas Young in his response to him.[35]

At the time of the struggle between the NAACP and the black press, during the late 1950s, the Virginia legislature was adopting a policy of "massive resistance" to school integration. Norfolk became the main battleground on which the fate of massive resistance as an official policy was decided.[36] The heated verbal exchanges inside Young's Norfolk office during the late 1950s in many ways mirrored the NAACP's strategy in the South and reflected the local black community's fears and uncertainties over desegregation.

Young favored a conservative approach. He believed that the white South was unprepared for a militant assault on school segregation. He reasoned, and research confirms, that the white leadership in the South anticipated an end to the separate-but-equal doctrine.[37] He argued that the white South realized that there was no legal way to avoid desegregation except to abandon the public school system entirely. He accurately predicted that school integration would provoke a reshuffling of the population, an abandonment of public schools in the black community, and the dismissal of black public schoolteachers. Moreover, the black community, in Young's view, was unprepared for integration. Accordingly, he organized the Hampton Conference of 1958 to prepare blacks for integration.

Robert Roberton, president of Norfolk NAACP, and black attorneys Victor Ashe and J. Hugo Madison assumed a more moderate position. They favored increased legal action and an enlarged black electorate. They suggested an alignment with Norfolk's school superintendent J. J. Brembaker, Norfolk's state senator Robert F. Baldwin, and other white moderates to end tuition grants as an instrument to circumvent integration. However, concommitant with this view was the knowledge that black political power was necessary to stop the harassment of black teachers and the insistence of state officials that they be given the NAACP's membership list. Roberton, Ashe, and Madison complained of harassment from delegate John Boatwright, chairman of the Committee on Offenses against the Administration of Justice, who had summoned them to explain the NAACP's financial contributions to cases filed in civil court. Vivian Mason favored selective integration. The "pioneers," she observed, should represent the best talent in the black community. Winston Douglass, Samuel Coppage, G. W. C. Brown, Joe Jordan, and Edward Dawley called for full integration. Jordan was Young's nemesis and often referred to him as "the white man's boy." He allegedly distributed leaflets that claimed that white businessmen, not Young, owned the *Guide*. His position was always the opposite of Young's. According to Thomas Dabney, who was present at many of the caucuses, Gartrell J. Gaines was even more radical than Jordan. Gaines favored miscegenation—"everybody marry someone white."[38]

When twenty-one black students were admitted to seven formerly all-white secondary schools in Norfolk and Arlington County on February 2, 1959, their enrollment effectively defused important psychological support of the resistance movement.[39] The token black pioneers in Norfolk were instructed by Young, Mason, and others to extend warmth and friendship to their classmates and to ignore hostile attitudes from their peers. Young recited the words of Charles Borland, who upon the appointment of black policemen in Norfolk said: "You are pioneers, and pioneers cannot afford to make mistakes."

As the nation's attention was captured by the impending constitutional crisis in Little Rock, Arkansas, during the summer of 1957, black Norfolkians were aware of the importance of the case, but at the moment they were overwhelmed by local issues that directly affected their lives, especially on Sundays.

In August 1957 the Virginia Alcoholic Beverage Control Board (ABC) announced plans to establish a liquor store in the 1500 block of Brambleton Avenue, next to the property of the Grace Protestant Episcopal Church.[40] Norfolk's black religious community was outraged. Black attorney Hilary H. Jones, Jr., a Grace vestryman, was retained by Grace Church as its legal representative. At the meeting of the city council on August 20, 1957, Young, Jones, Rector Richard B. Martin of Grace Church, junior warden of Grace Church C. A. Palmer, along with scores of angry blacks, appeared before the city council and "protested vigorously" against the establishment of the store. Jones spoke first. The council's president, Mayor Duckworth, quickly responded that the council lacked "authority" to act. Palmer retorted that the council was "guardian of the law of this city." He was "bitterly opposed" to the liquor store and found it "demoralizing." There was applause as the publisher of the *Guide* rose to speak. Young pointed out that the ABC Board was an agency of the state. He recited the history of Grace Church and presented a petition containing 250 names of persons opposed to the liquor store.[41]

After a long discussion, the council expressed its opposition to the proposed liquor store and instructed the city attorney and city manager to draft a letter of protest to the Virginia ABC Board in Richmond, with Young's petition attached. The council instructed Young to "take this matter up" with the city's representatives to the state legislature. In their letter City Manager Thomas F. Maxwell and City Attorney Leonard H. Davis called the proposed store "detrimental" and expressed "surprise" at its planned location. They urged the ABC Board to "reconsider" and to relocate the proposed store.[42]

184

Meanwhile, Young led a black delegation to Richmond on August 26, 1957, to meet with ABC officials. Black petitioners and J. H. Kellam, president of the Brambleton Civic League, lobbied Colonial Stores Incorporated, the previous owner of the property. J. W. Wood, vice president, noted that he lacked control over the property's use. Besides, he wrote, the sale of the property was an effort "to improve the neighborhood"; the proposed liquor store would be a "great improvement" over the former condition of the property. He lamented that more law violations had occurred at Colonial's Brambleton Avenue store than in "all" of its seventeen other locations."[43]

Despite these efforts, the board rejected the city's and black petitioners' requests to relocate the liquor store because its operation would not "adversely affect or interfere with the normal orderly affairs of the church." The board noted that the proposed liquor store was "one full block" from the church, and it expressed confidence that Norfolk's police could control or eliminate "panhandlers." The board promised to erect a fence and to staff the store with "experienced Negro personnel entirely," including the manager and assistant manager. Although the board had entered into a firm ten-year lease, it did promise to conduct a periodic review of the store's operation. The Grace congregation was stunned. The Sunday after the ABC Board's decision, the Grace Episcopal Church was filled to overflowing with concerned worshipers from other area churches. Josephine Young remembered Rector Martin's sermon. He characterized the ABC Board as the "Devil." "The devil is not a person with a tail and a pitchfork," Martin shouted. "The devil is a force, the devil is a being." The normally placid congregation responded with shouts of "Amen," "Go a'head on," "Preach." After Martin's address, he along with other teary-eyed members of the congregation bellowed out at the top of their voices: "Yield not to Temptation, for yielding is sin."[44]

The controversy over the liquor store, conflicts over municipal services, and the strain of massive resistance combined to impair relations between Young and city officials. Young complained about city hall's insensitivity to the black community while city officials worried about worsening race relations. In February 1961 Young and Mayor Duckworth had a rather heated telephone exchange. Young abruptly hung up the phone but later apologized. Mayor Duckworth agreed to "overlook" the incident.[45]

Young's inability to reverse the ABC Board's decision was in many ways symbolic of the decline of his status and leadership. Many black Norfolkians agreed that he could have negotiated a better settlement ten years earlier. In February 1961, as the civil rights movement began to have an impact on Norfolk, Mayor W. Fred Duckworth confidentially asked Young to name a few "outstanding colored citizens" in whom he had confidence. The people on Young's list, whom he described as "all conservatives," included Lyman B. Brooks, provost of Norfolk State College; Thomas W. Young, president of the Guide Publishing Company; J. J. Freeman, pastor of Queen Street Baptist Church; Willie Mae Watson, elementary supervisor in the Norfolk public school system; and Richard B. Martin, rector of Grace Episcopal Church.[46]

In October 1960, "after a careful study of the issues and men," the *Journal and Guide* endorsed John F. Kennedy for the presidency in a front-page editorial.[47] Young characterized Kennedy as "dynamic, and brilliant." Kennedy "spoke forthrightly" of equal opportunity, fair housing, and black civil rights. But Young never lived to see the fruition of Kennedy's dream or the promised political breakthrough. He died in Norfolk on October 9, 1962, at the age of seventy-eight. President Kennedy telegraphed his "heartfelt sympathy." Young's funeral was held in the Grace Episcopal Church. Josephine Young remembered that "white people almost filled the church." Former governor Colgate Darden, who was present, recalled that "everybody who was somebody in Virginia attended." Young was buried in a local black cemetery.

Plummer Bernard Young, Sr., was a man of his time, place, and station. He was a passionate freedom fighter in his own way, and he believed in the equality of all men. His conservative approach to improving race relations and his motto of "Build Up—Don't Tear Down" served as a model for aspiring black journalists and earned him the respect of prominent whites as well. Although Young's conservative political and social perspectives were often contrary to those of the New South's emerging black middle class, everyone regarded him as a "conciliator," "a race man," a person the mayor called upon if a "black presence" was needed. From 1910 to 1962 Young and his *Journal and Guide* epitomized black strategy and ideology in the American South. Because of the work of Young and his contemporaries, the American South has moved closer to the American creed.

Conclusion

P. B. Young recognized the significance of the printed word and often considered writing his own autobiography in order to influence the course of history. Helen King Bainbridge, an editor for William Morrow publishers in New York, negotiated with him for several years to publish his memoirs. "I never was successful in persuading Mr. Young to take the time from his crowded schedule to embark on an autobiography," she later wrote. Bainbridge described Young as "a man of great stature" and characterized her inability to secure his autobiography "one of the major failures of my publishing career."[1] However, Young left a full legacy and record of his lifetime in the pages of the Norfolk *Journal and Guide* and his personal papers.

The *Guide* is still in existence. Following the death of P. B. Young, Sr., in October 1962, his son Thomas W. Young served as publisher until his untimely death on September 6, 1967. His sudden death complicated the operations of this business long held in the family, setting into motion the forces that led to its decline and ultimately its forced sale.

P. B. Young, Sr.'s last will and testament revealed that he died almost broke. He left his wife Josephine $3,000, P. B. Young, Jr., $200, and his faithful house servant Mary Drake $100. The will shows that Young desperately wanted the *Guide* to remain a family business. It specifically states that the terms of the trustees, advertising manager John Belden and managing editor John Q. ("Rover") Jordan, "shall continue during the lifetime of Thomas W. Young or until the youngest of my grandchildren . . . reaches the age of 25." At the time of Thomas Young's death, the grandchild closest to age twenty-five was Davis Young, the son of P. B. Young, Jr. But Davis Young never considered the *Guide* as a "career option" and is the vice president of a bank in Boston. He recalled that his grandfather had groomed his brother, Thomas Davis Young, to assume a position of leadership at the *Guide*. Unfortunately, Thomas Davis Young, a pioneer marine aviator, died after a plane crash in 1962. His death and that of his uncle five years later changed the *Guide*'s history.

Jordan, Belden, and another friend, Southall Bass, served as trustees for the underaged stockholders. Belden, Jordan, and Bass found the *Guide* heavily in debt and in desperate need of qualified employees. Nevertheless, the *Guide* continued to appear and never missed an issue. Finally, however, the trustees had to confront what Jordan called "reality." In November 1972, with the youngest of P. B. Young's grandchildren of sufficient age, the trustees sold the Norfolk *Journal and Guide* to Bishop L. E. Willis, a black Norfolk businessman and a national leader of the Church of God in Christ. For the first time in over sixty years the *Guide* was no longer legally affiliated with the Youngs of Norfolk. According to Jordan, the legal agreement obligated the Guide Publishing Company to retain career employees such as himself, Belden, Bass, Thomas Dabney, and Mrs. Undine Young, who was the wife of P. B. Young, Jr., and the *Guide*'s social editor.

Most Norfolkians never noticed the change. Bishop Willis retained John Jordan as editor-in-chief, and the basic image of the *Guide* and its editorial policy remained unchanged. Bishop Willis increased the circulation and advertising staffs and vigorously pushed sales campaigns. He sold the outdated hot metal presses and composition equipment and closed down the mechanical department. For the first time in its history, the printing of the *Guide* was farmed out to an independent printer in North Carolina.

A few months after his purchase of the *Guide*, Bishop Willis became the chief executive officer of the black Atlantic National Bank. Because of his increased banking responsibilities, Bishop Willis sold the *Guide* to one of Norfolk's most prominent black attorneys, J. Hugo Madison, in November 1973. Publisher Madison's tenure was brief; ill health led him to sell the *Guide* to Milton A. Reid, a black Baptist minister and a former disciple of Martin Luther King, Jr., on April 1, 1974. Thus, within a span of eighteen months the third oldest and largest black business in the South had three separate owners. The changing ownership of the *Guide* mirrors a problem that is characteristic not only of the black press but of other black businesses as well. It would seem that after the original owners die, their entrepreneurial spirit is not passed to the next generation. Publisher Milton Reid still owns the *Guide;* a short time after his acquisition of the paper, however, he unsuccessfully sued attorney Madison because the *Guide* was a "financial quagmire" and an April Fool's joke. Meanwhile, the *Guide's* reputation suffered, and the paper faced extinction. Nevertheless, Reid did save the *Guide*, and in 1977, owing in part to Reid's dream and P. B. Young's legacy, Dr. Carlton B. Goodlett, a wealthy San Francisco black psychiatrist and newspaper publisher, made a financial contribution to the Guide Publishing Company and assumed the chairmanship of the board. Goodlett and Reid shared common objectives, the most important of which was to extend the legacy of P. B. Young and the Norfolk *Journal and Guide*.

By 1980 the *Guide* was on the road to recovery. It was the first black newspaper in America to install computerized typesetting. Also the Guide Publishing Company became a common stock company, which revitalized and generated community support and produced more revenue. In 1981 the *Guide* left its dilapidated headquarters on Church Street and purchased modern facilities for a quarter-million dollars on Princess Anne Road without a cosigner.

Most Norfolkians attached no special significance to the *Guide's* move from Church Street to Princess Anne Road. Undoubtedly, many regarded urban renewal, the removal of black businesses, and the proposed revitalization of blighted Church Street as "A New Move Forward," and indeed it was. But at the same time, the *Guide's* move from Church Street not only reflects the struggle of black entrepreneurs in America but, to some degree, explains why black Americans remain economically "the boat stuck at the bottom." Church Street as the center of black life in Norfolk was revitalized out of existence a few years ago. What happened to its black businesses? Most did not relocate but instead closed. More important, what happened to the business owners themselves and the economic foundations that their parents and grandparents nurtured and transformed during the pre–World War II years? Also, why is it that the black business community was unable to transfer generations of economic self-help and economic nationalism into visible and viable symbols of black capitalism after the 1960s? A detailed explanation has yet to be written, but urban migration, desegregated housing, and changes in education and public accommodation seem to be probable causes. Small profit margins and the lack of black consumer support also were factors. Thus, after nearly ninety years, the *Guide* is still struggling for professional respectability and financial security. Its total paid weekly circulation in October 1985 was 24,178, well below the figure it achieved during the Great Depression.

The Grace Episcopal Church is still in existence, and Undine Young, the wife of P. B. Young, Jr., and Marguerite Young, the wife of Thomas W.

Young, are still members. The "Grace Church," as it is affectionately known, and Bute Street's First Baptist Church are still pillars in the black community. Their membership include the descendants of Norfolkians whom Young first met when he arrived in Norfolk in 1907. Norfolk's black religious community must accept some responsibility for the demise of the *Guide*. The black church as been home to such community forces as the Negro Forward Movement, the Negro Organization Society, the Negro Elks, the Society of King David, and the Negro Chamber of Commerce. It is a pivotal force in the community. Had the church acted more energetically on the ideals of the Negro Forward Movement, the *Guide* would have emerged as a potent symbol of black capitalism during the 1950s. Instead, lacking that support, it entered an economic slump from which it may never recover.

After the *Brown* desegregation decision of 1954, Young often remarked, "Neither side is ready for integration." Of course, in one sense Young was wrong, for preparation for full citizenship is unnecessary. But his implied meaning has merit. He saw the walls of segregation "tumbling," but he recognized that the black leadership had not sufficiently sensitized black youth to the implications of their own experience, to the need to continue the struggle. Accordingly, the black press must reeducate each generation instead of building on the entrepreneurial spirit of past generations. Black businesses are now stigmatized as "insignificant and unworthy" because black consumers and black youth are ignorant of the historical traditions of their Church Streets.

Young himself and the South's other black leaders must bear some responsibility for their failure to devise a strategy or an instrument to perpetuate their ideals about self-help and racial solidarity. Young, Shepard, and others failed to see the coming technological revolution. They failed to realize that computerization would impair the effectiveness of the black press. Also, Young was, in the words of former editor-in-chief John Jordan, "urging when he should have been demanding." Young was too cautious and too concerned with his own image. He was so consumed with his own philosophy of success that he neglected to find a way to soldify the economic and political objectives for which he had worked. Young and his contemporaries knew that changes were coming in the biracial system but seemed unsure how to proceed. They did not have a strategy that looked beyond May 1954. Seemingly, they were as confused in victory as the white South was in defeat. They were too trusting and too paternalistic. They underestimated the strength and character of white racism, and, more important, they overestimated the influence of white liberals and their own power and ability to provoke changes within the biracial system. But Young, J. E. Shepard, and others were genuinely loyal to the race. They were not only "able and safe Negro leaders," they deemed themselves to be men of honor and integrity as well.

There is no evidence that Young was ever involved in a personal scandal; he was never arrested or even scolded severely by his liberal white friends. Yet he was a complex man beneath the gentlemanly veneer. Young was not always a gentleman, but he was a "dignified," predictable, cautious, and practical man. Perhaps three words from P. B. Young's basic philosophy best epitomize his overall character: arbitration, negotiation, and compromise. The biggest risk he ever took was his purchase of the lodge's *Journal and Guide* in 1910.

Notes
Selected Bibliography
Index

Notes

Chapter 1

1. U.S. Department of Commerce, Census Office, *Tenth Census (1880)* (Washington, D.C.: Government Printing Office) (hereafter cited as U.S. Census, 1880).

2. Records of the Bureau of Refugees, Freedmen, and Abandoned Lands, North Carolina, Halifax County, 1866–68, Record Group 105, box 38, National Archives, Washington, D.C. (hereafter cited as Freedmen Records, RG 105).

   Forty-one blacks brought to Halifax County during the war petitioned the Freedmen's Bureau in December 1866 to return them to their Canton, Miss., homes (Letters Sent, Received and Orders, Halifax County, vol. 119, July 1866–June 1867, p. 205, ibid.). See also Eric Anderson, *Race and Politics in North Carolina, 1872–1901* (Baton Rouge: Louisiana State University Press, 1981); Robert Engs, *First Freedom: Black Hampton, Virginia, 1861–1890* (Philadelphia: University of Pennsylvania Press, 1979); Joel Williamson, *After Slavery: The Negro in South Carolina during Reconstruction* (Chapel Hill: University of North Carolina Press, 1965); Leon Litwack, *Been in the Storm So Long* (New York: Alfred A. Knopf, 1979).

3. U.S. Department of Commerce, Census Office, *Eighth Census (1860), Agriculture of the United States* (Washington, D.C.: Government Printing Office).

4. Interview, James Robinson, aged 95, Littleton, N.C.; Helena Harris, aged 85, Littleton, N.C.; and Roger Boyd, aged 93, Halifax, N.C., Sept. 1979.

5. U.S. Census, 1880; ibid., agriculture schedule, p. 30.

6. Freedmen Records, RG 105; Records of the Superintendent of Education for the State of North Carolina, Bureau of Refugees, Freedmen, and Abandoned Lands, 1865–70, microfilm M844, rolls 15, 16; Charles William

Dabney, *Universal Education in the South* (Chapel Hill: University of North Carolina Press, 1936), 1: 433–526.

7. Halifax County Marriage Register, 1872–95, Halifax County Courthouse, Halifax, N.C.; Thomas D. Clark, *The Southern Country Store* (Norman: University of Oklahoma Press, 1964), pp. vii, 199; interview, James Robinson, Littleton, N.C., April 12, 1979; Dr. Willis Wilcox, Account Book 1873—, Halifax County Historical Society, Halifax, N.C.; storekeeper's log, Halifax Antiques, Main Street, Halifax, N.C.

8. Halifax County Commissioners, Minute Book, 1873–83, Halifax County Courthouse, Halifax, N.C.

9. Anderson, *Race and Politics in North Carolina*, pp. 54, 62; *The United States Official Register, 1877* (Washington, D.C.: Government Printing Office, 1978), p. 666.

10. Anderson, *Race and Politics in North Carolina*, pp. 81, 196, n. 21.

11. *People's Advocate* (Raleigh), Nov. 19, 1879; H. L. Suggs, *The Black Press in the South, 1865–1979* (Westport, Conn.: Greenwood Press, 1983), 257–87.

12. William Patrick Burrell, *Twenty-Five Years' History of the Order of the True Reformers* (Richmond, 1909), pp. 36–38, 95–111; Walter B. Weare, *Black Business in the New South: A Social History of North Carolina Mutual Life Insurance Company* (Urbana: University of Illinois, 1973), p. 14.

13. Burrell, *The True Reformers*, p. 29. The July 25, 1900, edition of *True Reformer* is only known extant copy.

14. Elsie M. Lewis, "The Political Mind of the Negro, 1865–1900," *Journal of Southern History* 21 (May 1955): 189–202.

15. T. Thomas Fortune, *Black and White: Land, Labor, and Politics in the South* (New York: Ford, Howard, 1884), pp. 116–18; Elsie M. Lewis, "The Political Mind of the Negro, 1865–1900," in Charles Wynes, ed., *The Negro in the South since 1865* (Tuscaloosa: University of Alabama Press, 1967), pp. 35–36; interview, James Robinson, Littleton, N.C., April 12, 1979; Helen G. Edmonds, *The Negro and Fusion Politics in North Carolina, 1894–1901* (Chapel Hill: University of North Carolina Press, 1951), p. 20; J. G. de R. Hamilton, *Reconstruction in North Carolina* (New York: Columbia University Press, 1941), p. 665.

16. Hugh Victor Brown, *A History of the Education of Negroes in North Carolina* (Raleigh: Irvin Press, 1961), pp. 26–27.

17. Interviews, James Robinson, Littleton, N.C., Helena Harris, Littleton, N.C., Roger Boyd, Halifax Co., N.C., Sept. 1979.

18. Interview (phone), Robinson, May 1979; anniversary editions of the Norfolk *Journal and Guide*.

19. Inverviews, Robinson, Littleton, N.C., Harris, Littleton, N.C., Boyd, Halifax Co., N.C., and Cupe Austin, aged 90, Halifax, N.C., Sept. 1979.

20. Interview, Robinson, Littleton, N.C., Sept. 1979.

21. Interview, Harris, Littleton, N.C., Sept. 28, 1979; J. Carlton Hayden, *Black Episcopalians* (in progress); interview, J. Carlton Hayden; Morgan State University, Baltimore, Oct. 3, 1979.

22. *True Reformer,* July 25, 1900; Edmonds, *The Negro and Fusion Politics in North Carolina,* p. 51.

23. Young to Alumni Secretary, St. Augustine College, March 31, 1954, P. B. Young, Sr., papers, in possession of the author, Clemson, S.C.; (hereafter cited as Young Papers) *Impressions of Saint Augustine's School, Raleigh, North Carolina* (Hartford; Church Mission Publishing Company, March 1906).

24 *St. Augustine's Annual Catalogue, 1899–1900, and Thirty-Ninth Annual Catalogue, 1905–1906,* both in archives, St. Augustine's College, Raleigh, N.C.

25. Interview, Robinson, Littleton, N.C., Sept. 1979.

Chapter 2

1. *Norfolk and Portsmouth Directory* (Norfolk, 1907); Frank Eberle, ed., *The Story of Norfolk, City of Great Opportunities* (Norfolk: Board of Trade, 1908); Col. William H. Stewart, *History of Norfolk County, Virginia, and Representative Citizens, 1637—1900* (Chicago: Biographical Publishing Co., 1902), pp. 180–85; George P. Phenix, "A Graphic Study of School Divisions in the State of Virginia regarding Blacks and Whites, 1908–1909," Young Papers.

2. *A Decade of Decay during the Brick and Mortar Administration: A History of Church Street* (pamphlet, n.d.); Norfolk *Virginian-Pilot,* June 15, 1958; City of Norfolk, Industrial Commission, *Norfolk, Virginia: Commercial, Industrial, Historical, Geographical, Social* (Norfolk, 1910); interview, E. R. Archer, Norfolk, July 14, 1977.

3. Eileen Southern, *The Music of Black Americans* (New York: W. W. Norton, 1971), pp. 300–330.

4. Interview, Charles Morris, Jr., Norfolk, July 22, 1979; *What Hampton Graduates Are Doing, 1868–1904* (Hampton: Hampton Institute Press, n.d.), p. 38.

5. See W. E. B. Du Bois, ed., *Economic Cooperation among Negro Americans* (Atlanta: Atlanta University Press, 1970), no. 12, p. 144; W. H. Brown, *The Education and Economic Development of the Negro in Virginia* (Charlottesville: University of Virginia Press, 1924), pp. 102–4, 175.

6. Brown, *Education and Economic Development of the Negro;* Norfolk, *Emancipation Celebration: Souvenir Program Booklet, Sixty-Second Anniversary* (Norfolk, 1925); William S. Dodd, "Negro Life Insurance," *Twelfth*

Annual Report of the Hampton Negro Conference (Hampton, Va.: Hampton Institute Press, 1908).

7. W. E. B. Du Bois, ed., *The Negro in Business* (Atlanta: Atlanta University Press, 1899), no. 4, p. 38.

8. Papers of the National Association for the Advancement of Colored People, box 818, MSS Division, Library of Congress, (hereafter NAACP Papers).

9. Virginius Dabney, *Richmond: The Story of a City* (New York: Doubleday, 1976), p. 272; *Journal of Asian and African Studies* 60 (July 1974): 180–90.

10. Dabney, *Richmond*, p. 272; *Southern Workman* 36 (Jan.–Dec. 1907): 503.

11. Norfolk *Journal and Guide*, Oct. 17, 1916 (hereafter referred to as *Guide*).

12. Mrs. Casper Titus, "Work Being Done for Girls in Southern Cities," *Hampton Negro Conference Number Two* (Hampton: Hampton Institute Press, July 1898), p. 75.

13. *Souvenir Book, 1883–1953* (Norfolk: Grace Episcopal Church, Nov. 21, 1953); interview, Father Joseph Green, Rector, Grace Church, June 1980; see also Hortense Powdermaker, *After Freedom: A Cultural Study in the Deep South* (New York: Atheneum, 1968), pp. 223–85; and Carter G. Woodson, *The History of the Negro Church* (Washington, D.C.: The Association for the Study of Negro Life and History, 1921).

14. Minutes of the Vestry, 1903–28, Parish Register, Grace Episcopal Church, Norfolk.

15. Andrew Buni, *The Negro in Virginia Politics, 1902–1965* (Charlottesville: University Press of Virginia, 1969), pp. 32–33; Henry C. Ferrell, Jr., *Claude A. Swanson of Virginia: A Political Biography* (Lexington: University Press of Kentucky, 1987).

16. Buni, *Negro in Virginia Politics*, pp. 37, 40; Ann Alexander, "Black Protest in the New South: John Mitchell and the Richmond *Planet*, 1863–1929" (Ph.D. diss., Duke University, 1972); Richmond *Planet*, July 4, Oct. 17, 1908.

17. Lester Rubin, William S. Swift, and Herbert R. Northrup, *Negro Employment in the Maritime Industries* (Philadelphia: University of Pennsylvania, 1974), pp. 26–28; see also Lorenzo Green and Carter G. Woodson, *The Negro Wage Earner* (Washington, D.C.: The Association for the Study of Negro Life and History, 1930), pp. 143, 332.

18. Young to Booker T. Washington, Dec. 18, 1909, Booker T. Washington Papers, box 400, MSS Division, LC.

19. H. L. Suggs, in 75th anniversary edition of *Guide*, Oct. 25, 1975; Suggs, *Black Press in the South*, pp. 257–87.

20. For the following account, see ibid., and issues of July 19, Oct. 4, Nov. 22, 1931, Jan. 4, 9, 1932, Dec. 22, 1933, Oct. 12, Dec. 28, 1935, Nov. 23, Dec. 23, 28, 1940; *The 1936 News Index of the Journal and Guide* (Norfolk, 1937); unpublished addresses: "The Negro Press in a Changing World"

(March 1946), "The Norfolk Journal and Guide: A Brief History" (n.d.), "The Extent and Quality of the Negro Press" (Aug. 1933), "The Negro Press" (n.d.), all Young Papers; Suggs, *Black Press in the South*, pp. 379–421; Suggs, history of the *Guide*, in 75th anniversary edition of the *Guide*, Oct. 25, 1975, and the 84th anniversary souvenir booklet (March 1984). The January 14, 1905, extant issue of *Lodge Journal and Guide* is in possession of the author.

21. "Guide Publishing House" (feature), *Guide*, Feb. 3, 1917; "Notes from the Field" (column), ibid., April 7, June 2, Sept. 1, 1917.

22. Ibid., Feb. 24, 1917, Nov. 25, 1922.

23. Minutes of the Vestry, 1903–28, Parish Registry, Grace Episcopal Church, Norfolk.

Chapter 3

1. P. B. Young to Booker T. Washington, April 19, 1904, Washington to Young, April 24, 1904, Washington Papers, box 296.

2. Clippings, Hampton Institute Scrapbook Collection, Peabody Special Collection, Hampton Institute, Hampton, Va.; Booker T. Washington, "The Negro and Labor Unions," *Atlantic Monthly* 3 (June 1913): 756–67.

3. "Negro Organization Society," clippings, Peabody Special Collection, 235, vol. 2; interview, J. Rupert Picott, executive director, Association for the Study of Negro Life and History, Richmond, Dec. 31, 1979.

4. New York *Evening Post*, May 2, 1913; Newport News *Daily Press*, May 10, 1913; Young to Washington, Oct. 13, 1913, Washington Papers, box 929.

5. Richmond *Times-Dispatch*, Nov. 8, 1913.

6. Newport News *Daily Press*, Oct. 12, 1913, in Peabody Special Collection, 235, vol. 2; New York *Evening Post*, Nov. 7, 1913.

7. Richmond *Times-Dispatch*, Nov. 8, 1913, in Peabody Special Collection, 236, vol. 2; Newport News *Star*, Aug. 22, 1914.

8. Clippings, Washington Papers, box 514.

9. Norfolk *Virginian-Pilot*, Nov. 11, 1914; See also H. L. Suggs, "P. B. Young of the Norfolk *Journal and Guide:* A Booker T. Washington Militant, 1904–1928," *Journal of Negro History* 64 (Fall 1979): 365–376.

10. Suggs, "Young and the Norfolk *Journal and Guide*," pp. 365–76.

11. "Get Together Conference" (feature), *Guide*, Nov. 18, 1914, in Peabody Special Collection, 236, vol. 1.

12. Clippings, Washington Papers, box 1062; clippings, Young Papers.

13. Emmett Scott to Young, May 3, 1915, Washington Papers, box 943.

14. Virginia State Constitution of 1902, section 31.

15. August Meier and Elliott Rudwick, *Along the Color Line: Explorations in the Black Experience* (Urbana: University of Illinois Press, 1976), pp. 85, 93; reprint of *Proceedings of the National Negro Conference* (New York): Arno Press, 1969), p. 1; B. Joyce Ross, *J. E. Spingarn and the Rise of the NAACP, 1911–1939* (New York: Atheneum, 1972); Charles Flint Kellogg, *A History of the NAACP, 1909–1920* (Baltimore: Johns Hopkins University Press, 1967); John Hope Franklin and August Meier, *Black Leaders of the Twentieth Century* (Urbana: University of Illinois Press, 1982), pp. 85–103; Louis Harlan, *Booker T. Washington: The Wizard of Tuskegee, 1901–1915* (New York: Oxford University Press, 1983), pp. 359–78.

16. "Is the Negro Expecting Too Much?" (editorial), *Guide*, June 21, 1913.

17. Application for charter, Jan. 22, 1917, Norfolk Branch file, NAACP Papers, box G208; *Guide*, Jan. 27, 1917; Meier and Rudwick, *Along the Color Line*, pp. 94–119.

18. Letters and documents, Young Papers; interview with Mrs. Josephine Young, Norfolk, Oct. 24, 1975; call letter, March 1917, Norfolk Branch file, NAACP Papers, box G208.

19. Clippings (n.d.), Young Papers; "Movement for Better Streets" (editorial), *Guide*, March 24, 1917.

20. National Urban League Papers, ser. 6, box 86, LC; scrapbook, Urban League, ser. 14, boxes 1 and 2, ibid.; *Guide*, Sept. 9, Oct. 21, 1916.

21. Clippings (n.d.), *Guide*, Young Papers.

22. Ibid.

23. Editorials, *Guide*, Nov. 25, 1916, March 10, 24, April 21, 1917.

24. Ibid.; editorial and letter, ibid., March 17, 1917; "Mrs. Washington on Labor Question" (feature, front page), ibid., Nov. 25, 1916.

25. "N.C. Colored Farms Conference," "North Wants Reliable Labor," "Old Eastern Association . . ." (features), ibid., Oct. 13, 1917, Nov. 4, Dec. 2, 1916.

26. Ibid., March 24, 30, April 7, 1917.

27. "Norfolk Longshoremen Paid Substantial Wages," ibid., April 7, 1917.

28. "Prosperity Ahead for Hampton Roads Towns" (feature), Richmond *Times-Dispatch*, April 29, 1917.

29. Clipping (n.d.), Richmond *Planet*, Young Papers.

30. Ibid.: see also Suggs, "Young of the Norfolk *Journal and Guide*," pp. 365–76.

31. Eugene Levy, *James Weldon Johnson: Black Leader, Black Voice* (Chicago: University of Chicago Press, 1973), pp. 187–92; *The Autobiography of W. E. B. Du Bois*, ed., Herbert Aptheker (New York: International Publish-

ers, 1968), p. 274; *Guide*, Jan. 12, 1918; Washington *Bee*, Nov. 16, 1918; Chicago *Defender*, Oct. 24, 1914; New York *Age*, Feb. 8, 1919; *Crisis*, July 1918.

32. NAACP Papers, box C 428.

33. Richmond *News-Leader*, Oct. 18, 1918.

34. U.S. Department of Commerce, Bureau of the Census, *U.S. Census of Population, 1930, City and County Data Book, Negro Population, 1790–1915* (Washington, D.C.: Government Printing Office, 1918).

35. Edward O. Smith, *History of the Newport News Shipbuilding and Dry Dock Company from October 1880 to December 31, 1934* (Newport News, Va., 1939; rep. 1965), p. 160; *Guide*, Sept. 22, 1917; "A Word to Our Readers" (editorial), ibid., Dec. 2, 1916.

36. *Guide*, May 5, 1917.

37. Ibid., July 21, Aug. 11, 1917.

38. Ibid., Aug. 18, 1917.

39. "An Ounce of Prevention" (letter to the editor), Norfolk *Virginian-Pilot*, Aug. 9, 1917; see also William M. Tuttle, Jr., *Race Riot: Chicago in the Red Summer of 1919* (New York: Atheneum, 1980).

40. *Guide*, Dec. 11, 1917, March 2, 30, 1918, St. Louis *Argus*, Nov. 11, 1917, Savannah *Tribune*, Dec. 12, 1917, Jan. 5, 1918, Richmond *Planet*, Sept. 1, 1917, Philadelphia *Tribune*, Sept. 2, 1917, Brooklyn *Eagle*, Dec. 12, 1917, Peabody Special Collection, vol. 6; see also Arthur E. Barbeau and Floretta Henri, *The Unknown Soldiers: Black American Troops in World War I* (Philadelphia: Temple University Press, 1974), pp. 178–79.

41. "The National Disgrace and Shame" (editorial), *Guide*, Aug. 2, 1919, in Robert T. Kerlin, *The Voice of the Negro, 1919* (New York: E. P. Dutton, 1910; rept. Arno Press, 1968), pp. 75–99; National Urban League Papers, ser. 13, box 77; "Let Us Reason Together" (editorial), *Crisis*, Sept. 1919; New York *Age*, May 24, 1919; Washington *Bee*, July 26, Aug. 16, 23, 1919; Savannah *Tribune*, July 26, Aug. 2, 16, 1919.

42. Norfolk City Council, Record Book, 2, Mar. 4 to Aug. 28, 1919; Norfolk *Virginian-Pilot*, July 22, 26, 1919; Norfolk *Ledger-Dispatch*, July 22, 26, 1919.

43. Theodore Kornweibel, *No Crystal Stair: Black Life and the Messenger, 1917–1928* (Westport, Conn.: Greenwood Press, 1975), p. 73.

44. Peabody Special Collection, 247, vol. 1.

45. "Bolshevikism and Race Rioting" and "Negro Will Not Again Be Tame" (editorials), *Guide*, Aug. 9, Nov. 29, 1919; Andrew Buni, *Robert L. Vann of the Pittsburgh* Courier: *Politics and Black Journalism* (Pittsburgh: University of Pittsburgh Press, 1974), pp. 106–8.

46. *Guide*, Mar. 6, 18, 1919, Aug. 21, 1920, in Peabody Special Collection, 230, vol. 9.

47. Arnold Taylor, *Travail and Triumph: Black Life and Culture in the South since the Civil War* (Westport, Conn.: Greenwood Press, 1976), pp. 57–58.

48. *Crisis*, Aug., Sept. 1919; Brooklyn *Eagle*, Sept. 1919.

49. Peabody Special Collection, 153, vol. 6; *Guide*, Dec. 1, 1917.

50. William Avery to Governor Henry C. Stuart, June 20, 1916, Gov. Henry C. Stuart Papers, box 35, Virginia State Archives, Richmond.

51. "The South Waking Up" (editorial), *Guide*, April 13, 1918, in Peabody Special Collection, 253, vol. 6.

Chapter 4

1. *Guide*, Aug. 12, 1922, Jan. 20, Feb. 3, 1923; Suggs, "P. B. Young of the Norfolk *Journal and Guide*, 1910–1962," lecture, Western Carolina Univ., Cullowhee, N.C., May 1975.

2. *Guide*, Dec. 20, 1930.

3. Suggs, "P. B. Young of the Norfolk *Journal and Guide*, 1910–1962."

4. *Guide*, March 31, April 7, 1923.

5. Ibid., Jan. 27, Feb. 19, March 10, 24, 1923.

6. The *Guide* has what Young called "a substantial number" of white subscribers during this period.

7. "Unlimited Supply of Black Labor Keeps Norfolk Commerce and Industry Moving" (feature), *Guide*, Aug. 12, 1922.

8. "The National Association of Women Wage Earners" (editorial), ibid., April 23, 1921; Nannie Burroughs's speech, Young Papers.

9. "The South Waking Up" (editorial), *Guide*, April 13, 1918, in Peabody Special Collection, 253, vol. 6.

10. Alexander, "Black Protest in the New South," pp. 185–361.

11. "Colored Insurgent Movement Fails" (feature), Washington *American*, March 19, 1910, p. 1.

12. *Guide*, April 9, 16, July 30, Oct. 15, 1921; *Virginian-Pilot*, Oct. 25, 1921.

13. Monroe N. Work, ed., *Negro Year Book: An Annual Encyclopedia of the Negro, 1921–1922* (Tuskegee: Negro Year Book Publishing Co., 1921), pp. 39–40; *Guide*, Oct. 8, 15, 1921.

14. *Guide*, July 30, Oct. 8, 15, 1921; Work, *Negro Year Book, 1921–1922*, pp. 13–16.

15. *Guide*, Oct. 8, 1921.

16. Buni, *Negro in Virginia Politics*, p. 87; *Guide*, Dec. 3, 1921.

17. *Guide*, Oct. 30, 1926.

18. Ibid., July 2, 18, Dec. 5, Aug. 8, 12, 15, 1925; *Autobiography of W. E. B. Du Bois*, p. 273; see also Tony Martin, *Race First: The Ideological and Organizational Struggle of Marcus Garvey and the UNIA* (Westport, Conn.: Greenwood, 1976); Elliott M. Rudwick, *W. E. B. Du Bois: Propagandist of the Negro Protest* (New York, Atheneum, 1968), p. 229; Levy, *James Weldon Johnson*, p. 231.

19. Levy, *James Weldon Johnson*, pp. 276–78; Kornweibel, *No Crystal Stair*, pp. 231–34.

20. Hans Schmidt, *The U.S. Occupation of Haiti, 1915–1934* (Rutgers, N.J.: Rutgers University, 1971), pp. 56, 60; Rayford W. Logan, *Haiti and the Dominican Republic* (New York: Oxford University Press, 1968); Rayford W. Logan, "Haiti: The Native Point of View," *Southern Workman* 58 (Jan. 1929): 36–40; James A. Padgett, "Diplomats to Haiti and Their Diplomacy," *Journal of Negro History* 25 (July 1940): 265–330.

21. Johnson, *Along This Way: The Autobiography of James Weldon Johnson* (New York: Viking Press, 1933), pp. 358–60; "Keeping Faith with Haiti" (editorial), *Guide*, Oct. 17, 1931.

22. Schmidt, *U.S. Occupation of Haiti*, pp. 7, 149; "James Weldon Johnson Confers with President Harding" (feature), *Guide*, April 9, 1921; Johnson, *Along This Way*, pp. 320–21; Richard B. Sherman, *The Republican Party and Black America: From McKinley to Hoover, 1896–1933* (Charlottesville, Va.: University Press of Virginia, 1973), pp. 145–47.

23. *Guide*, Aug. 18, 1923; Sherman, *Republican Party and Black America*, p. 203.

24. *Guide*, Feb. 2, 16, 1924.

25. Ibid., Aug. 18, 1923, June 21, 1924, March 21, 1925.

26. Ibid., March 1, Nov. 1, 1925.

27. "The Washington Conference," ibid., Nov. 28, 1925; Washington *Tribune*, Nov. 14, 1925; interview, William Walker, publisher of Cleveland *Call* and *Post*, Washington, D.C., March 17, 1978.

28. "President Told Race to Insist on Full Citizenship" (feature), *Guide*, Nov. 21, 1925, pp. 1, 14.

29. Raymond Wolters, *The New Negro on Campus: Black College Rebellions of the 1920's* (Princeton, N.J.: Princeton University Press, 1975), pp. 28, 340–41; *Guide*, Feb. 7, 21, 1925.

30. Wolters, *New Negro on Campus*, pp. 28, 340–41; *Crisis* 28 (1925); *Guide*, May 16, July 25, Oct. 31, 1925.

31. *Guide*, May 16, 23, July 25, 1925, Oct. 15, 22, 29, Nov. 12, 1927; *Nation*, 125 (Nov. 2, 1927).

32. White to Young, Oct. 15, 1926, Administrative file, NAACP Papers, box C271.

33. Thomas W. Young to Walter White, Oct. 18, 1926, Jan. 21, 1927, and Memorandums of Conference on NYU Discrimination, Feb. 9, 1927, ibid.

34. Thomas W. Young to Walter White, May 12, 1927, James Weldon Johnson to E. George Payne, Sept. 24, 1927, and National NAACP News Release, Oct. 31, 1929, ibid., box G208; clippings, Young Papers; New York *Amsterdam News and Star*, Dec. 31, 1927; Brooklyn *Eagle*, Dec. 31, 1927.

35. Robert W. Bagnall to Charles Tucker, Norfolk, Aug. 8, 1921, G. Hamilton Francis to Robert W. Bagnall, Nov. 2, 1921, Aug. 6, 1925, Bagnall to Young, Sept. 18, 1925, Bagnall to Rev. Richard H. Bowling, Oct. 25, 1925, NAACP Papers, box G208.

36. Bagnall to David Edwards, Nov. 12, 1925, Norfolk NAACP to William Pickens, Dec. 18, 1925, ibid.

37. Young to Bagnall, Sept. 23, 1925, G. W. C. Brown to Bagnall, April 19, 1926, Bagnall to David Edwards, April 16, 1926, and Press release, "Virginia Segregation Law Declared Unconstitutional," Feb. 26, 1926, ibid.; Darlene Clark Hine, *Black Victory: The Rise and Fall of the White Primary in Texas* (Millwood, N.Y.: KTO Press, 1979), p. 234.

38. *Guide*, Jan. 9, 16, 23, 1926; broadside, n.d., and David Edwards to Walter White, April 3, 1926, Edwards to James Weldon Johnson, Feb. 16, 1926, NAACP Papers, box G208.

39. Edwards to Walter White, April 3, 1926, Edwards to James Weldon Johnson, Jan. 15, July 3, 1926, Bagnall to Edwards, April 16, 1926, NAACP Papers, box G208.

40. "The Carrsville Case" (editorial), *Guide*, May 11, 18, 1929; William Andrews to P. B. Young, May 27, 1929, Young to Andrews, June 7, 1929, Young Papers.

41. *Guide*, March 31, April 12, Oct. 27, 1923.

42. Letter to Chicago *Defender* from Norfolk resident (no name), June 22, 1922; Young to William Andrews, May 24, 1929, Andrews to Young, May 27, 1929, Young to James Weldon Johnson, May 20, 1929, "The Carrsville Case" (editorial), *Guide*, May 18, 1929, "Klan Holds Demonstration at Carrsville" (editorial), Norfolk *Ledger-Dispatch*, May 16, 1929, all in Norfolk Branch file, NAACP Papers, box G208.

43. Clipping, Young Papers; Norfolk *Virginian-Pilot*, March 13, 1950; *Guide*, Jan. 11, 1930.

44. Hine, *Black Victory*, pp. 72–89; Richmond *Planet*, March 12, 1927; New York *Age*, March 12, 1927.

45. Administrative file, NAACP Papers, box C202; Ross, *J. E. Spingarn*, pp. 111–22; Buni, *Robert L. Vann*, pp. 148–58.

46. *Guide*, Nov. 14, 1926; Richmond *Planet*, Oct. 23, 1926; Chicago *Bee*, Oct. 23, 1926; Philadelphia *Tribune*, Oct. 23, 1926.

47. Hine, *Black Victory*, p. 84; telegram from James E. Shepard to Governor Henry C. Stuart and William Anthony Avery to Gov. Stuart, June 20, 1916, Stuart Papers, box 35; *Guide*, Feb. 6, 1926.

48. Robert Bagnall to Rev. B. W. Harris, Feb. 20, 1930, Harris to Bagnall, Feb. 25, March 3, April 9, 1930, NAACP Papers, box G208.

Chapter 5

1. *Guide*, Oct. 20, Nov. 10, 1928, Dec. 20, July 5, 1930, April 21, Sept. 15, Dec. 1, 1934.

2. Interview, Dr. Samuel Coppage, Norfolk, Dec. 30, 1972; Kornweibel, *No Crystal Stair*, p. 234; Buni, *Robert L. Vann*, p. 179; Rudwick, *W. E. B. Du Bois*, p. 262; *Crisis* 35(1928): 416, 418, 336.

3. *Guide*, Nov. 8, 1928.

4. "Conference Fails to Endorse Either Smith or Hoover" (feature), ibid., Sept. 8, 1928.

5. Ibid., Nov. 8, 1928.

6. "A Glance Backward" (editorial), ibid., March 16, 1929.

7. Ibid., Nov. 3, 10, 17, 1928, March 16, 1929.

8. Ibid., March 16, 1929.

9. Ibid., Nov. 10, 1928; Buni, *Negro in Virginia Politics*, pp. 104–5; Donald J. Lisio, *Hoover, Blacks, and Lily Whites: A Study of Southern Strategies* (Chapel Hill: University of North Carolina Press, 1985), pp. xiii–xiv; Ralph J. Bunch, *The Political Status of the Negro in the Age of FDR* (Chicago: University of Chicago Press, 1973), p. 36; Ross, *J. E. Spingarn*, p. 147.

10. Bunch, *Political Status of the Negro*, pp. 36–37; *Guide*, March 26, June 4, July 30, Oct. 1, 8, Nov. 19, May 28, 1932, March 21, 1936, March 28, 1938.

11. Harold F. Gosnell, *Negro Politicians: The Rise of Negro Politics in Chicago* (Chicago, 1935), pp. 29, 163–85; *Guide*, Sept. 4, 1930, June 30, 1931, March 12, 1932.

12. "De Priest for Political Independence" (editorial), *Guide*, June 3, 1931.

13. Richard I. Watson, Jr., "The Defeat of Judge Parker: A Study in Pressure Groups and Politics," *Mississippi Valley Historical Review* 50 (Sept. 1963): 213–34; *Guide*, Jan. 18, 19, April 5, 19, May 10, 1930; Sherman, *Republican Party and Black America*, pp. 240–41; Buni, *Negro in Virginia Politics*, pp. 109–11.

14. Sherman, *Republican Party and Black America*, pp. 245–47; "War Department and Gold Star Mothers" and "Political Emancipation" (editorials), *Guide*, May 10, May 24, 1930; ibid., June 7, 1930.

15. Dan Carter, *Scottsboro: A Tragedy of the American South* (Baton Rouge:

Louisiana State University Press, 1969), pp. 399–413.

16. *Guide*, Feb. 21, 1931, Jan. 16, 23, Sept. 3, 1932; U.S. Department of Commerce, Bureau of Census, *Negroes in the United States, 1920–1932* (Washington, D.C.: Government Printing Office, 1935), pp. 297–309; Taylor, *Travail and Triumph*, p. 169; see also Herbert Gutman, *The Black Family in Slavery and Freedom, 1750–1925* (New York: Pantheon Books, 1976), table 11–12, pp. 48–58.

17. "After Commencement What?" (editorial), *Guide*, May 28, 1932; ibid., Sept. 3, 1932.

18. *Guide*, April 18, May 16, 1931; Raymond Gavins, *The Perils and Prospects of Southern Black Leadership: Gordon Blaine Hancock, 1884–1970* (Durham, N.C.: Duke University Press, 1977), p. 52; Raymond Wolters, *Negroes and the Great Depression: The Problem of Economic Recovery* (Westport, Conn.: Greenwood Press, 1970), pp. ix, 3–4, 83–86; John Williams, "Struggles of the Thirties in the South," in Bernard Sternsher, ed., *The Negro in Depression and War: Prelude to Revolution, 1930–1945* (Chicago: Quadrangle Books, 1969), pp. 166–78.

19. "After the Depression" (editorial), *Guide*, March 26, 1932.

20. News article and "The Cleaners Controversy" (editorial), ibid., April 23, 1932.

21. "An Opportunity for Action" and "Using Purchasing Power" (editorials), ibid., Jan. 3, 1931, April 30, 1932.

22. Robert L. Factor, *The Black Response to America: Men, Ideals, and Organization from Frederick Douglass to the NAACP* (Reading, Mass.: Addison-Wesley, 1970), p. 226.

23. *Guide*, Feb. 6, 13, March 5, Sept. 3, 24, 1932.

24. Wolters, *The New Negro on Campus*, pp. 341–48; *Guide*, Jan. 17, 1931, Feb. 6, March 5, Sept. 3, 24, 1932, Nov. 28, Dec. 12, 1936, Jan. 3, 23, 1937, Nov. 4, 1939.

25. *Guide*, "Increasing Suicides" (editorial), Feb. 9, 1935.

26. Clippings, Young Papers.

27. *Guide*, July 19, Nov. 22, 1931, Jan. 4, 9, 1932, March 1, July 1, Dec. 22, 1933, Dec. 28, 1935, Jan. 3, 23, 30, 1937, March 28, 1938, Nov. 23, Dec. 23, 28, 1940.

28. Ibid., March 16, Oct. 12, Dec. 28, 1935; financial statement, Dec. 1930, Young Papers.

29. "A Next Move Forward" and "Partisan vs. Non-Partisan" (editorials), *Guide*, Sept. 20, 1930, Dec. 12, 1931; Louise Overacker,"The Black Struggle for Participation in Primary Elections," *Journal of Negro History* 30 (Jan. 1945): 54–61; Lee Alilunas, "Legal Restrictions on Blacks in Politics," ibid., 15 (April 1940): 153–202; Robert E. Martin, *Black Disfranchisement in Virginia* (Washington, D.C.: Howard University Press, 1938).

30. Clippings, Young Papers; *Guide*, April 30, Oct. 1, 8, 1932.

31. "Political Independence Needed" (editorial), *Guide*, Oct. 8, 1932.

32. Ibid., April 18, 25, 1931; clipping, Young Papers.

33. Clipping, Young Papers; *Guide*, Feb. 13, 1932.

34. Clipping, *Guide*, March 5, 1932, and untitled speech delivered before Norfolk Social and Benefit Organization, Feb. 1932, Young Papers.

35. Oscar De Priest, speech, "Independent Voters League," Feb. 27, 1932, and Young memo to Attorney Walter Davis, president, Independent Voters League, Young Papers.

36. Clipping, ibid.; "Howard's President Declares He Is Not a Communist" (feature), *Guide*, June 10, 1932.

37. *Guide*, Jan. 5, 12, March 2, 16, 23, 1935; interview, Southall Bass, Norfolk, Nov. 1978.

38. *Guide*, June 20, Sept. 12, 1931; Sept. 24, Oct. 8, Nov. 5, 1932; "Political Emancipation" and "How We Should Vote" (editorials), ibid., May 24, 1930, May 28, 1932.

39. "Amazing Political Sophistry," "Time for a New Deal," "We Should Take Part," "Political Parties and Issues Are Reviewed by Editor" (editorials), ibid., June 4, July 30, Aug. 6, Oct. 1, 1932; clipping, Oct. 1, 1932, and speech (undated), Young Papers.

40. Buni, *Negro in Virginia Politics*, p. 111; *Guide*, May 10, 24, 1930, Sept. 24, Oct. 8, Nov. 5, 1932; John G. Van Deusen, "The Negro in Politics," *Journal of Negro History* 21 (July 1936): 273.

41. Buni, *Negro in Virginia Politics*, pp. 111–12; "Mr. Roosevelt Elected" and "President Roosevelt's Inaugural Address" (editorials), *Guide*, Nov. 19, 1932; March 11, 1933.

42. Buni, *Robert L. Vann*, p. 194; clippings (n.d.), Young Papers.

Chapter 6

1. "President Roosevelt's Inaugural Address" (editorial), *Guide*, March 11, 1933.

2. Edwin Nourse, Joseph Davis, and John D. Block, *Three Years of the Agriculture Adjustment Administration* (Washington, D.C., 1937); Wolters, *Negroes and the Great Depression*, p. 7, pp. 1–34; Taylor, *Travail and Triumph*, pp. 71–80; Ross, *J. E. Spingarn*, p. 150; *Guide*, Jan 4, 1932, Dec. 1, 15, 1934, March 16, 23, April 13, Sept. 7, 21, 1935; see also David Eugene Conrad, *The Forgotten Farmers: The Story of Sharecroppers in the New Deal* (Urbana: University of Illinois, 1965), pp. 64–82; Paul E. Mertz, *New*

Deal Policy and Southern Rural Poverty (Baton Rouge: Louisiana State University Press, 1978).

3. John Hope Franklin, *From Slavery to Freedom*, 3d ed. (New York: A. A. Knopf, 1967), pp. 534–35; Pittsburgh *Courier*, July 8, 1933.

4. *Guide*, Aug. 19, 1933.

5. Interview, Dr. Samuel Coppage, Norfolk, April 1974; Arthur F. Raper and Ira De A. Reid, *Sharecroppers All* (New York: Russell and Russell, 1971), pp. 98–102; *Guide*, Aug. 12, 19, 26, Oct. 28, 1933, March 9, 23, 1935; Chicago *Defender*, March 23, 1935; Buni, *Robert L. Vann*, pp. 209–11.

6. Wilma Dykeman and James Stokely, *Seeds of Southern Change: The Life of Will Alexander* (New York: W. W. Norton, 1962), pp. 216, 238.

7. Project Descriptions, Region IV, Virginia, October 1936, and Joseph H. B. Evans to John O. Walker, Sept. 15, 1937, Papers of the Farm Security Administration, General Correspondence File, 1935–40, box 249, Farm Security Administration Records, National Archives, Washington, D.C., Record Group 96 (hereafter cited as FSA, RG96).

8. *Guide*, Feb. 20, 1937.

9. Dykeman and Stokely, *Seeds of Southern Change*, pp. 220–21; Newport News *Daily Press*, June 7, 1937; "Aberdeen Homestead" (editorial), *Guide*, June 12, 1937.

10. William Littlejohn to G. S. Mitchell, Dec. 11, 1940, William Thompkins to G. S. Mitchell, June 25, 1941, John P. Murchison to Young, March 29, 1934, Young to Murchison, March 30, 1934, Jack Bryan to Mitchell Thompson, Oct. 13, 1942, Leonard Tracy to Thompson, May 25, 1942, L. Herbert Henegan to Young, Jan. 16, 22, 1943, and clippings, *Guide*, Sept. 28, 1940, FSA, RG96.

11. Mary McLeod Bethune to P. B. Young, Dec. 7, 1938, William H. Hastie to Young, June 12, July 14, 1941, Young Papers; Franklin, *From Slavery to Freedom*, p. 532; "A Good Appointment," "A Plea for Integration," "Advancement" (editorials), *Guide*, Oct. 28, 1933, Nov. 17, 1934, Jan. 18, 1936; Young to Mary McLeod Bethune, June 21, 1935, Mary McLeod Bethune Papers, Amistad Research Center, Tulane University, New Orleans.

12. "Senator Byrd" (editorial), *Guide*, Nov. 4, 1933; J. Harvie Wilkinson III, *Harry Byrd and the Changing Face of Virginia Politics, 1945–1966* (Charlottesville: University Press of Virginia, 1968), p. 6.

13. *Guide*, Nov. 4, 1933; "Breaking a Gentlemen's Agreement" (editorial), ibid., Oct. 28, 1933.

14. Ibid.; Norfolk *Virginian-Pilot*, Nov. 4, 1933; "Forty Acres and a Mule" and "Next Tuesday's Election" (editorials), *Guide*, Nov. 3, 1934.

15. Frank Freidel, *F.D.R. and the South* (Baton Rouge: Louisiana State University Press, 1965), pp. 48, 72, 80.

16. *Guide*, Sept. 12, 1936, Dec. 24, 1938; Charles Henry Martin, "Negro Thought on the National Recovery Administration" (M.A. thesis, Tulane University, 1968).

17. William E. Leuchtenburg, *Franklin D. Roosevelt and the New Deal, 1932–1940* (New York, 1963), p. 185; Van Deusen, "Negro in Politics," p. 273; Lawrence Sullivan, "The Negro Vote," *Atlantic Monthly*, Oct. 1940, p. 480; *Guide*, Nov. 17, 1934; Richmond *Planet*, Nov. 17, 1934; John G. Van Deusen, *The Black Man in White America* (New York: 1944), pp. 134–36.

18. Buni, *Negro in Virginia Politics*, pp. 106–15; *Guide*, Nov. 17, 1934; Richmond *Planet*, Nov. 17, 1934; Van Deusen, *Black Man in White America*, pp. 134–36.

19. Buni, *Robert L. Vann*, p. 211; *Guide*, Nov. 7, 1936; Buni, *Negro in Virginia Politics*, pp. 113–17; see also Leuchtenburg, *Roosevelt and the New Deal*; Franklin, *From Slavery to Freedom*, pp. 512–32; Arthur M. Schlesinger, Jr., *The Age of Roosevelt: The Politics of Upheaval* (Boston: 1960), pp. 425–38.

20. *Guide*, Oct. 17, 31, Nov. 7, 1936, Jan. 30, 1937; Norfolk *Virginian-Pilot*, Nov. 4, 5, 1936; Buni, *Negro in Virginia Politics*, pp. 116–17.

21. Buni, *Negro in Virginia Politics*, pp. 122–23; *Guide*, Nov. 14, 1936, March 27, 1937.

22. William B. Crawley, *Bill Tuck: A Political Life in Harry Byrd's Virginia* (Charlottesville: University Press of Virginia, 1978), p. 12; Raymond Pulley, *Old Virginia Restored: An Interpretation of the Progressive Impulse, 1870–1930* (Charlottesville: University Press of Virginia, 1968), p. 84; V. O. Key, Jr., *Southern Politics in State and Nation* (New York: A. A. Knopf, 1949), pp. 20, 489–527; Gunnar Myrdal, *An American Dilemma: The Negro Problem and Modern Democracy* (New York: Harper and Row, 1944), p. 476; *Guide*, Jan. 9, 1937, Jan. 22, Aug. 13, 1938, Sept. 23, 1939.

23. "Unless We Vote" (editorial), *Guide*, March 27, 1937; ibid., April 3, June 11, July 2, Nov. 12, 1938, April 7, June 3, Sept. 23, 30, Nov. 4, 11, 25, Dec. 1, 1939, July 6, 1940; Virginius Dabney, *Below the Potomac* (New York: D. Appleton-Century, 1942), pp. 127–38.

24. Crawley, *Bill Tuck*, p. 8; Key, *Southern Politics*, p. 23; *Guide*, July 29, Aug. 19, 1939, April 13, July 27, 1940.

25. Freidel, *F.D.R. and the South*, pp. 80–81; Leuchtenburg, *Roosevelt and the New Deal*, pp. 252–54; *Guide*, April 16, Oct. 1, 1938, Jan. 20, 1940.

26. *Guide*, Oct. 12, 19, 1940; Buni, *Robert L. Vann*, pp. 292–98; NAACP Annual Conference file, NAACP Papers, box B-8; Baltimore *Afro-American*, Oct. 19, 1940.

27. *Guide*, Oct. 12, 19, 26, 1940; see also Richard Bardolph, *The Negro Vanguard* (New York: Rinehart, 1959), p. 261.

28. Norfolk *Virginian-Pilot*, Nov. 7, 1940; Young to Claude A. Barnett, Nov. 7, 1940, Claude A. Barnett Papers, Chicago Historical Society, Chicago.

29. "Both Right and Left" (editorial), *Guide*, March 28, 1936.

30. Interviews, John Belden, John Jordan, and pharmacist David Schwartz, Norfolk, Oct. 1975; *Guide*, March 16, Oct. 12, Dec. 28, 1935; financial statement, Dec. 1930, Young Papers.

31. The Richmond, Hampton-Phoebus, and Portsmouth editions were established in 1932, the Washington-Baltimore in 1933, and the special Virginia edition in 1934.

32. Interview, Norfolk, July 12, 1977; see also William H. Chafe, *Civilities and Civil Rights; Greensboro, N.C., and the Black Struggle for Freedom* (New York: Oxford, 1980), p. 5.

33. ". . . Journalist Repels Disturber" (feature), *Guide*, May 28, 1932; ibid., Dec. 19, 1931.

34. Ibid., Jan. 18, 1936.

35. "Destructive Lawlessness" (editorial), ibid., Jan. 26, 1935; "Newport News Numbers Players Hit for Thousands" (feature), ibid., March 25, 1933; see also ibid., Feb. 20, Oct. 15, 1932, March 11, 25, 1933, Aug. 11, Dec. 15, 1934, Jan. 26, 1935, Feb. 11, 18, 1939.

36. ". . . Crime Wave" (editorial), ibid., June 10, 1933; Norfolk City Council, Record Books 2–31, March–Aug. 1919 to Sept.–Dec. 1930; *Guide*, Feb. 11, 1939.

37. "Our Local Crime Problem" and "Good Police Work" (editorials), *Guide*, Feb. 11, 18, 1939.

38. "Good Police Work" (editorial), ibid., Feb. 18, 1939; ibid., Feb. 11, 1939; *U.S.Census, 1930, WPA Housing Survey*, Norfolk, 1936, Hampton University Archives, Hampton, Va.

39. Frank Sullivan, "The Norfolk Redevelopment and Housing Authority: Its Origin, Achievements, and Objectives," July 15, 1966, Records of the Norfolk Redevelopment and Housing Authority, Norfolk (hereafter cited as NRHA); Frank Sullivan, "Norfolk Destroys Slums," *Commonwealth*, June 1952, pp. 35–36; pamphlets, *Norfolk* (1957) and *This Is It* (1946), published by Norfolk Redevelopment and Housing Authority; Norfolk City Council, Record Books, Jan. 1930–Dec. 1940.

40. NRHA records; Norfolk City Council, Record Book, Jan.–Dec. 1935; Norfolk *Virginian-Pilot*, Jan. 24, 1935.

41. NRHA records; Norfolk *Virginian-Pilot*, Jan. 24, 1935, May 18, 1936, June 28, 1939; clippings (n.d.), Young Papers.

42. Robert C. Weaver, address in Norfolk, March 20, 1967, NRHA records.

43. "Dropping Women from Relief" (editorial), *Guide*, May 11, 1935; ibid., May 18, 1935; Young to H. G. Parker, May 11, 1935, Young Papers.

44. *Guide*, Aug. 15, 30, 1931, Jan. 7, 28, Oct. 22, Nov. 12, Dec. 3, 1932, Feb. 11, March 18, 1933.

45. *Guide*, March 23, 30, May 11, 18, 1935.

46. *Guide*, July 6, 1935.

47. "Our $7,000 Tax Raise" (editorial) and "Citizens Holding Mass Meeting" (feature), ibid., Feb. 6, 1932; clippings (n.d.), Young Papers.

48. Young to Thomas P. Thompson, Sept. 4, 1935, Thompson to Young, Sept. 5, 1935, Norfolk City Council, Record Book.

49. Paul Wilstach, *Tidewater Virginia* (Indianapolis: Bobbs-Merrill, 1929), p. 102; pamphlet, *Agriculture and Food Production in Norfolk* (Norfolk: Industrial Commission, 1912); "The Great Wall" and "Proving Our Case" (editorials), *Guide*, Feb. 11, 1933; Thomas J. Wertenbaker, *Norfolk: Historic Southern Port* (Durham: Duke University Press, 1931), pp. 27–46.

50. "Municipal Budget, the Schools, and Branch Libraries" (editorial), *Guide*, March 25, 1933; "City Council Meeting" (feature), ibid., April 1, 1933; Norfolk City Council, Record Book, April 1933.

51. *Guide*, Feb. 6, 20, 27, April 2, May 7, Sept. 3, 1932; "Time for a New Deal" (editorial), ibid., July 30, 1932.

52. Ibid., Feb. 6, 20, Sept. 10, 1932.

53. Clipping (n.d.), Norfolk *Virginian-Pilot*, Young Papers; "The Beach on the Brink" and "A Legal and Moral Victory" (editorials), *Guide*, Feb. 6, March 12, 1932; Norfolk City Council, Record Book, March–April 1932.

54. Interview, John Jordan, John Belden, and Southall Bass, Norfolk, July, Oct. 1974, July 1977; P. B. Young, Sr., "The Extent and Quality of the Negro Press," *Southern Workman* 62 (Aug. 1933): 328.

55. *Guide*, Feb. 25, March 18, 1933; Nov. 16, 23, 1935.

56. "Long Needed Relief Near" and "New Probe in Shockett Death" (editorials), ibid., Sept. 14, 28, 1935, April 23, 1932; ibid., June 1932.

57. Ibid., March 21, 1931, Jan. 6, 1940.

58. Ibid., Sept. 24, 1932, Dec. 16, 1933, Sept. 15, 1934.

59. "Education by the Press" (editorial), ibid., July 20, 1935; see also "The More Considerable Press" (editorial), ibid., Jan. 9, 1932.

60. Ibid., Sept. 24, 1932, Oct. 6, 1934, March 23, 1935.

61. Interview, Thomas Dabney, Norfolk, July 1977; "Nansemond County Training School—A Correction" (editorial), *Guide*, Feb. 16, 1935.

62. "Defending Our Liberalism" (editorial), *Guide*, June 10, 1933; see also Virginius Dabney, *Liberalism in the South* (Chapel Hill: University of North Carolina Press, 1932), p. 411.

Chapter 7

1. Young was one of the few "able and safe Negro leaders" identified by Hamptonian William Avery in a letter to Virginia governor Henry Stuart, June 20, 1916, Stuart Papers, box 35.

2. "Editor Pleads for Quickened Social Justice" (feature), *Guide*, April 25, 1931.

3. *Southern Regional Council 30th Annual Meeting* (pamphlet), Young Papers; New York *Times*, March 16, 1930; Will Alexander to CIC members, May 1, 1935, Frank Porter Graham Papers, folder 67, Southern Historical Collection, University of North Carolina, Chapel Hill.

4. P. B. Young to L. R. Reynolds, Aug. 31, 1939, Reynolds to Jonathan Daniel, Aug. 31, 1939, Frank Barfield to Reynolds, Sept. 7, 1939, Records of the North Carolina Commission on Interracial Cooperation, folder 8, box 1, Southern Historical Collection (hereafter cited as NCCIC).

5. Report, Annual Meeting, Commission on Interracial Cooperation, North Carolina and Virginia, April 18–19, 1934, Young Papers; Memoranda on Executive Committee Meeting (n.d.), Howard Odum Papers, folder 320, box 16, Southern Historical Collection. The paper was later published in the *Southern Workman*, August 1933, and reprints wre distributed by CIC members throughout the South.

6. Notes, Executive Committee, Odum Papers, box 16, folder 347; interview, confidential source, Durham, N.C., June 1976; "Jim Crowism at Its Worse," "Our Inhumane Hospitals," "But the Problem Remains," "Does Some Good" (editorials), *Guide*, Aug. 15, Nov. 21, Dec. 19, 1931, Jan. 13, 1934.

7. Untitled address, Atlantic Christian College, Wilson, N.C., June 23, 1933, Young Papers; interview, David Suggs, uncle of author and lifetime resident of Wilson, N.C., July 1977; see also "Editor Addresses North Carolina White College" (feature), *Guide*, July 1, 1933.

8. Memo, "Critical Situation in North Carolina," Sept. 15, 1933, Odum Papers, folder 320; "North Carolinians Aroused" (editorial), *Guide*, Nov. 25, 1933.

9. Spaulding to N.C. Newbold, Sept. 12, 1934, Odum Papers, box 16, folder 355; *Guide*, Dec. 9, 1933, Jan. 13, 1934; clippings, *Carolina Times*, NCCIC, box 3823.

10. "North Carolinians Aroused" (editorial), *Guide*, Nov. 25, 1933; ibid., Jan. 13, Sept. 12, 1934.

11. Memo (n.d.), Odum Papers, box 17, folder 387; *Guide*, Nov. 9, 1935.

12. "Progress in Race Relations," "Some Methods of Reducing Race Prejudice" and "Let Us Understand Each Other" (editorials), *Guide*, April 25, June 15, Sept. 7, 1935.

13. "Negro Destiny in the South . . ." (speech, n.d.), by Mordecai Johnson, Young Papers; interview, President James Ellison, Virginia Union University, Richmond, Sept. 1977.

14. Interview, Southall Bass, Norfolk, June 1978.

15. *Guide*, March 13, 1934; Young to Graham, Dec. 4, 1936, Graham Papers, box 9033, folder 542.

16. Thomas A. Krueger, *And Promises to Keep: The Southern Conference for Human Welfare, 1938–1948* (Nashville: Vanderbilt University Press, 1967), pp. 18–27; Edwin Lee Plowman, "An Analysis of Selected Strategies Used by Southern Regional Council in Effecting Social Change in the South," Graham Papers; George Tindall, "The Significance of Howard W. Odum to Southern History: A Preliminary Estimate," *Journal of Southern History* 24 (Aug. 1958): 300; "A Little Ahead of the Political South" (editorial), *Guide*, Dec. 3, 1938; Odum to Charles Johnson, Nov. 14, 1938, Odum Papers, box 21.

17. Chicago *Defender*, Dec. 10, 1938; *Guide*, Dec. 3, 1938; Krueger, *And Promises to Keep*, pp. 26–39.

18. Clippings (n.d.), Montgomery *Advertiser*, Montgomery *Journal*, Louisville *Courier-Journal*, and New York *Times*, Young Papers; editorial, *Guide*, Dec. 17, 1938; Buni, *Negro in Virginia Politics*, p. 117.

19. Myrdal, *American Dilemma*, 471.

20. Krueger, *And Promises to Keep*, p. 119.

21. "Going Forward Together," "The Changing South," "A Common Destiny" (editorials), *Guide*, April 23, 30, 1938, Dec. 24, 1938, March 4, 1939; Chicago *Defender*, Dec. 10, 1938.

22. Governor James H. Price to L. R. Reynolds, July 18, 28, 1939, Reynolds to Price, July 27, 1939, Young to Price, Aug. 7, 1939, and clipping, *Guide*, Aug. 12, 1939, Governor James H. Price Papers, Virginia State Archives Richmond.

23. Clipping (n.d.), Young Papers.

24. Reynolds to Jonathan Daniels, Aug. 31, 1939, clipping (n.d.), "Free to Move," Raleigh *News and Observer*, Young to Reynolds, Aug. 31, 1939, Reynolds to Frank Barfield, Aug. 31, 1939, NCCIC, box 1, folder 8.

25. Frank Barfield to L. R. Reynolds, Sept. 7, 1939, Reynolds to Barfield, Sept. 9, 1939, Young to Reynolds, Sept. 11, 1939, ibid.; clippings (n.d.), ibid., box 2, misc.; recollections confirming Barfield's interpretations, Henry Martin Suggs, uncle of the author and a landowner and lifetime resident of Ayden, N.C., near Kinston, and tobacco farmers Charlie Suggs and Sidney Suggs, also uncles of the author and lifetime residents of Pitt County, N.C.

26. Reynolds to James Price, June 26, 1941, Reynolds to Gouber B. Ambler, June 27, 1941, clipping, *Guide*, June 28, 1941, NCCIC, box 1.

27. Interview, John Belden, Norfolk, July 1979; *Guide*, June 29, Aug. 24, Nov. 9, 16, Oct. 19, 1935.

28. *Guide*, Nov. 9, 1935; interview, John Jordan, Norfolk, March 1977.

29. "Justice Vindicated" (editorial), *Guide*, March 5; ibid., April 2, Oct. 15, 29, 1932, Jan. 28, 1933.

30. "How Negroes Are Made Scapegoats in Crime" (feature), ibid., Aug. 20, 1927; ibid., Oct. 29, 1932.

31. Carter, *Scottsboro*, pp. 399–413.

32. *Guide*, Jan. 2, 9, 1932, Jan. 15, April 8, 15, 22, 29, 1933.

33. Ibid., April 22, 1933.

34. Buni, *Robert L. Vann*, p. 236; "Negro Editors on Communism: A Symposium of the American Negro Press," *Crisis* 39 (April–May 1932): 117; Wilson Record, *The Negro and the Communist Party* (Chapel Hill: University of North Carolina Press, 1951), pp. 86–87; see also Mark Naison, *Communists in Harlem during the Depression* (Champaign: University of Illinois Press, 1983).

35. Will Alexander to Walter White, Sept. 30, 1930, NAACP Papers, group 1, ser. C, box 310; "An Alabama Harper Case" and "Darrow, the Communist and Scottsboro" (editorials), *Guide*, May 23, 1931, Jan. 9, 1932.

36. Assistant Secretary of the National NAACP to Dr. J. M. Tinsley, Aug. 14, 1933, NAACP Papers, group 1, ser. C, box 310.

37. "Our Eternal Vigilance" (editorial), *Guide*, Dec. 5, 1931; interview, Thomas Dabney, Norfolk, Feb. 1977.

38. Interview, Thomas Dabney, Norfolk, Feb. 1977; "Hundreds Attend Protest Meetings; Scottsboro Main Topic" (feature), *Guide*, Oct. 22, 1932; see also ibid., Aug. 15, 1931, April 30, 1932.

39. "ILD Speaker Assails NAACP for Inaction" (feature), *Guide*, Feb. 23, 1935; ibid., Aug. 15, 1931, April 30, Oct. 22, 29, 1932, Jan. 1, 1935.

40. "War in Alabama," "Tension in Alabama," "Scottsboro Extra," "What Scottsboro Means to America," and "Verdict at Decatur" (editorials), ibid., July 25, Aug. 29, 1931, April 1, 8, 15, March 25, 1933.

41. "An Opportunity for Fair Minded People to Act," "The Court Intervenes," "Penalizing Greatness of Character" (editorials), ibid., July 1, 1933, June 30, 1934.

42. Sylvia Feningston to Arthur Spingarn, June 24, 1930, Silvian Feningston to Walter White, June 24, 1930, Will Alexander to Walter White, Sept. 30, 1930, NAACP Papers, group 1, box 310.

43. "Jury System Attacked in Gordon Case" (feature), *Guide*, Aug. 12, 1933; Virginius Dabney's column in Richmond *Times-Dispatch* reprinted in *Guide*, May 13, 1933.

44. Common Law Order Book, March 3, 1930–March 2, 1931, Norfolk Corporation Court (now Norfolk Circuit Court), pp. 515, 549; statement of William Harper, Jan. 8, 1931 (original confession), Norfolk Corporation Court; Norfolk *Virginian-Pilot*, Jan. 8, 1931.

45. Common Law Order Book, March 3, 1930–March 2, 1931, Norfolk Corporation Court, pp. 515, 520, 549; memorandum, Wilkins to Andrews, digest of William Harper–Dorothy Skaggs case, Sept. 9, 1931, Norfolk Branch file, 1929–June 1933, NAACP Papers, box 310.

46. Affidavit, *Commonweath* vs. *William Harper,* Norfolk Corporation Court, March 1931 (affidavits filed Jan. 31, 1931); Common Law Order Book, March 3, 1930–March 2, 1931, Norfolk Corporation Court.

47. Walter White to W. T. Mason, July 31, 1931, assistant secretary to Norfolk Branch, Sept. 11, 1931, and clippings (n.d.), Norfolk Branch file, 1929–June 1933, NAACP Papers, box 310. "Give Harper a Chance" (editorial), *Guide,* Feb. 7, 1931, clippings (n.d.), *Guide,* Young Papers.

48. Memorandum, Harper-Skaggs case, Young Papers; *Guide,* March 14, 1931; Norfolk Corporation Court, Records, 1931.

49. Norfolk Corporation Court, Records, 1931.

50. *Commonwealth of Virginia* vs. *William Harper,* March 5, 1931, Norfolk Corporation Court; *Guide,* Feb. 14, 28, March 7, 1931; "Justice Vindicated" (editorial), ibid., July 11, 1931.

51. "Harper Accuser Confesses . . . ." (feature), *Guide,* Feb. 28, 1931.

52. Robert W. Bagnall to Rev. R. W. Harris, Feb. 20, April 2, 1930, Harris to Bagnall, Feb. 25, March 3, April 30, 1930, Norfolk Branch file, 1929–June 1933, NAACP Papers, box 310.

53. Robert Bagnall to Eugene West, Dec. 16, 1931, Walter White to W. T. Mason, July 31, 1931, clippings and "Is Justice Blind" and "No Room for Injustice Here" (editorials), *Guide,* March 14, 21, 1931, Young Papers.

54. Clippings and "The Skaggs Case Once More" (editorial), Petersburg *Progress-Index,* July 23, 1931, and clippings (n.d.), Roanoke *World-News,* Norfolk *Virginian-Pilot,* Richmond *Times-Dispatch,* Young Papers.

55. "Happy Outcome near Travesty" (editorial), *Guide,* May 2, 1931.

56. "Harper Accuser Guilty . . . Gets Five Years" and "Justice Vindicated" (editorials), ibid., July 11, 1931.

57. Charles Houston, "The Crawford Case . . . ," and Martha Gruening, "Is NAACP Retreating?" *Nation,* June 27, July 4, 1933; "Trying Crawford Case in Press" (editorial), *Guide,* July 7, 1932.

58. Clippings, *Daily Worker,* Nov. 1, 1933, and "Crawford Loses a Round" (editorial), *Guide,* Oct. 21, 1933, Young Papers.

59. Press release, NAACP, May 25, 1933, Assistant Secretary, NAACP, to Rev. E. A. P, Cheek, May 20, 1933, Asst. Secretary, NAACP, to Rev. E. W. Wainwright, May 18, 1933, NAACP Papers, group 1, box C332; White to Mrs. L. Marian Poe, June 22, 1933, ibid., box G208.

60. Eugene West to Walter White, Aug. 15, 1933, White to West, Aug. 23, 1933, ibid., box G208.

61. *Guide,* June 17, 24, Oct. 21, 28, 1933.

62. Walter White to D. S. Freeman, Nov. 1, 10, 1933, Douglas Southall Freeman Papers, box 94, LC.

63. Freeman to White, Dec. 9, 18, 1933, White to Freeman, Dec. 4, 1933, ibid.

64. "The Crawford Case" (editorials), *Guide,* Nov. 18, Dec. 23, 1933; ibid., May 13, Oct. 21, Dec. 23, 30, 1933; White to Freeman, Dec. 22, 1933, Freeman Papers, box 94.

65. *Guide,* Feb. 17, 1934; interview, John Jordan, Norfolk, June 1975 and July 1977.

66. "Rape and Race" (editorial), *Guide,* March 25, 1939.

67. Richmond *Times-Dispatch,* Aug. 10, 1933; Roy Wilkins to Dr. J. M. Tinsley, Aug. 14, 1933, NAACP Papers, box G210.

68. Eugene West to Walter White, April 15, 1935, W. P. Milner to White, March 25, 1935, NAACP Papers, box G210.

Chapter 8

1. Sternsher, *Negro in Depression and War,* p. 229; E. Franklin Frazier, *The Negro in the United States,* rev. ed. (New York: Macmillan Co., 1957); Numan Bartley, *The Rise of Massive Resistance* (Baton Rouge: Louisiana State University Press, 1969), p. 3.

2. Roi Ottley, *New World A-Coming: Inside Black America* (Boston: Houghton Mifflin Co., 1943), p. 111; Sterling Means, *Ethiopia and the Missing Link in African History* (Harrisburg, 1945), p. 120.

3. Brice Harris, Jr., *The U.S. and the Italo-Ethiopian Crisis* (Stanford: Stanford University Press, 1964), pp. 1–4, 73; William Scott, "Black Nationalism and the Italo-Ethiopian Conflict, 1934–1936," *Journal of Negro History* 63 (April 1978): 118–33; "Riches Causes Fight" and "Italians Bomb Abyssinia" (features), *Guide,* Dec. 29, 1934; ibid., Jan. 5, 1935; "Clear Road for Mussolini" (editorial), ibid., July 13, 1935.

4. "Onward Christian Soldiers" (editorial), *Guide,* July 27, 1935; ibid., Aug. 10, 17, 24, 31, Oct. 5, 12, 1935.

5. "War Seems Nearer and Nearer" (editorial), ibid., Aug. 17, 1935; ibid., July 27, 1935; Harris, *U.S. and the Italo-Ethiopian Crisis,* pp. 1, 20.

6. *Guide,* Jan. 5, July 6, 13, 20, 27, Aug. 10, 17, 24, 31, Sept. 21, Oct. 3, 1935; Buni, *Robert L. Vann,* pp. 244–48.

7. Scott, "Black Nationalism and the Italo-Ethiopian Conflict, 1934–1936," p. 120; *Crisis* 63 (Sept. 1935): 273; Harris, *U.S. and Italo-Ethiopian Crisis,* p. 41.

8. "The League's Dilemma," "On the War Front," "Outlawed by Aggression" (editorials), *Guide,* Oct. 12, Dec. 21, 1935, Jan. 25, 1936.

9. Clippings, *Guide,* Philadelphia *Tribune,* Baltimore *Afro-American,* Young Papers; Scott, "Black Nationalism and the Italo-Ethiopian Conflict, 1934–

1936," pp. 118–20; Buni, *Robert L. Vann*, p. 244; New York *Times*, Oct. 4, 1935, p. 6.

10.   "Hitler On March," "Dangerous Precedent," "The Outlook for War," "A Crazy Quilt," "Law and Order" (editorials), *Guide*, March 19, June 18, Aug. 27, Sept. 3, 1938; see also ibid., April 16, 23, July 9, 1938; "The Last Resort," "Communist Menace," and "American Security" (editorials), ibid., May 28, Oct. 1, 1938.

11.   "Our Foreign Policy" (editorial), ibid., March 4, 1939; see also ibid., May 27, Aug. 12, Sept. 9, Dec. 16, 1939.

12.   "What an Editor Does in His Spare Time" (editorial), ibid., Sept. 5, 1942; "*Guide* Editor on Honor Roll," "The War on Home Front Goes On," "The War and Peninsula Negroes" (features), ibid., Jan. 6, 1940, March 13, April 17, 1943.

13.   Herbert Feis, *The Road to Pearl Harbor* (Princeton, N.J.: Princeton University Press, 1950), pp. 307–41; James MacGregor Burns, *Roosevelt: The Soldier of Freedom, 1940–1945* (New York: Harcourt Brace, 1970), pp. 161–63; *Guide*, Dec. 13, 20, 1941.

14.   *Guide*, Jan. 24, 1941.

15.   Ibid., Feb. 17, Nov. 2, 1940; Jack D. Foner, *Blacks and the Military in American History* (New York: Praeger, 1974), pp. 132–37; clippings (n.d.), Young to Barnett, Nov. 7, 1940, Young Papers; pamphlet, *The Hampton Conference on the Participation of the Negro in National Defense, Hampton, Virginia, November 25–26, 1940*; Richard M. Dalfiume, *Desegregation of the U.S. Armed Forces: Fighting on Two Fronts, 1939–1959* (Columbia: University of Missouri Press, 1969), pp. 105–31; Lee Finkle, "The Conservative Aims of Militant Rhetoric: Black Protest during World War II," *Journal of American History* 60 (Dec. 1973): 692–713; "President's Inaugural" (editorial), *Guide*, Jan. 25, 1941.

16.   "Discrimination in Defense Programs" and "Map Drive against Defense Discrimination" (editorials), *Guide*, Jan. 4, 1941.

17.   "Social Equality . . ." and "Missed the Point" (editorials), ibid. Feb. 1, 1941; ibid., March 1, 15, 22, April 12, May 24, 1941; Richard Polenberg, *War and Society: The United States, 1941–1945* (New York: J. B. Lippincott, 1972), p. 115.

18.   William H. Harris, *Keeping the Faith: A. Philip Randolph, Milton P. Webster, and the Brotherhood of Sleeping Car Porters, 1925–37* (Urbana: University of Illinois Press, 1977); Herbert Garfinkel, *When Negroes March: The March on Washington Movement in the Organizational Politics for FEPC* (Glencoe, Ill.: Free Press, 1959), pp. 37–61; Gavins, *Perils and Prospects*, p. 102; "Pilgrimage to Washington" (editorial), *Guide*, June 14, 1941.

19.   Burns, *Roosevelt: The Soldier of Freedom*, pp. 123–24; *Guide*, March 29, April 26, June 21, 28, July 5, 1941; "Constructive Protests Pay Dividends" (editorial), ibid., June 28, 1941.

20. Rayford W. Logan, ed., *What the Negro Wants* (Chapel Hill: University of North Carolina Press, 1944); H. L. Suggs, "P. B. Young and the Norfolk *Journal and Guide*" (Ph.D. diss., University of Virginia, 1976), p. 365; Gavins, *Perils and Prospects*, esp. pp. 128–60; *Southern Conference on Race Relations* (pamphlet, Durham, N.C., Oct. 20, 1942) in Young Papers; interview with Benjamin Mays, Washington, D.C., May 10, 1978.

21. *Guide*, July 4, Aug. 8, 15, Oct. 3, 7, 31, 1942.

22. P. B. Young to Horace Mann Bond, Jan. 3, 1943, Horace Mann Bond Papers, Countee Cullen Archives, Atlanta University, Atlanta (hereafter cited as Bond Papers, CCA); Young to Ames, Feb. 4, 1943, Jessie Daniel Ames Papers, box 3686, Southern Historical Collection; Young to Paul Mallon, Jan. 25, 1943, Mallon to Young, Jan. 27, 1943, papers of the Commission on Interracial Cooperation, Countee Cullen Archives, Atlanta University (hereafter cited as CIC Papers, CCA); Paul Mallon, "News behind the News," *Virginian-Pilot*, Jan. 28, 1943.

23. Young to H. L. McCrorey, March 15, 1943, J. M. Ellison Papers, private collection, Richmond.

24. Young to Shepard, March 9, 1943, Young Papers; Ames to Shepard, Jan. 15, 1943, Dabney to Ames, Jan. 21, 1943, Ames Papers, box 10, SHC; *Southern Conference on Race Relations* (pamphlet, Durham, Oct. 20, 1942); Shepard to Luther P. Jackson, March 4, 1943, Luther P. Jackson Papers, Virginia State University, Petersburg; clipping, "Fact-Finding Conference . . . ," Augusta (Ga.) *Herald* (n.d.), Young Papers; "Southern Leadership" (editorial), Houston *Informer*, May 29, 1943; see also *Durham Fact-Finding Conference* (pamphlet, Durham, 1929), in Peabody Collection, Hampton Institute; Claude Barnett Papers, Chicago Historical Society.

25. Confidential source, Durham, N.C.

26. Ames to Dabney, Feb. 10, 16, 1943; Dabney to Ames, Jan. 21, Feb. 18, 1943, Ames to Shepard, Jan. 15, 1943; Ames Papers, box 2, folder 11, SHC.

27. Young to H. L. McCrorey, March 15, 1943, Ellison Papers; Young to Horace Mann Bond, Feb. 25, March 1, 1943, Bond Papers, CCA; Young to Luther P. Jackson, Jan. 13, Feb. 4, 11, 1943, Jackson Papers; Ames to Dabney, Feb. 16, 1943, Hancock to Ames, Jan. 24, 1943, Ames Papers, box 2, folder 11, SHC.

28. Young to Shepard, March 9, 1943, Jackson Papers; Young to Shepard, Feb. 24, 1943, Shepard to Young, Feb. 25, 1943, Ames Papers, box 2, folder 11, SHC.

29. Shepard to Young, Feb. 25, 1943, Ames Papers, box 2, folder 11, SHC; Shepard to Jackson, March 4, 1943, Jackson Papers; Bond to Young, March 1, 1943, Bond Papers, CCA.

30. *Transcript of Proceedings of Conference of White Southerners on Race Relations*, held at Piedmont Hotel, Atlanta, April 8, 1943, CCA; Ames to Young, March 13, 1943, Ames to Dabney, Feb. 5, 10, 1943, Hancock to Ames, Jan. 28, 1943, Ames Papers, box 2, folders 10, 11, SHC.

31. *Transcript, Conference of White Southerners*, CCA; *The Durham, Atlanta Richmond Statement*, pamphlet published by Commission on Interracial Cooperation, Atlanta, CIC Papers, CCA; *Guide*, April 17, 24, 1943; Atlanta *Journal*, April 11, 1943; Richmond *Times-Dispatch*, April 11, 1943; Chicago *Defender*, May 1, 1943; New York *Amsterdam News and Star*, May 1, 1943.

32. S. Y. Austin to H. T. Quillian, April 26, 1943, Young Papers.

33. *The Durham, Atlanta, Richmond Statement;* Young to Ames, June 11, 28, 1943, Hancock to Ames, July 5, 1943, Ames Papers, box 2, folder 15, SHC.

34. Hancock to Ames, June 25, 1943, Ames to Dabney, July 1, 1943, Young to Ames, July 10, 1943, Ames to Young, July 12, 1943, Hancock to Ames, July 5, 1943, Ames Papers, box 2, folder 16, SHC; Charter, Southern Regional Council, Inc., Jan. 6, 1944, and Minutes, Executive Committee, SRC, Feb. 16, 1944, SRC Archives, Atlanta; Odum to Young, Jan. 1, 1944, Young to Odum, Jan. 6, 1944, Odum Papers, box 26, folder 549, SHC.

35. Marvin Schlegel, *Conscripted City: Norfolk in WWII* (Norfolk: Norfolk War History Commission, 1951), pp. 193–95, 281, 322–24; Polenberg, *Americans at War*, pp. 107–8; Nancy Armstrong, *The Study of an Attempt Made in 1943 to Abolish Segregation of Races on Common Carriers in State of Virginia*, University of Virginia Phelps-Stokes Fellowship Papers, no. 17 (Charlottesville, 1950), pp. 63–68; Virginius Dabney, "Nearer and Nearer the Precipice," *Atlantic Monthly*, Jan. 1944, pp. 94–100; see also Thomas J. Wertenbaker and Marvin Schlegel, *Norfolk: Historic Southern Port* (Durham, N.C.: Duke University Press, 1962).

36. "No Defense Housing" (editorial), *Guide*, April 12, 1941; ibid., July 12, 1947.

37. Address, Robert Weaver, Norfolk, March 20, 1967, NRHA Records; Sullivan, "Norfolk Redevelopment and Housing Authority," p. 6.

38. Sullivan, "Norfolk Redevelopment and Housing Authority," part 2, 1st sec., pp. 1–2; Frank Sullivan, "Norfolk Destroys Slums," *Commonwealth*, June 1952, pp. 35–36.

39. H. J. Dillehay to P. B. Young, March 8, 1941, Young Papers; Young to W. H. Stillwell, April 1, 1941, NRHA.

40. Minutes, NRHA Records, Sept. 10, 1942.

41. Ibid., July 24, 1944, Oct. 8, 1945.

42. J. Blan Van Urk, "Norfolk—Our Worst War Town," *American Mercury* 56 (Feb. 1943): 144–51; Schlegel, *Conscripted City*, pp. 99–102, 317–22; *Guide*, March 13, Oct. 23, 1943, March 11, Oct. 28, 1944, March 3, Aug. 18, 1945.

43. Schlegel, *Conscripted City*, pp. 99–102, 317–22.

44. "We Want Police Officers" and "Negro Police Officers" (editorials), *Guide*, April 10, 1943, Jan. 27, 1945; Norfolk *Virginian-Pilot*, May 10, 1945.

45. Norfolk *Virginian-Pilot*, Nov. 9, 1945; *Guide*, Nov. 17, 1945; Newport News *Daily Press*, April 8, 1946; interview, Rev. Charles Satchel Morris, July 1977, Norfolk.

46. President Franklin Roosevelt to Young, June 30, 1943, Young to Roosevelt, July 3, 1943, Francis J. Haas to Marvin H. McIntyre, June 29, 1943, Franklin D. Roosevelt Papers, Roosevelt Library, Hyde Park, N.Y.

47. FEPC members to Roosevelt, Jan. 31, 1944, ibid.

48. Minutes of the Fair Employment Practice Commission, Oct. 18, 1943, office file Carol Coan, March 1944, and memos, staff reports, Division of Review and Analysis, Records of the Fair Employment Practice Commission, National Archives, Washington, D.C. (hereafter cited as FEPC, NA); Washington *Star*, Sept. 13, 1944; New York *Times*, May 5, 1945; Chicago *Defender*, Jan. 20, 1945; *Journal of Negro Education*, Summer 1943 and Fall 1943.

49. Minutes, Dec. 27, 1943, and Jan. 15, 1944, Meetings, Division of Review and Analysis, FEPC, NA; *Summary of Evidence with Findings and Recommendations*, case no. 42, ibid.

50. "War on the Home Front" (editorial), *Guide*, Dec. 4, 1943; clippings, Young Papers; reprinted articles, *Guide*, Oct. 16, 30, Nov. 6, 20, Dec. 4, 11, 18, 25, 1943, Jan. 1, 8, 22, 1944; full text of FEPC opening statement in Portland, Ore., ibid. Nov. 20, 1943; picture of Young and FEPC, ibid., Nov. 27, 1943.

51. Roosevelt to Young, Feb. 16, 1944, Young Papers.

52. *Guide*, July 24, Aug. 14, 28, Sept. 11, 18, 1943.

53. Ibid., June 19, 26, 1943, July 17, 1944.

54. Ibid., June 19, 26, July 10, 24, Aug. 14, 18, 1943.

55. Ibid., Feb. 5, 12, 1944; see also Ulysses Lee, *The Employment of Negro Troops: The United States Army in World War II* (Special Studies) (Washington, D.C.: Office of the Chief of Military History, 1966), pp. 450–96.

56. *Guide*, June 26, 1943; "99th Convinces Skeptics" (editorial), ibid., Feb. 5, 1944; "An Analysis of the Achievements of the 99th" (feature), ibid., "Ninety-Ninth Squadron" and "Experiment Proved," *Time*, Aug. 3, Sept. 20, 1943; see also Charles E. Francis, *The Tuskegee Airmen: The Story of the Negro in the U.S. Air Force* (Boston: Bruce Humphries, 1955); Richard J. Stillman, *Integration of the Negro in the U.S. Armed Forces* (New York: Frederick H. Praeger, 1968); Alan M. Osur, *Blacks in the Army Air Force during World War II: The Problem of Race Relations* (Washington, D.C.: Office of Air Force History, 1977); Lawrence J. Paszek, "Negroes and the Air Force, 1939–1949," *Military Affairs* 31 (Spring 1967): 1–9.

57. *Guide*, Feb. 12, 26, May 6, 1944.

58. Ibid., May 13, June 3, 17, 1944.

59. Ibid., May 27, June 10, 1944; telegram, July 1, 1944, Young Papers; see also George W. Goodman, "The Englishmen Meet the Negro," *Common Ground*, Autumn 1944.

60. *Guide*, Aug. 19, 1944.

61. Ibid., Sept. 2, 9, 23, 1944.

62. Interview, Wade McCree, Washington, D.C., June 17, 1978.

63. Lee, *The Employment of Negro Troops*, pp. 536–79; Milton Bracker, "Americans Lose Ground in Italy," New York *Times*, Feb. 14, 1945; Milton Bracker, "Negro Courage Upheld in Inquiry," New York *Times*, March 15, 1945; John Cabot Smith, New York *Herald-Tribune*, March 15, 1945; "A Behavior Pattern," *Newsweek* 25 (March 26, 1945): 37; see also "The Luckless 92nd," ibid., 25 (Feb. 26, 1945): 34–35.

64. "Somebody's Gotta Go!" (editorial), Chicago *Defender*, March 24, 1945; Michigan *Chronicle*, March 24, 1945; New York *People's Voice*, March 24, 1945; see also Lee, *The Employment of Negro Troops*, p. 578; Lester M. Jones, "Editorial Policy of Negro Newspapers of 1917–18 as Compared with That of 1941–42," *Journal of Negro History* 29 (Jan. 1944): 24–37.

65. "Too Much Ado about the 92nd Division Episode" (editorial), *Guide*, April 14, 1945; "Remove General Almond" (editorial), Baltimore *Afro-American*, March 24, 1945; for similar opinion, see Philadelphia *Tribune*, March 31, 1945; Pittsburgh *Courier*, March 31, April 7, 1945; Lee, *The Employment of Negro Troops*, p. 578.

66. *Guide*, July 22, 1944.

67. Ibid., Aug. 26, Sept. 9, Oct. 21, 1944.

68. Ibid., Nov. 11, 1944; "Growing Awareness of America's Major Problem" (editorial), ibid., Dec. 9, 1944.

69. Ibid., Dec. 9, 1944.

70. Ibid., Dec. 9, 1944, Jan. 6, 13, Feb. 3, 1945.

71. "We Discuss a Complaint" (front-page editorial), ibid., Oct. 7, 1944; L. D. Riddick, "The Negro Policy of the U.S. Army, 1775–1945," *Journal of Negro History* 34 (Jan. 1949): 9–29.

72. John D. Stevens, "Black Correspondents of World War II Cover the Supply Routes," *Journal of Negro History* 57 (Fall 1972): 395–406; "Are Negroes Fighting in This War?" (editorial), *Guide*, Oct. 21, 1944.

73. *Guide*, June 15, 22, 1946; "What Lies behind Atomic Bomb Test in Lonely Desert?" (editorial), ibid., Feb. 17, 1951.

Chapter 9

1. Interviews, Mrs. Josephine Moseley Young, Norfolk, March 11, June 18, 1977, April 2, 1980.

2. Folder, Guide Business Reports, 1942–45, Young Papers.

3. Memo, "Organizational Meetings . . . ," Willkie Foundation, Nov. 18, 1946, Agnes E. Meyers Papers.

4. "The Negro Press Changing World," March 1, 1946, Young Papers; *Guide*, March 9, 1946.

5. Young to Freeman, Feb. 21, March 6, 1946, Freeman to Young, Feb. 22, 1946, and to P. B. Young, Jr., March 27, 1946, Douglas Southall Freeman Papers; Pittsburgh *Courier*, June 17, 1950.

6. "A General Improvement in Race Relations" and "Race Progress Noted in Norfolk in 1946" (editorials), *Guide*, May 11, 1946, June 18, 1947.

7. William Cooper to Luther P. Jackson, May 22, 1946, and clippings, "Rights and Duties in a Democracy," May 11, 1946, Jackson Papers; *Guide*, Jan. 12, 1946.

8. P. B. Young, "The Political Status of Negroes in Virginia" (speech, ca. 1946), Young Papers (a similarly titled speech by Young, "The Political Status of Negroes in Virginia," was delivered before Richmond Negro Forum Council, under auspices of Alpha Phi Alpha Fraternity, Fall 1940, reprinted in *Virginia Education Bulletin*, Nov. 1940, pp. 37–38); interview, Benjamin Mays, Washington, D.C., Aug. 1977; *Guide*, Feb. 1, 1947.

9. Lenwood G. Davis, "Miles Mark Fisher: An Analysis," March 5, 1980, Helen G. Edmonds History Colloquium, White Rock Baptist Church, Durham, N.C.; Morton Sosna, *In Search of the Silent South: Southern Liberals and the Race Issue* (New York: Columbia University Press, 1977), p. 139; "The South Advances in Interracial Accord" (editorial), *Guide*, Feb. 1, 1947; ibid., May 11, 1946, Jan. 18, 1947.

10. Luther P. Jackson, *Sixth Annual Report: The Voting Status of Blacks in Virginia* (Richmond: Quality Printing Company, 1945); Jackson, *Eighth Annual Report: The Voting Status of Blacks in Virginia, 1947–1948* (Richmond: Quality Printing Company, June 1948); "Indifference vs. Discrimination" (editorial), Newport News *Daily Press*, May 9, 1945.

11. "On Selling Race down the River" (editorial), *Guide*, Jan. 13, 1945.

12. Interview, Josephine Young, Norfolk, May 1980; Jackson to Woodson, May 19, 1944, Woodson to Jackson, May 23, 1944, Woodson to Jackson, July 21, 1945, Jackson Papers.

13. "On Selling the Race down the River," "The Ole Colored Man and the Council Race," "Mere Protest Useless for Voteless People" (editorials), *Guide*, Jan 13, 1945, April 13, 1946, June 7, 1947; Norfolk City Council, Records.

14. Young to Governor Colgate W. Darden, Jr., Feb. 11, 1944, Young Papers; interview, John Belden, Norfolk, June 1975.

15. *Guide*, June 15, 1946, June 22, 28, 1947; Buni, *Negro in Virginia Politics*, p. 153; Ashe to Jaffe, May 4, 1946, Young Papers.

16. Campaign memorabilia, Young Papers.

17. Jackson to Young, Aug. 16, 1947, Young Papers, Jackson, *Seventh Annual Report, Voting Status, 1946;* Jackson, *Eighth Annual Report, Voting Status of Negroes in Virginia, 1947–1948;* Richmond *Times-Dispatch,* Aug. 7, 1947; see also column "Rights and Duties . . . ," *Guide,* Aug. 16, 1947.

18. Buni, *Negro in Virginia Politics,* pp. 159, 161–62; *Guide,* Feb. 7, March 13, Nov. 13, 1948. "Wallace and the Negro" (editorial), ibid., March 20, 1948; see also Emile B. Ader, *The Dixiecrat Movement* (Washington, D.C., 1955).

19. "Post Election Observations" (editorial), *Guide,* Aug. 6, 1949.

20. "Walls of Racial Prejudice Are Crumbling" and "Developments in the Campaign for Civil Rights" (editorials), ibid., April 3, 1948; Crawley, *Bill Tuck.*

21. Thomas C. Reeves, *The Life and Times of Joe McCarthy* (New York: Stein and Day, 1982), pp. 204–10.

22. Dorothy Butler Gilliam, *Paul Robeson: All-American* (Washington, D.C.: New Republic Book Company, 1976), pp. 137, 141, 143; statement of Thomas W. Young to the House Un-American Activities Committee, Washington, D.C., July 13, 1949, Young Papers.

23. Young to Guy B. Johnson, March 28, Nov. 30, 1945, Harold Trigg to Young, April 30, 1946, Dec. 5, 1946, Feb. 17, 1947, Young to Trigg, April 19, 1947, Young Papers.

24. Young to Beecher, Oct. 1, 1946, ibid.

25. Ibid.; Payroll Records, 1942 (Summary), and folder, *Guide* Business Reports, 1942–45, ibid.; interview, Juanita Yeates Moore, Norfolk, Oct. 15, 1975; interviews, twenty long-term former employees, Norfolk, Oct. 1975, Nov. 1980.

26. Interview, Thomas Dabney, Norfolk, March 12, 1977; P. B. Young, Jr., to Dabney, July 15, 1947, Young Papers; Associated Negro Press News Release, Nov. 17, 1947, Barnett Papers.

27. Interview, *Guide* employees, Norfolk, July 15, 1977.

28. "The History and Achievement of Washington Memorial and Development Plans for the Industrial Training Center," Lenoir Chambers Papers, SHC.

29. Phillips to Harry Truman, April 4, 1946, Tuck to Dabney, May 1, 2, 8, 1946, Phillips to Dabney, Oct. 1, 1946, Virginius Dabney Papers, University of Virginia Library, Charlottesville.

30. 80th Cong., 1st sess., H.R. 3814, June 12, 1947; Dabney to Young and Foster, June 18, 1947, Young to Dabney, June 21, 1947, Dabney Papers.

31. Malcolm Griffin to Dabney, July 8, Aug. 6, 8, 1947, Dabney to Griffin, Aug. 7, 1947, Dabney Papers.

32. Flier, Booker T. Washington Birthplace Memorial, Phillips to Thomas W. Young, April 17, 1951, Young to Dabney, June 8, 1951, Young Papers.

33. See, for example, James P. Spencer to S. J. Phillips, March 29, 1952, ibid.

34. Joseph C. Otterbein to Young, March 20, 1952, F. W. Evans to Young, March 25, 1952, Thomas Young to Sue R. Slaughter, Sept. 3, 1952, ibid.

35. Sue Slaughter to Thomas Young, Aug. 25, 1952, ibid.

36. Clippings, Roanoke *Times*, Feb. 5, 1954, Roanoke *World News*, Jan. 19, 1954, *Guide*, Jan. 22, 1955, ibid.; "Interior Secretary Rejects Booker T. Washington Monument Idea" (feature), *Guide*, Feb. 11, 1956.

37. *Guide*, June 17, July 8, Oct. 7, 1950, Jan. 13, 27, Feb. 10, 1951; Peter Henriques, "John S. Battle and Virginia Politics: 1948–1953" (Ph.D. diss., University of Virginia, 1971), pp. 177–87.

38. *Guide*, Feb. 10, 1951.

Chapter 10

1. Henry S. Rorer's *History of Norfolk Public Schools, 1681–1968* (n.d.), copy in Young Papers.

2. Herbert Aptheker, ed., *The Education of Black People: Ten Critiques, 1906–1936* (New York: Monthly Review Press, 1973), pp. x, 5, 15; Atlanta *Constitution*, May 31, 1906; New York *Times*, May 31, 1906; clippings (n.d.), Young Papers.

3. *Guide*, Dec. 16, 1933, Nov. 17, 1934.

4. W. E. B. Du Bois, ed., *The Negro Common School* (Atlanta, 1901; rept. New York: Arno Press, 1968), p. 114.

5. "This School Needs This Name" (front-page editorial), *Guide*, Sept. 7, 1935, p. 1; "Honoring Man and School" (editorial), ibid., Sept. 14, 1935.

6. Ibid., Sept. 21, 1935, p. 8.

7. "Virginia Union's Norfolk Extension" (editorial), Norfolk *Virginian-Pilot*, reprinted in *Guide*, Sept. 21, 1935, p. 8.

8. *Guide*, June 15, June 29, Aug. 10, 1935; "Norfolk's Junior College" (editorial), ibid., Sept. 14, 1935.

9. Ibid., June 15, Oct. 19, 1935.

10. "More Pay for Teachers," "Courageous Band of Educators," "To the Teachers" (editorials), ibid., June 20, 1931, Sept. 10, 1932, March 18, 1933.

11. "Buckingham County Citizens Want and Get Education" (feature), ibid., Sept. 12, 1931; ibid., May 9, June 6, Dec. 5, 1931, Jan. 16, Oct. 8, 1932.

12. Records, reports, pamphlets, statistics from the Office of the State Superintendent of Education, Young Papers; *Guide*, Jan. 23, 1932.

13. "Separate but Equal," "Virginia and Education," "Reduction of Teachers Salaries" (editorials), *Guide*, Jan. 16, 23, Feb. 13, 1932; *Southern Workman*, Feb. 1932; Norfolk City Council, Records, Jan. 1932.

14. Clippings, "Our Educational Dilemma . . . ," *Guide*, and clippings from Richmond *Times-Dispatch*, Norfolk *Ledger-Dispatch* (n.d.), Young Papers; "The Troubled Educational Waters" (editorial), *Guide*, Sept. 28, 1935; ibid., Oct. 5, 1935.

15. David Lanley to Walter White, July 13, 1936, White to Daisy E. Lampkin, Feb. 28, 1938, Marshall to P. B. Young, Sr., Oct. 19, 31, 1938, Young to Marshall, Oct. 22, 1938, Legal file, NAACP Papers, box D91.

16. "Let the School Board Reconsider" (editorial), Norfolk *Virginian-Pilot*, June 27, 1939; Richmond *Times-Dispatch*, Dec. 8, 1940; *Virginia Journal of Education*, Jan. 1941; *Virginia Teachers Bulletin*, Jan. 1941; see also "Equal Education Decision," and "Negro Grads Ability" (editorials), Norfolk *Virginian-Pilot*, Dec. 15, 19, 1938.

17. P. B. Young, Jr., to Marshall, April 5, 1938, Thomas Young to Marshall, Nov. 16, 1938; Marshall to Charles Houston, Dec. 6, 1938; Marshall to P. B. Young, Sr., July 21, Oct. 11, Sept. 25, 1939, Legal file, NAACP Papers, box D91.

18. Confidential source, Norfolk.

19. Leo Ransom to Marshall, Nov. 1, 6, 1940, Alfred Anderson to Marshall, Nov. 6, 1940, Olive Hill to Marshall, Nov. 6, 1940, Marshall to White and Wilkins, Nov. 7, 1940, memo, Marshall to White and Wilkins, Nov. 8, 1940, Legal file, NAACP Papers, box D91; "U.S. Court of Appeals on Equalization of Teachers Salaries," *Virginia Teachers Bulletin*, Nov. 1940, pp. 9–15.

20. Marshall to Ransom, Jan. 9, 1941, telegrams, Marshall to Ransom, Nov. 4, 15, 1940, and Marshall to Hastie, Nov. 6, 1940; Legal files, NAACP Papers, box D91.

21. Memo, Marshall to White and Wilkins, Nov. 8, 1940, ibid.; confidential interviews with three *Guide* employees.

22. Marshall to Wilkins, Nov. 12, 1940, J. Henry Clayton to Marshall, Nov. 16, 1940, Walter Williamson to Marshall, Dec. 3, 6, 12, 1940, White to Gilliam, March 5, 1941, Legal files, NAACP Papers, box D91; see also Oliver Hill to Leo Ransom, Jan. 31, 1941, ibid.

23. Marshall to Hastie, Nov. 28, 1940, ibid.

24. Carl Murphy to Marshall, Nov. 19, 1940; White to Hastie, Dec. 4, 1940, Marshall to Leo Ransom, Jan. 9, 1941, Ransom to Wilkins, Feb. 6, 1941, ibid.

25. Gilliam to Marshall, Feb. 23, 1940, Feb. 18, 1941, Gilliam to White, Nov. 12, 1940, March 8, 1941, ibid.

26. Memo, E. Frederic Morrow to National Office, Oct. 11, 1939, Gilliam to White, Nov. 12, 1940, ibid.

27. "How Long, Oh, Lord, How Long!!" (editorial), *Guide*, Dec. 8, 1945.

28. Marshall to S. F. Coppage, Dec. 13, 1945, Legal file, NAACP Papers, box D91; Augustus M. Burns III, "Graduate Education for Blacks in North Carolina, 1930–1951," *Journal of Southern History* 46 (May 1980): 195–218; Richard Kluger, *Simple Justice: The History of* Brown *v.* Board of Education *and Black America's Struggle for Equality* (New York: A. A. Knopf, 1976), pp. 212–13; P. B. Young to James E. Shepard, Dec. 14, 1938, Shepard to Governor C. R. Hoey, Dec. 15, 1938, Young Papers; David L. Corbitt, ed., *Addresses, Letters, and Papers of Clyde Roark Hoey, Governor of North Carolina, 1937–1941* (Raleigh, N.C., 1944), p. 38; "Orioles Hear Editor Young" (feature), *Guide*, Dec. 24, 1938.

29. Clipping, "The Equal Education Decision" (editorial), Norfolk *Virginian-Pilot*, Dec. 15, 1938, Young Papers; *Guide*, Dec. 10, 17, 24, 1938; Morton Sosna, *In Search of the Silent South*, pp. 126–27.

30. *Guide*, Feb. 25, March 4, 11, 1939; see also "Academic Freedom" (editorial), ibid., June 6, 1936.

31. "Equality Decisions Are Definite Gains, But Suits Will Continue" (editorial), ibid., June 10, 17, 1950.

32. Interview, Colgate Darden, Norfolk, July 15, 1977; *Guide*, July 15, 22, 1950; Marshall to Young, April 12, 1939, Ransom to Marshall, April 14, 1939, Young to Marshall, April 15, 1939, Legal file, NAACP Papers, box D-91.

33. Clippings (n.d.), Richmond *News-Leader*, Norfolk *Ledger-Dispatch*, Roanoke *World-Times*, Richmond *Times-Dispatch*, Young Papers; *Guide*, May 19, June 9, 1951; interviews, John Jordan, Thomas Dabney, Norfolk, July 1977.

34. Young to Swanson, June 14, 1951, Young Papers.

35. Interview, Colgate Darden, Norfolk, July 15, 1977.

36. *Guide*, May 14, 1949, June 10, 1950, March 7, Oct. 10, 1953.

37. Interview, John Jordan, Norfolk, June 1975; Bob Smith, *They Closed Their Schools* (Chapel Hill: University of North Carolina Press, 1965).

38. Interview, John Jordan, Norfolk, June 1975.

39. *Guide*, March 7, July 4, 1953, April 24, July 3, 10, Aug. 28, May 22, 1954; Kluger, *Simple Justice*, pp. 256–84.

40. *Guide*, May 22, Aug. 28, Nov. 27, 1954.

41. Henry Lewis Suggs, "Tidewater Virginia's Editorial Response to Change in the Bi-Racial System, 1945–1955," *Virginia Social Science Journal*, Nov. 1980, pp. 40–47; Derrick Bell, "Learning from the *Brown* Experience," *Black Scholar*, Sept./Oct. 1979, pp. 9–17.

Chapter 11

1. Interview, Josephine Young, Norfolk, July 1977.

2. Young to C. A. Harrell, May 21, 1951, Harrel to Young, May 23, 1951, Frederick Huette to Decker, May 25, 1951, Decker to Harrell, June 14, 1951, Young to Decker, July 3, 1951, Young to W. Fred Duckworth, Aug. 28, 1952, Young to Henry H. George III, Sept. 9, 1952, unsigned letter to Duckworth, Aug. 29, 1952, George to Young, Sept. 4, 1952, Jan. 27, June 16, 1953, Young Papers.

3. George to Young, Dec. 10, 21, 1953, Young to George, Dec. 22, 1953, ibid.

4. P. Bernard Young, Jr., to Division of Water Supply, Dec. 9, 1953, Young to George, Jan. 30, 1954, R. W. Fitzgerald to George, March 23, 1954, George to Young, March 25, 1954, ibid.

5. George to Young, July 22, 1955, P. Bernard Young, Jr., to W. H. G. Chase, Aug. 26, 1957, ibid.

6. Interview, Josephine Young, Norfolk, July 1977.

7. Ibid., interview, Louis and Phillip Bress, Norfolk, July 1977.

8. Interview, Colgate Darden, Norfolk, July 15, 1977.

9. Clippings (n.d.), Young Papers; interview, John Jordan, Norfolk, July 1976, March 1977.

10. Ibid.

11. H. L. Suggs, "A Social History of the Black Press in America, 1900–1962" (lecture), Howard University, Fall 1979.

12. Ibid.

13. Barnett to Thomas W. Young, Feb. 13, 1950, P. B. Young to Barnett, Nov. 10, 1950, Barnett to P. B. Young, Nov. 21, 1950, Young Papers.

14. Young to Nannie Helen Burroughs, Aug. 31, 1954, Nannie Helen Burroughs Papers, LC; *Guide*, July 29, 1950, July 7, 1951, March 28, 1953; "Virginia Tech Accepts First Black Student" (feature), *Virginian-Pilot*, Sept. 11, 1953.

15. Clippings (n.d.), Young Papers.

16. Interview, Maceo Dailey, Washington, D.C., April 20, 1982.

17. Remarks by P. B. Young, chairman, Howard Board of Trustees, Oct. 25, 1943, Young to Johnson, March 4, April 7, 1952, Johnson to Young, March 5, 1952, Young Papers.

18. Johnson to Young, March 28, 1952, Barnes to Johnson, March 27, 1952, Young to Johnson, April 7, 1952, ibid.

19. Washington to Johnson, Sept. 8, 1952, Young to Washington, Sept. 10, 1952, ibid.

20. Johnson to Washington, April 1, 1952, Washington to Johnson, Sept. 8, 1952, Young to Washington, Sept. 10, 1952, ibid.

21. Emmett E. Dorsey to Young, Jan. 10, 1955, Rayford Logan to Young, March 29, 1955, Young to Logan, April 6, 1955, ibid.

22. Johnson to Young, Jan. 20, 1953, and legal brief, Edward Jackson v. Mordecai Johnson and Howard University, ibid.

23. Young to J. L. Johnson, April 15, 1954; Young to Mordecai Johnson, April 15, 23, 1954, Mordecai Johnson to Young, April 21, June 28, 1954, J. B. Clarke to Young, June 1, 1954, ibid.

24. Johnson to Young, June 28, 1954, Young to Johnson, July 6, 1954, ibid.; *Congressional Record,* June 8, 1954.

25. Johnson to Young, May 19, 1955, Young to Johnson, May 23, 1955, Young Papers.

26. Roy Wilkins to Edward T. Clayton, April 18, 1956, May 29, 1957, Wilkins to Simeon Booker, Feb. 1, 1957, General Office file, NAACP Papers, box 177.

27. Clipping, "The NAACP, Where Does It Go from Here" (feature), Pittsburgh *Courier,* July 28, 1958, other clippings, Wilkins to Murphy, July 23, 1958, memo, Thomas Young to P. B. Young, Aug. 6, 1958, Young Papers. Roy Wilkins, *Standing Fast: The Autobiography of Roy Wilkins* (New York: Viking Press, 1982) does not record the controversy between himself and the black press.

28. Baltimore *Afro-American,* July 26, 1958; *Pittsburgh Courier,* July 28, 1958; Wilkins to Murphy, July 23, 1958, Young Papers.

29. Memo, Moon to Wilkins, Aug. 6, 1958, E. Washington Rhodes to Wilkins, Aug. 8, 1958; Young to Wilkins, Aug. 11, 1958, William Walker to Wilkins, Aug. 13, 1958, Young Papers; Washington *Post and Times Herald,* Jan. 7, 1958.

30. Wilkins to Young, Aug. 14, 1958, Young Papers.

31. Ibid.

32. Young to Wilkins, Aug. 18, 1958, Moon to Tom Young, July 20, 1954, and Tom Young to Moon, July 12, 1954, Young Papers; Suggs, *Black Press in South,* preface.

33. Young to Wilkins, Aug. 18, 1958, Young Papers.

34. Walker to Wilkins, Aug. 13, 1958, ibid.

35. Memo, John A. Morsell to Wilkins, Aug. 24, 1958, Wilkins to Young, Aug. 21, 1958, ibid.

36. Luther J. Carter, "Desegregation in Norfolk," *South Atlantic Quarterly* 58 (Autumn 1959): 507–20.

37. Suggs, "Tidewater Virginia's Response to Change in the Bi-Racial System," pp. 40–47.

38. Interviews, Vivian Mason, Norfolk, Feb. 28, 1981, J. Hugo Madison, Norfolk, March 10, July 14, 1977.

39. Carter, "Desegregation in Norfolk," p. 507.

40. Hilary H. Jones, Jr., to John D. Corbell, Aug. 15, 1957, Young Papers.

41. Norfolk City Council Records, Aug. 20, 1957.

42. Ibid.; Thomas F. Maxwell to Virginia ABC Board, Aug. 22, 1957, Young Papers.

43. J. W. Wood to J. H. Kellam, Aug. 27, 1957, John W. Hardy to Maxwell, Aug. 30, 1957, Young Papers.

44. John W. Hardy to Rev. Richard B. Martin, Jan. 3, 1958, ibid.; interview, Josephine Young, Norfolk, July 1977.

45. Young to Duckworth, Feb. 1, 1961, Duckworth to Young, Feb. 3, 1961, Young Papers.

46. Ibid.

47. "We Endorse Kennedy" (editorial), Oct. 8, 1960, *Guide*.

Conclusion

1. Helen King Bainbridge to author, Sept. 19, 1977.

Selected Bibliography

Manuscript Collections

Amistad Collection, Tulane University, New Orleans: Papers of Mary McLeod Bethune.

Chicago Historical Society, Chicago: Papers of Claude A. Barnett.

Countee Cullen Collection, Woodruff Library of Atlanta University, Atlanta: Papers of Horace Mann Bond; Council on Interracial Cooperation.

Duke University Library, Durham, N.C.: Papers of Charles N. Hunter; Robert Algeron Myrick; Anne Biddle Pope.

Halifax County Historical Society, Halifax, N.C.

Johnston Memorial Library, Virginia State University, Petersburg: Papers of J. M. Gandy; Luther P. Jackson; Virginia Negro Teachers Association.

Library of Congress: Papers of Mary McLeod Bethune; Nannie Helen Burroughs; Henry Flood; Douglass Southall Freeman; Agnes Meyers; National Association for the Advancement of Colored People (NAACP); National Urban League; Booker T. Washington; Walter White (NAACP); Carter Woodson.

Moorland-Spingarn Research Center, Howard University, Washington, D.C.: Papers of Campbell C. Johnson; Kelly Miller; Peter Marshall; Joel Spingarn; Gregory Swanson; Judge Waties Waring.

National Archives, Washington, D.C.: U.S. Census 1800–1910; U.S. Census Agriculture Schedule (1880); Records of the Bureau of Refugees, Freedmen, and Abandoned Lands, 1865–70; Records of the Fair Employment Practices Commission (FEPC); Records of the Farm Security Administration; Records of the Federal Bureau of Investigation (1920–30); Records of the Resettlement Administration; Records of the Superintendent of Education for the State of North Carolina.

Norfolk City Hall: Record Book, Norfolk City Council, 1900–1940: Records of the Norfolk Redevelopment and Housing Authority.

Peabody Special Collection, Hampton University, Hampton, Va.: Papers of the Negro Organization Society; T. C. Walker; and Hampton University Scrapbook Collection.

Roosevelt Library, Hyde Park, N.Y.: Papers of President Franklin Delano Roosevelt.

Schlesinger Library, Radcliffe College, Cambridge, Mass.: Charlotte Hawkins Brown Collection.

Southern Historical Collection, Library of the University of North Carolina at Chapel Hill: Papers of Jessie Daniel Ames: Lenoir Chambers; Commission on Interracial Cooperation; Frank Porter Graham; Guy Johnson; North Carolina Commission on Interracial Cooperation; Howard Odum.

Southern Regional Council, Atlanta.

Truman Library, Independence, Mo.: Papers of Harry S. Truman.

University of Massachusetts, Amherst: W. E. B. Du Bois Collection.

University of Virginia Library, Charlottesville: Papers of Harry Byrd, Sr.; Virginius Dabney.

Virginia State Archives, Richmond: Papers of Governors Harry Byrd, Jr., Westmoreland Davis, John Pollard, James H. Price, and Henry Stuart; Virginia Commission on Interracial Cooperation.

Others: Papers of Thomas Dabney (Virginia Union University, Richmond; James M. Ellison (in the possession of Mrs. James M. Ellison, Richmond); Louis I. Jaffe (in the possession of Mrs. Louis I. Jaffe, Norfolk); John Q. Jordan (in the possession of the author); James E. Shepard (private collection, Durham, N.C.); P. B. Young, Sr. (in the possession of author); Grace Episcopal Church Archives, Norfolk.

Interviews (selective listing)

With Southall Bass, Norfolk, July 1974, July 1977, and over subsequent years; John Belden, Norfolk, July 1974, July 1977, and over subsequent years; Roger Boyd, Littleton, N.C. April–August 1979; Louis and Phillip Bress, Norfolk, July 14, 1977; Clarence Bunch, Norfolk, July 1974; Governor Colgate Darden, Norfolk, July 15, 1977; Helena Harris, Littleton, N.C. April–August 1979; John Q. Jordan, Norfolk, July 1974 and over subsequent years; Carl Jacox, Norfolk, July 1974, July 1977; J. Hugo Madison, Norfolk, July 14, 1977; Benjamin E. Mays, Atlanta, July 9, 1977; James Robinson, Littleton, N.C. April–August 1979; H. C. Young (nephew of P. B. Young, Sr.), Norfolk, July 13, 1977; Mrs. Josephine

Young, Norfolk, June 18, March 11, 1977, April 2, 1980, and over subsequent years.

Letters Received (selective listing)

Freddye G. Ashford, Librarian, Lincoln University of Missouri, Jan. 14, 1981; Helen King Bainbridge, former editor, William Morrow, Sept. 19, 1977; Gilbert Gude, Director, Library of Congress, Congressional Research Service, June 7, 1979; Lawrence D. Hogan, Jan. 27, 1976; Milton A. Reid, publisher, Norfolk *Journal and Guide*, Nov. 12, 1975; Mrs. Josephine Young, Norfolk, May 21, 1979.

Newspapers

Atlanta *Constitution;* Columbia, S.C., *State;* Greenville, N.C., *Daily Reflector;* Newport News, Va., *Star;* New York *Times;* Norfolk *Journal and Guide;* Norfolk *Ledger-Dispatch;* Norfolk *Virginian-Pilot;* Raleigh, N.C., *News and Observer;* Richmond *News-Leader;* Richmond *Planet and Afro-American;* Richmond *Times-Dispatch;* Washington *Post.*

Index